ACKNOWLEDGEMENTS

There are an awful lot of incidents covered and people mentioned who have played a part in my life, but I would like to give a special acknowledgement to Geraldine Davis, who has worked with me over a number of years, and continues to provide help and guidance. I'd also like to acknowledge the help given to me by Keeley Bennett, who worked as my secretary for some time and somehow managed to keep me in order, while providing support and loyalty; and to thank my lawyer, Bernard Clarke, who has offered sound advice to an often headstrong client. I would like to thank the boxing media and have to say I wouldn't have missed the bust-ups or the good times on some of those transatlantic trips for anything. I must also thank the boxing fans with whom I've always had a great relationship, and realise that without them and their support of the sport I would be out of a job.

Finally, my special thanks go to my wife Tracey, daughters Emma, Sophie and Libby, and to Kevin Brennan's wife Lynda and their children, James and Rachel. Both families had to suffer some tantrums and bad behaviour that went with the writing of this book, but I hope that in the end they will feel it was all worthwhile.

NO BALONEY

FRANK MALONEY

WITH KEVIN BRENNAN

MAINSTREAM
PUBLISHING
EDINBURGH AND LONDON

This edition, 2004

First published in Great Britain in 2003 by
MAINSTREAM PUBLISHING COMPANY (EDINBURGH) LTD
7 Albany Street
Edinburgh EH1 3UG

ISBN 1 84018 898 7

A catalogue record for this book is available from the British Library

Typeset in Badhouse and Berkeley
Printed and bound in Great Britain by
Cox & Wyman Ltd

CONTENTS

world. 'And don't drink for the next month.' I agreed, with my fingers crossed behind my back.

The first time I went down the Gym (Maloney's Fight Factory) I was like a kid in a sweet shop. It was perfect. No fancy machines, no fancy anything, just boxers quietly training. Even the name was like something out of a 1930s American movie. In fact so was Frank. He reminded me of one of the urchins in *Angels with Dirty Faces*. And to be honest I felt I was walking into a gang's hide out. They were a tight unit. Frank and his brother Eugene – the bosses – the staff they employed and the fighters they trained. The swearing, the machismo and the subjects talked about, would suggest that these people would not make the greatest role models, yet all the boxers were polite and respectful. They weren't aggressive bruisers, they were student athletes trying to make someone proud of them. Frank mainly. I decided to make him proud too.

I started my first training session sprightly and confidently. It wasn't as hard as I expected. Eighteen minutes later, as I collapsed on the floor gasping for breath and begging to stop, I remember Frank with his last attempt at rousing me saying, 'You're not acting like a boxer.' I replied, 'I'm not a fucking boxer, I'm a fucking comedian.' That made him laugh. I'd proved my point. I'm still a comedian but I felt like a boxer for a few minutes on 9 December 2002. A fat one.

The next day Frank called from Russia and said he was proud of me. I did it.

Ricky Gervais

1. THE PUNCHING PRIEST

HAD THINGS WORKED OUT DIFFERENTLY I MIGHT HAVE FOUND MYSELF WITH A church to look after in some far off place rather than the heavyweight champion of the world.

It may seem strange now to think that I once had ambitions to be a missionary Catholic priest with the Mill Hill Fathers, but the idea was genuine enough, even if it did take only a matter of weeks before I realised my talents would be better suited to something else.

It probably upset my parents and grandparents who were proud to think that their little Francis had what was needed to become a priest. But I think they soon got over their disappointment and came to realise that their loss was the church's gain. There was no way I would have had the dedication or enthusiasm to see it through, and when the Holy Fathers politely suggested that I might not be cut out for the task, I felt a rush of relief run through me.

I'd been very serious about the whole thing and because of my background the Church played a big part in my life from the day I was born. I suppose I must have been about 13 when this all happened, and as a kid growing up in Peckham, south London, there was still a big wide world out there that held all sorts of mysteries for me.

It's funny to think I was so serious about the priesthood, but it was something I found fascinating because of all the religion that surrounded me. My mum and dad didn't go overboard about it, but being a Catholic was very much part of our lives. The idea of becoming a priest didn't seem that outlandish, but the short experience I had soon persuaded me to look elsewhere for my true vocation in life.

It wasn't so much a lack of religious belief that was the stumbling block, it was realising I would have to forget about the pleasures of getting to know all about the opposite sex. Even at that very early age the thought of a life of celibacy certainly didn't appeal to me!

I think the idea of being a priest came from hearing missionaries talk when they visited my school. For some reason they had a big effect on me, and their lifestyle, together with the stories they told, seemed pretty exciting. There was also a bit of gentle persuasion from my headmaster, Mr Timmins, who himself later became a Christian Brother. It seemed to spark my imagination and I would come home bursting with enthusiasm for the whole thing.

I'd already been on a trip to Lourdes as an 11 year old and that had left its mark on me as well. I suppose I was exposed to quite a bit of religion, because I was also an altar boy at St James's, our local church, which meant being on duty for weddings and funerals. I actually used to look forward to the funerals more, because for some reason or other you got paid extra money.

My parents probably knew my grand plans to become a priest would be nothing more than a five minute wonder, but they were quite happy to go along with the idea, and I was shipped up to a seminary in Freshfield, Liverpool.

I don't exactly know what I was expecting, but it was certainly a disappointment to me when I was shown a big dormitory and told that was where I'd be staying while I was up there. It wasn't long before I realised the whole thing was not my scene at all, but when I tried to talk to one of the other boys about it he seemed very reluctant to say anything to me. It was only some time later that I found out he was on a retreat, which meant he was expected to stay silent and concentrate on studying the Bible.

I eventually did talk to one of the other boys who was much more into it and clued up about what was expected. Once he told me what was going on I quickly decided I should start to look elsewhere for something to do with the rest of my life.

Although it was a pretty serious place I'm afraid I couldn't help being my usual cheeky self and I managed to play tricks on the other lads, like swapping all their clothes over in the dormitory at night when they were asleep. I was also into trying to make a bit of extra cash by selling sweets to the other kids, which probably didn't go down too well either. Apart from being told there were no girls involved in any of the activities, I think it was the quietness of the place that really got to me. So I headed back to south London a wiser young man, but still without any kind of idea about what I wanted to do with my life.

Things were very carefree for me and I suppose I got up to all the usual pranks kids of my age were into. I had arrived in this world, kicking and screaming on 23 January 1953, the son of a pretty typical working-class Irish couple, Thomas and Maureen. Mum came from County Wicklow and Dad from Roscrea. They had settled in south London, bringing up a family that consisted of me and two brothers, Eugene who was three years younger and Vince who came along four and a half years after I made my first appearance.

I was born in Lambeth Hospital just around the corner from the Elephant and Castle, and in the shadow of the Oval cricket ground. For the first few years of my life the family lived in a one bedroom flat in Gipsy Hill with my mum and dad sleeping in the front room on a makeshift bed.

It was the place where my youngest brother Vince was born and where I got my first real taste of school, although I did have some experience of the education system in Ireland for a time, where I spent six or eight weeks in a pretty strict environment trying to come to terms with learning all the subjects using Gaelic.

We went there because my parents had been told by our landlord in London that we had to move out of the flat. I was really excited by the prospect, because I'd spent so many fantastic holidays in Dublin and in the Tipperary countryside during my very early years. I would have been quite happy to have stayed in Ireland had I been a farmer's son working on the land, but once schoolwork reared its ugly head things didn't seem quite so rosy.

As you can imagine this wasn't exactly easy for a kid of seven, particularly as I'd spent most of my time in London since being born, and apart from the language problem there was also the physical threat from stick-wielding nuns. It really was a very stern set-up and certainly not the sort of school I was suited to. The nuns ran the place with a rod of iron, or to be more precise, a rod of wood.

I couldn't believe it when I first saw the Mother Superior walking around the school with a great big stick, and she would lash out with it whenever she thought a pupil was doing something wrong. On one particular occasion she ended up getting a bit more than she bargained for with me, and when she tried to give me a swipe I somehow managed to get hold of the lethal weapon and break it. The incident didn't go down too well and only added to the general feeling that my brother Eugene and I would be better off back in London. After about six weeks there I just couldn't take it any more and to be honest, I don't think the nuns could either. They must have been just as relieved to see the back of us as we were to wave goodbye to them.

We soon settled back into south London life and the family moved to a large Victorian house in Camberwell Grove which had been converted into a couple of flats. It all seemed very grand to us at the time and was a real step up from our last accommodation. We all had our own bedrooms, and the really big thing was having a family bathroom. I was sent to a local school called St Joseph's, which happily was a much nicer and friendlier place to be than the almost prison-like regime I'd experienced in Ireland.

By that time the real sporting love of my life was not boxing but football. I couldn't get enough of it and played matches every day with the other kids in the playground. I was also hooked on Millwall Football Club after being taken there by my dad to see a game at the tender age of three. Some of the most vivid memories I have as a kid come from that time: going to home games at the Den, which wasn't very far from our house. It was a ground with a unique atmosphere and also a place with a bit of a reputation for having some supporters who were real hard cases.

It was a love affair that has lasted to this day, and although the club have since moved grounds and the old style terraces are a thing of the past, Millwall are still a unique club as far as I'm concerned with fanatical support. I've bought shares in them over the years, more through loyalty than in any hope of making money, and have a season ticket these days. I go to as many games as I can and there's no doubt the club will always be in my blood.

As you can imagine for someone who is now fully grown and stands just 5 ft 3 in., I wasn't exactly the biggest kid at school, but I still joined in all the sporting activities and gave as good as I got. I had a happy childhood, with my mum working as a waitress and Dad employed on the construction side of things by British Rail.

My parents were a big part of my life and we were a close-knit family. I must admit it was a devastating feeling, some years later when I was a teenager of 19, to wake up one morning and find out my mum and dad were splitting up. In the end they got divorced, but both have continued to play big roles in my life.

Mum was always very protective of her family and none more so than her little Francis. For 11 years of my childhood that was my name, and it wasn't until I went to the Sacred Hearts Secondary School that I was first called Frank by Mr Timmins. I've used the name ever since and liked the sound of it right from the start because it made me feel a bit more grown up. I always thought it sounded like a character out of a Hollywood gangster movie: 'Frankie Maloney' the tough guy. It was important to me back then, particularly as I was still being dressed in shorts to go to school. My mum has done a lot of good things for me over the years, but dressing me in shorts until I was about 13 years old was not one of them!

Although I was never a big kid at school I soon learned how to look after myself and was never afraid to have a go if I got involved in a fight with a boy who was bigger and stronger than me. I got up to the usual things that might be expected, including running around the streets causing all sorts of havoc with a group of mates.

It was all harmless stuff really, especially when you compare it to what goes on with some youngsters these days. I used to love anything to do with sport and it was during my time at Sacred Hearts that I first encountered what were to become the two loves of my life – boxing and women – although not always in that order.

The first girl I was ever really friendly with was called Margaret

Dooley. She used to leave messages on my school desk and I had my leg pulled by friends because of them. She was nothing like the girls I was later attracted to. Margaret was small and had dark hair, but I soon began to discover the saying that 'blondes have more fun' seemed to be right as far as I was concerned, or at least I had more fun with them. In fact, my first bit of crude fondling involved a rather cheeky blonde girl who one day invited me to explore the delights of her body while we were under the school stage.

It was a case of grope and hope on my part, with a French kiss thrown in for good measure. Going under the stage was a regular thing at school for many kids who wanted to avoid lessons or even have the odd crafty smoke of a cigarette. Ironically, quite a few years later I was invited back to my old school to give a speech and stood right on top of the very place where that fairly innocent sexual encounter had taken place.

I first laced on a pair of boxing gloves when our PE teacher, Mr Sally, decided to organise a tournament. When I entered the competition there were a lot of people who laughed and said I was too small to box, but I was confident I could prove them wrong. I eventually got into the ring with a kid called Ray Callaghan who was about 5 ft 6 in. with red hair and physically a lot bigger than me.

Unfortunately there was no fairytale ending to my ring debut because I lost on points and ended up crying because I was so disappointed. But the boxing bug had bitten and from that day it was a sport I began to get more and more involved in. The idea of being able to box regularly led to me joining a local amateur club with the glamorous name of Dog Kennel Hill, or DKH as they were known.

From that moment boxing started to play a considerable part in my life, but at the time I suppose I saw it as nothing more than another sport I enjoyed taking part in. I certainly wasn't the sort of kid who immediately had dreams of one day becoming a world champion. I was just happy to go to a club regularly for the training, and at the same time learn how to box and take care of myself in the ring.

Little did I realise at the time that the fight game would play such a big part in my life and that I'd go on to earn my living from it. In those days the only financial reward that concerned me was the weekly pocket money Mum dished out, the paper round I did, a milk round and the cash I managed to claim as an altar boy.

Even at that stage I was keen to start making some money, so Eugene and I dabbled in all sorts of jobs to try and top up the coffers. I can remember washing cars fairly regularly and we also tried our luck with a stall in the local market selling anything we could lay our hands on. It was usually a load of old junk that other people had thrown out of their houses, but we were happy to get it and more than pleased to take it away for them.

I can't say I was too academic and school was never a favourite place of mine. For a long time I found it a struggle to come to terms with things other children seemed to find easy, and it wasn't until much later that I discovered the reason for a lot of my learning difficulties was the fact that I suffered from dyslexia.

My school career ended at the tender age of 15, which in those days was the earliest you could leave. Despite my lack of qualifications I'd enjoyed all the sporting activities and by the time I left, my footballing abilities almost gave me the chance to play for Wimbledon, who were then a non-league outfit.

I had a trial for them one snowy Saturday morning and played on the wing in what I thought were very difficult conditions. The guy who was running the game was nice when it came to discussing my efforts, and said that maybe I was a little too small. He told me to come back and have another game when I'd grown a bit, but little did he know that by then I'd virtually reached my full height anyway!

With one sporting avenue closed to me, my dad decided it might be a good idea to pursue another in a profession where my lack of inches could actually prove to be a real advantage. He had always been interested in horse racing and a friend of his, a Rotherhithe bookmaker called Eddie Reid, told him there was a stable in Epsom who were always looking to take on youngsters as apprentice jockeys.

Dad had already spelled things out to me in no uncertain terms about how he thought it was time I started to look for a 'proper' job, and to him the idea of his son becoming a jockey fitted nicely into that category.

As far as he was concerned I had started to spend too much time with my mates and some local girls hanging around the streets of Peckham, as well as going to favourite weekend haunts like the Savoy Rooms in Catford. Getting me away from all of that must have seemed like the perfect solution to him at the time, so I was packed off to the famous green Downs of Epsom.

I must admit that becoming a jockey had some appeal to me and it seemed like a decent way of earning a living. Coupled with that was the fact that I knew many of the young jockeys took part in boxing tournaments, and the 'stablelads' show was an annual event on the London amateur boxing scene. I was eager to sample life as an apprentice, but my views on becoming a part of the sport of kings changed rapidly.

Don't get me wrong, I think Epsom is a lovely place with lots to offer, but I quickly found out that was certainly not the case if you were trying to make it as a jockey. My dreams of becoming the next Lester Piggott were shattered faster than it took me to muck out a stable. I couldn't wait to leave the place after having to endure what I considered to be nothing more than slave labour for about six weeks.

It might not have seemed that bad to some of the other apprentices, but to me it was the kind of regime that was not only unfair, but also demeaning in the way we were all treated. The whole place just seemed to rub me up the wrong way, and it wasn't long before I swapped the green acres of Epsom for the more familiar grey brickwork of Peckham and south London.

Throughout this time I'd been sharpening up my boxing skills by regularly training at the DKH club, and I'd also started to have properly regulated amateur bouts for them. I got encouragement from my first contest, which I won, and I managed to maintain the unbeaten run in my next seven bouts. But it wasn't all about success and I can vividly remember losing a novice contest to a kid from the Arbour Youth Club in east London. The thing that stands out in my memory was the fact that he looked so much bigger than me. He was also perfectly kitted-out with a vest in his club colours, while I was just a skinny little kid with a white vest, shorts, and plimsolls on my feet instead of proper boxing boots.

I'm not saying the way I was dressed stopped me from winning, but it certainly made me feel a little inferior to him, because he looked the part more than I did. From that moment on I decided to take boxing a bit more seriously and Mum and Dad were generous enough to cough up the money for me to invest in a pair of boxing shorts and boots. DKH was a great club and allowed me to get a real taste of the sport.

I took part in the London Federation of Boys' Clubs Championships, losing to Dave Smith from Eltham, once at Café Royal and then at the Hilton Hotel, both times on points. He was a solid boxer who looked good even at that very early age, and he later went on to become a very decent professional.

I also took part in the junior ABAs, where I met a youngster called Jimmy Flint from Bethnal Green's famous Repton Boxing Club in a bout which took place in Luton. The fight was short and sweet – at least it was for him. All I can recall of the contest was the opening bell, a few punches being thrown by both of us, and then waking up in the back of the van that had taken me to Luton for the tournament.

Flint knocked me spark out, and it was the first time I'd ever experienced anything like it. The kid seemed to be able to hit like a mule, although I apparently helped his cause by committing the cardinal boxing sin of walking straight onto his punch. It may have been the first time I'd experienced the shock of an unexpected whack, but it wasn't to be the last and in the years that have followed there have been quite a few – all out of the ring and one of them from a woman!

The lady in question was the partner of boxer Kirkland Laing, who was a gifted but erratic Jamaican fighter. I was promoting him on a show in north London against one of my own up-and-coming fighters called Kevin Lueshing. We'd increased security at the venue on the night because I was having trouble with a former business partner I'd barred from the show. Kevin eventually won the fight and I was sitting at ringside feeling pleased with his victory when I felt an almighty left hook explode onto the side of my face, and the next thing I heard was a woman screaming at me.

'You've robbed Kirkland,' she shouted. 'You've set him up.'

The security people ran over and took her away before apologising for the fact that they'd let her get to me. They'd thought she just wanted to give a sympathetic hug to Kirkland and never dreamed she was hell-bent on giving me a clump instead.

The guy who had been banned from that show was someone called Ambrose Mendy and on another occasion at Crofton Park Leisure Centre he got rather upset and decided to lash out, catching me in the face.

While Ambrose was no heavyweight, someone else who decided violence was the best way to settle a grievance with me certainly was. His name was Billy Aird, a likeable Scouser who fought professionally in the 1970s and 1980s before becoming a pub landlord in south London. He was also a boxing manager and promoter who staged shows in the same sort of places I did on the small hall circuit.

He had a boxer named Johnny Melfah who'd left Bill and switched to my camp. It was all good local fun and I decided to get some publicity out of it by playing up the angle that Johnny hadn't made much money during his time with Aird. We even stunted up a picture for a newspaper of Melfah on a park bench saying he couldn't afford to pay his rent. I think Billy got an apology from the paper but it left a bitter taste in his mouth and he had a go at me one day when we were both at a boxing show.

Billy's always been a passionate guy and when he started to clench his fist I knew what was coming and managed to turn away just as his punch glanced off the side of my face. If he'd managed to catch me properly I would have been out cold, but I managed to stay on my feet.

'If that's how hard you punch, Bill, it's no wonder you never did anything as a heavyweight!' I told him.

As far as I was concerned that was the end of the matter, but my headstrong younger brother Eugene got to hear about it, and along with a friend of his, paid Billy a visit at his pub. A few strong words were exchanged, but Billy and I are able to laugh about the whole thing now.

The shock I received from the Luton episode didn't put me off the fight game and Jimmy Flint went on to win all sorts of titles and establish himself as one of the hardest punching featherweights around. The incident also made me realise I needed to start making a bit more progress. Fortunately, I met a trainer called Gerry Hogan, who looked after fighters at the Polytechnic Club in Regents Street and also the Fisher Club in Bermondsey.

Fisher had strong Catholic ties and made an annual trip to the Downside Monastery and public school in Somerset where we'd compete against the boys at boxing, football and rugby. The first time I went, we won the boxing event and I got a stoppage victory in a bout with one of their kids, but we lost the football and rugby matches.

It was a great trip for all of us because it was so different to our usual environment, but we made the big mistake of getting well and truly stuck into the local scrumpy cider and were soon out of our heads on the stuff. We started to run riot with all the alcohol inside us, raiding the dormitories and ringing the famous monastery bells. Apparently they were used each morning at 4 a.m. to call the monks to prayer but we started doing it at about 1 a.m. and they all began to get up!

We weren't looked on too kindly when we arrived for breakfast all nursing hangovers, and there were a few bruises on the public schoolboys that bore testimony to the fact that we had really got out of control the night before. Not surprisingly, the trip was cancelled the following year.

I trained at both clubs under Gerry and actually got through to a senior Feds Final at the London Hilton, where I met Dave Smith for the second time. I'd boxed and lost against him in my first Class 'B' Feds final at the Café Royal, and my second clash with Dave was just as disappointing for me, and once again I missed out when I was outpointed by him.

Although I loved my boxing, despite the disappointment, I was also heavily into football, playing for a club that was part of St James's church where I was an altar boy. The priest, Father Clements, was a nice man who encouraged me to take part in as many sports as I could, but it was always boxing and football that really held my interest.

Father Clements actually did a lot for the kids in the area, including starting a football league for local teams which really blossomed over the years and it certainly helped to keep the kids off the streets and give their lives more purpose. He would also organise day trips during the school holidays to places like Box Hill in Surrey, which we loved and looked forward to with a lot of anticipation. We were a bit boisterous on a train one year and got accused of being little hooligans by a rather snooty woman. Father Clements immediately spoke up for us saying we weren't hooligans, just excited young kids who were looking forward to having a day in the country. He earned a lot of respect from the boys who came into contact with him, and I'm sure he stopped quite a few from going off the rails.

As well as actually playing football I'd become a fanatical Millwall supporter by this time, going to all the home games and making as many away trips as I could. I continued to box after I'd left school having flunked every exam put in front of me. I just couldn't wait to get away and explore the great wide world outside the school gates.

After the unfortunate experience in Epsom my dad spoke to another of his friends, this time someone who was in the catering trade and he suggested I might like the idea of becoming a chef. So, equipped with the regulation outfit that included a hat which seemed bigger than me, I got a job in the West End of London at St Giles Court, in Shaftsbury Avenue, which was a Ministry of Defence establishment. At the same time I began attending Westminster Catering College to study for my City and Guilds certificates.

It seemed like a good opportunity for me, although I must admit that when I arrived I started to have my doubts, especially when I was told to start preparing about 600 sausages. As I was changing into my oversized trousers one of the second head chefs, a guy called Eric, made a crack about them being big enough for two people to get into. I thought no more about it and accepted his offer of a piece of string to help tie them up around my waist. A little while later when I was getting on with the brain-numbing job of rolling the sausages Eric appeared behind me, put his hand on my backside, and made some very strange remarks.

I couldn't believe what was happening, but pretty soon the initial shock was replaced by a raging anger, and I immediately reached for a knife that was close by. Before randy Eric could make his next move or get any more ideas about what he'd like to do with his own little sausage, I stuck the knife right into the back of the hand he was using to lean against the table I was working on.

His scream must have been heard by everyone in the building, and just to emphasise the point I was trying to make I warned him that if he tried anything like it again, I'd stick the knife very precisely up another part of his anatomy. Not surprisingly, after that little incident Eric decided to leave me alone to continue my apprenticeship, and I was taken under the wing of a female West Indian cook who remained a friend and went on to work for me at a later date. I actually began to enjoy catering, particularly when I was given the opportunity to learn the management side of things.

With the job came some money and because of my new-found wealth I was quick to start experiencing some of the more enjoyable pleasures of life, even if I was only 15 at the time. Although my brother Eugene was younger than me, he always seemed to have cash, and a lot of it came from some of the street scams he devised which I helped him with on occasions.

I can remember the time we sold a whole batch of stuff outside London Bridge station one evening just before Christmas to some unsuspecting soul who took one look at what we had on offer and decided to buy all 12 boxes from us. The trouble was, as he later no doubt found out, only the top box contained any goods because the rest were full of junk. It was real 'Del Boy' stuff, just like the characters in the TV comedy, *Only Fools and Horses*, even down to the fact that we were doing a lot of this in Peckham where the series is set. But our scams were for real and happily for us we got money from them as well.

We had a stall selling anything and everything near East Street market and also did some trading out of suitcases, which was known as fly-pitching. Eugene and I would take it in turns to look out for the police, while the other would try to sell goods from the case as quickly as possible. We got caught out once because we weren't quick enough running away with the suitcase we were using to trade from. It meant having to appear at a Magistrates' court the same day and although we pleaded poverty he obviously wasn't going to be fooled. Instead, he fined us the amount we had in our pockets, which was an absolute bundle.

Getting up to little scams like that was all part of growing up and we were really no different to any of our mates that we hung around with. Although it was a bit like 'Del Boy' in many ways, I have to say that the way we learned to duck and dive and survive on the streets made us a lot shrewder than the TV character.

There was a kind of pecking order with the younger guys learning from the older ones, as you gradually became a part of the scene. As a kid we did things like nicking empty lemonade bottles from the crates at the back of shops where they sold them, then nipping round the front and taking them into the shop because you used to get some money back on the bottles. We later progressed to doing things like stripping lead off roofs, and taking scaffolding from building sites and selling it on to another.

Some of the guys around at the time always seemed to have money and they were very conscious of their appearance. Having stylish clothes meant a lot to them and their sense of dress and the amount of time they spent on it would have given David Beckham a run for his money. There was one guy called Bobby Scanlon who always seemed to have the best clothes, a nice car and great-looking women hanging around him. Although nobody could have claimed to have had a great formal education, the people I knew and had as friends were very street-wise. What they lacked in qualifications, they more than made up for in other ways and were always able to earn a very decent living.

While Eugene carried on 'ducking and diving,' I started to settle into my career in catering. I was also beginning to get really interested in girls. I'd had a few mild flirtations while I was at school, but they were nothing out of the ordinary, although one liaison did result in me getting the sharp end of my dad's tongue when he found me out with a girl one night enjoying a kiss and cuddle just around the corner from our home, when I should have been studying or sleeping.

Sometime before I had moved to my secondary school the family left Camberwell Green and set up home a short distance away in Peckham. The new place was a large house owned by St James's church and the downstairs area was used as a social club by them. It covered a huge area with a full-size snooker table, a basement room with a table-tennis table, and enough room outside to play things like badminton.

Having all those facilities made us very popular with our mates and they started to come around to our house on a regular basis. I was left in charge once when my mother and father went away to Ireland for a holiday, and was pressurised by a few of the 'chaps' to have a party on the Saturday night. Everything was going well until an argument broke out which ended in one of the windows being smashed. It was a disaster and I knew I'd be in real trouble with my parents, but the next day a friend of mine named Micky Griffin turned up with his dad and helped me clear up. They also installed some new glass and by the time my mum and dad got back, everything looked back to normal. I thought I was off the hook, but hadn't bargained for some nosy neighbours who told my dad everything. He also spotted the wet putty in the window frame, which was a dead giveaway, and I quickly realised the game was up.

Parties were a big thing and when you began to be invited to them, you really knew you'd arrived. We'd quite often bundle into cars at the end of a night out and drive off to a party someone was having. Some of the cars would have double the amount of people they should have had in them and there was never any thought about drinking and driving, because everyone did it back then and it was an accepted part of having a night out. I had to get into the boot of a car for my first experience of one of these parties because I was small enough to fit in and all the seats had been taken by other people. I was worried they might forget about me and kept shouting out to remind them just in case.

Cars were always very important to us and having them gave you a lot more freedom, although on one occasion we all decided to go for something a bit bigger after leaving a party in the early hours. Not being able to get a taxi, we decided to nick a bus out of the local garage to get us home and drove off in it before finally getting stopped by the police. They charged the guy who was driving, but the rest of us were luckier and got let off with a warning. There were also things like prize fights and dog fights organised above snooker halls. These were a regular part of the scene and we all used to go.

By this time I had resigned myself to the fact that I would not be playing football professionally for a living, and instead continued to turn out for my boys club. It was a combination of my love of football and women that led to me meeting my first wife when I was 17 and she was just 14.

I'd gone to a football club dance with Eugene and a mate of his called Tony Hudson, who boxed with us at the Fisher club. The two of them also played together for the same team. Tony, like Eugene, was a few years younger than me but both were real characters who were always the life and soul of any party.

They were very much alike in many ways and were to get into several scrapes together during the years that followed. While my youngest brother Vince was never any real trouble, Eugene had shown from day one that he could be a real handful. He never seemed to be a kid for long and although he was younger than me he just seemed very advanced for his age when it came to the ways of the world – or at least our little world. He was certainly the only kid around our way who was driving a car at the age of 14.

In fact, it wasn't just any old car; instead it was a gleaming white Bentley! I'll never forget the day my dad pulled me to one side and asked if I knew anything about Eugene having a car. I remember laughing, as I explained Eugene was just too young to be driving. But my father was deadly serious. He'd been told by some people in the area that they'd seen my tearaway brother driving around alongside Tony in a white Bentley, with some girls in the back seat. I genuinely thought the story was too far-fetched to be true, but just a few days later I happened to be walking along a road quite close to our home and there in front of me was a gleaming white Bentley, with my brother Eugene sitting proudly behind the wheel.

When I asked him what was going on he told me in a very matter-of-fact way that he and Tony had bought it with money from some 'bits and pieces' they'd been up to, but asked me not to tell our dad. He also offered to give me a ride in the car, but I declined, knowing what our father's reaction would be if he were to see his sons cruising around south London in a white Bentley.

Eugene always seemed capable of going that one step beyond anything I would ever dream of doing, and quite often it would lead to him getting into trouble.

Tony Hudson was often a willing accomplice in some of their schemes and on one occasion they had been up to no good in London and had their pockets full of certain things they shouldn't have had. They had both got jobs working for a diamond merchant and it didn't take them too long to work out a way to boost their weekly wages. You can just imagine how they felt when a policeman tapped them on the shoulder at Holborn Underground station.

The two of them froze, expecting the worst, but were then relieved to see the familiar face of a copper called Johnny Banham, who was a boxing trainer and coach to the Metropolitan Police team. All he wanted from them was their help in lining up for an identity parade that they were holding at the local Holborn Police Station. Not only were they happy to oblige, but they talked boxing with Johnny all the way there and back, as he politely dropped them at the station after they'd finished. The two of them couldn't stop laughing the whole way home on the train with their ill-gotten gains still tucked safely into their pockets.

The pair of them managed to make my love life a misery one evening when they turned up at our house drunk and giggling, just as I was beginning to get rather serious with a young lady on the sofa in our front room. When I asked them what the hell they were playing at, all they could do was laugh and then they started to throw what looked like tiny pieces of glass onto the table in front of me. I didn't know whether they were diamonds but they were obviously pretty precious to them, because when I picked up a fistful and threw them out the window, it immediately had a sobering effect on the pair.

They went scrambling down the stairs and into the garden trying to retrieve whatever I'd thrown through the window. As I looked out at them crawling around on hands and knees I had no sympathy and just thought it served them right. The only valuables I was interested in getting my hands on had by that time been well and truly covered up by the young girl on the couch, who was furiously trying to re-arrange her clothes following my fumbling attempt to remove them. To this day Eugene swears not all of those stones were recovered on the night, so there might still be some hidden treasure to be found in that Peckham garden.

Soon after we arrived at the football dance I spotted this terrific-looking girl who was just my sort: small, blonde and very pretty. She was also wearing hot pants, which were all the rage at the time, and they made her look even sexier. She was with four or five of her friends but I immediately went over and introduced myself. I found out that her name was Jackie and she was none other than Tony's little sister, which just went to show what a small world it was and one that would often prove to be difficult to live in at times during later years.

I suppose I shouldn't have been too surprised by the fact that we all knew of each other, because everybody seemed to know everyone else in Peckham. It wasn't exactly a big place and we tended to do the same sort of things. As I've said, you kind of graduated and progressed as you got older, but there were certain routines and rituals that almost everyone got involved in. I remember one particular fad among a lot of the boys was having a bull terrier dog and walking them on Peckham Rye. I had a white one called 'Peggy', and the idea was to have really flash collars for them.

The café at Peckham Rye railway station was also a favourite haunt for all of us. As well as serving food and drink you could usually find someone in there who could get you anything you wanted, from a decent pair of shoes to things like televisions and cars. I bet half the homes in Peckham got their TVs from the place!

Watching Millwall was a big part of regular life for most of the boys. As soon as I was old enough I started watching them home and away. The older guys were real role models on the terraces and when I first started to go there as a kid the club had a big following among the dockers, whose language left little to the imagination. Millwall supporters have always had a bit of a reputation, and I can recall the time the Northern Ireland striker, Derek Dougan, got a clump from one of the supporters down at the Den, because he obviously wasn't happy with what was going on. I was guilty of jumping the wall one day and giving the manager at the time, Benny Fenton, a mouthful of abuse because I didn't like the way the team was playing.

The club produced some real characters both on and off the field, and as fans we used to worship some of the players, who were heroes to all of us. The players and supporters had a great relationship and there was never any hint of the sort of big money that floats around the game these days. One of the players I watched at Millwall was a winger named Joe Broadfoot. He had a couple of spells with the club and I can remember him telling me some years later that part of the deal in one of his transfers was that he got £1,000 and two second-hand Mini cars. A bit different to some of the perks expected by today's Premiership stars!

I suppose it might have been easy for me to get caught up in the whole football hooligan thing had it not been for boxing. Going to matches was a very tribal thing and there was a definite buzz to being there with all of your mates. Although we didn't look for trouble, there was no hesitation on our part in getting stuck in and helping out if it did get a bit naughty. I did get worried once at a game when I was part of a mob of fans who went running down the Old Kent Road and managed to smash some car showroom windows, but we avoided being caught by the police.

As well as our nights out locally I would regularly go to the West End of London to shop for clothes at the weekends, and then go to some clubs at night. In 1966 I financed one of my shopping trips by cashing in on a cup final ticket. I'd managed to get my hands on a couple through the football club I played for and my dad managed. He'd won them in a draw and passed them on to me and a friend of mine so that we could go along for the big day at Wembley and watch the match between Everton and Sheffield Wednesday. But just as we got to the famous old stadium I was offered a lot more than the face value to part with the pair. My mate, Micky Griffin, was keen to see the match and wanted to hold on to his ticket, but the temptation of getting my hands on some easy money was too much for me to resist and I quickly said yes to the desperate supporter. I headed off to the West End to spend the money on clothes, before meeting up with Micky to find out what had happened and what the result was in case my dad asked me about the match.

Like so many young working-class kids of my age, the first experience I had of foreign travel was a two week holiday to Benidorm in Spain, which saw a few of us get kicked out of the hotel for being too rowdy, and ended with me feeling as though I needed a holiday when I got back to England because the trip had been so exhausting. The holiday had been all about booze, sex and sun.

Pubs were also very much part of the scene and drugs could be found fairly easily if you wanted them. Most people seemed keen on 'speed' because it kept people going and you could stay up all night without getting tired. I was never really into it, although I did try it once and I don't think I stopped talking for about two days. Thankfully not too many of my friends got into drugs, but a couple did unfortunately get hooked. Most of the guys I grew up with steered clear of them and we've all ended up doing very different things, like boxing, money broking and antique trading. A couple got on the wrong side of the law and spent some time in prison for various things, and unfortunately someone else committed suicide. We were just a typical bunch of young south London guys growing up in the 1960s and 1970s. I can look back on the time with a lot of affection, and the experiences I had gave me the sort of street education I wouldn't have missed for the world.

Things started to change for me around the time I met Jackie at the dance and my dedication to boxing began to tail off a bit. I drifted away from some of my mates as I became more and more serious with Jackie. I was working in the catering business, at the Adelphi Ministry of Defence building in London's Strand, and had just passed my City and Guilds exams.

My relationship with Jackie really started to flourish, and although there were other girls that I went out with, she became special and over the next year or so we began seeing a lot of each other. It didn't exactly meet with the approval of her family and I suppose they were a bit suspicious of me and what I might get up to. In the end Jackie and I began to drift apart and we saw less and less of each other, which was mainly due to her parents.

I continued to enjoy my job and some time later the Ugandan dictator, General Amin, started to make a name for himself throughout the world for all the wrong reasons, when he decided to expel Asians from his country. It meant an immediate influx of refugees arriving in Britain where many were put into camps which were scattered around the country. One of these Government-run camps happened to be in Honiton, Devon, and I was asked whether I fancied the idea of transferring there to become one of the chefs at the site which had about 900 people staying on it. It was a big step-up and also provided a good opportunity to show what I was capable of. I said yes straight away and was soon heading off on a train from Waterloo station in London down to Devon and the unknown wilds of the West Country.

When I first arrived I couldn't believe how quiet it all was compared to London, but that soon changed once I'd settled in. There wasn't much nightlife, except for an isolated pub where the management team and I spent a lot of our time in the evenings drinking, chatting amongst ourselves and flirting with the local girls.

To my surprise the biggest flirting came from an unexpected source one morning as I was getting ready to go to breakfast. I shared one of the cottages on camp with a manager and was just getting myself ready when the cleaning lady arrived. She was far from glamorous, and was probably older than my own mother, but that didn't stop her flirting and telling me just what I was missing chasing young girls, because older women could teach lads of my age so much.

Like so many other young guys it had always been a fantasy of mine to sleep with an older woman, and *The Graduate* is still one of my favourite movies, but my cleaning lady was more Nora Batty than Anne Bancroft and we didn't exactly sleep with each other; it was more like a grappling match.

Before I knew where I was her cleaning overalls were fluttering at her side and my trousers were dangling around my ankles as we fumbled with each other against the bedroom wall. Just as the activity was getting even more frenzied we heard the front door open and the voice of the manager I was sharing the cottage with.

She quickly told me that I would have to leave, which seemed a little strange seeing as how I was staying there, but then she explained that she'd been sleeping with this particular manager since the day he had arrived on camp. I gathered up some of the clothes that had dropped to the floor, and with my trousers still hanging around my ankles, I jumped through the bedroom window and crouched below, just as my colleague took up where he'd left off the night before with the cleaner. It was all so crazy that I had to laugh, but it also made me even more determined to become a manager. It was obvious the position had a lot more perks than I'd expected.

In terms of the job I was doing there I was quite pleased with myself, and after introducing some ideas of my own in the first few days, things began to go well as I stamped my mark on the whole operation. But it started to go dramatically wrong the day I decided to try and allow the refugees some greater scope in what went on by involving them in the catering.

NO BALONEY

My brilliant idea was to use the culinary skills of the people who were living in the camp and in doing so give their fellow refugees a taste of some real home cooking. Unfortunately, my master plan failed to take account of the deep religious divides that existed among so many of them, and instead of the taste of Asia that I'd hoped for in the dining area, I managed to incite a near riot!

The problem was that I somehow mixed up Hindu and Muslim dishes, handing them out without realising the strict code of eating habits that went with the different religions. It caused all sorts of problems, and the night actually ended with plates being thrown and arguments raging everywhere as I stepped out of the kitchen to see what all the noise was about.

We eventually managed to restore some calm and order, with a promise that the policy would not be continued and a reassurance that normal service would be resumed. But the disaster helped me learn an important lesson, and that was to find out first what people want instead of just wading in with ideas of my own. Despite all the fuss over that mealtime fracas, I managed to enjoy my time in Honiton and I still have fond memories of the two months I spent in Devon.

When I got back to London I took up my first managerial job, transferring to Gower Street and enjoying some of those perks that seemed to come with being the boss. I started having a fling with my supervisor who was a few years older than me, but certainly provided a decent enough incentive to get into work early.

I also had the chance to visit 10 Downing Street when Ted Heath was Prime Minister and I was one of the chefs sent there to help out with a banquet they had. Although things were going quite well for me professionally, it certainly wasn't the case when it came to my personal life. After returning from Devon, I discovered that my mum and dad's relationship had deteriorated. Mum had moved out of the house, and the priest who was in charge of the property gave Dad one month to leave.

My parents' split hit me hard and also stunned both of my brothers. As I've said, we had a fairly typical south London childhood with the family being a big thing for all of us, so you can imagine the shock the three of us felt when we found out that our mum and dad would be getting a divorce.

THE PUNCHING PRIEST

It seemed like one minute we were a normal family and then all of a sudden there was no house and no family home. I was about 19 at the time and it was a pretty devastating feeling. I was studying for some more City and Guilds catering qualifications, but my parents splitting up meant we all went our separate ways.

I had to move out of our house and eventually found a horrible flat in north London, just a stone's throw from the Arsenal Football Club in Highbury. Eugene moved out, made money and started to get into all sorts of mischief. He also soon became a father with the birth of the first of six children he was to have. He was only 16 at the time, but as I've said he wasn't a kid for long and soon began to have the sort of lifestyle and experiences of someone way beyond his years.

My little flat wasn't exactly in the most salubrious of locations, but I needed somewhere to stay and I also had to start looking after my kid brother Vince, who came to live with me and was still at school. The two of us shared the flat with a larger-than-life character called Alan Ferris, who was later to become godfather to my daughter. Having Mum and Dad split up was a tremendous shock to all of us, and maybe as the eldest it hit me even harder, but I was also beginning to start a new sort of life and the fact that I was working in a job I enjoyed helped to get me through things.

The flat was a real tip and it's amazing to think now just how bad the conditions were. I've often driven past it in recent years and wondered how we lived there. I'm surprised our landlady was allowed to rent it out in the first place, because it must have been close to being condemned as unfit to live in. She reminded me of a female version of Rigsby from the TV comedy show *Rising Damp*.

It was dirty and smelly, with mice running around as almost constant companions for the unfortunate souls like myself who happened to be living there, but it was all any of us could afford at the time. There was no real electricity and when you did have a bath, quite often the only thing to use as a light was a candle. Poor Vince must have wondered what hit him after the cosiness of the family home we all shared with our parents, but we just had to get on with things. Every day I would go off to work and Vince would make the trek across London to his school.

I'd done quite well with my job and moved into a low-grade

management position at a relatively young age, but I knew that promotion in the Civil Service was usually done on a seniority basis, which meant I would have to wait a long time before moving up the scale. So when the opportunity came to work for the Inland Revenue at Somerset House as a restaurant manager, I grabbed the chance with both hands. As well as a basic salary which was pretty good, my pay was performance related. I also managed to pull off a few deals that helped swell my bank account, and it was while working there that Jackie suddenly re-entered my life.

One day I answered the phone in my office and immediately recognised her voice on the other end of the line. We hadn't spoken or seen each other for over two years, but as soon as I heard her speak I knew I wanted to get her back into my life. I hadn't really had any serious girlfriends since we split up, just a series of fairly varied short-lived flings. I was running regular discos at Somerset House on Friday nights, so I asked Jackie if she wanted to come along and said I thought we had a bit of catching up to do. She agreed and I began to look forward to seeing her once more. The old feelings I had for her were still there and I got the impression she felt the same as I did.

She looked as pretty as ever when I saw her a couple of days later at the disco and that night we ended up staying at my flat. After that I knew Jackie still felt something for me, because she was willing to stay in the horrible hole I called home. We talked a lot and I discovered she was due to be married to someone else, but by the time morning arrived those wedding plans were out of the window and I was determined not to let her go again.

It wasn't too long before her parents found out she was seeing me once more, and they weren't too pleased. Her mum made it clear Jackie had two options as far as she was concerned. Either she stopped seeing me straight away, or she could move out of the family home. With a little gentle persuading from me, she took the brave decision to wave goodbye to her parents and move in with me. She even changed jobs and went to work near our flat in north London.

It was just before Christmas 1974 and I'd already made plans to be in Scotland for the holiday period, which meant poor Jackie was stuck in my flat crying herself to sleep, with only a few mice as companions. It was no surprise that she was constantly on the phone to me, but I couldn't get back because there was no public transport running until after Boxing Day. We were both desperate to see each other and I eventually got the first train out I could, bought a £50 ring in a second-hand jewellers in Holloway Road when I arrived back in London, and then popped the question on New Year's Day.

We decided to get married as quickly as possible and the whole thing was a very rushed affair as we tied the knot on 14 January 1975. The ceremony was followed by lunch at the Adelphi, which was generously paid for by my employers. Ironically, it was also the same building where I'd had a few of my previous conquests during the time I'd been away from Jackie, but I put those thoughts behind me as we all celebrated. After that it was back to the flat where we partied late into the night thanks to some great organisation from Vince and Alan.

We had quite a few people at the hastily arranged reception, including my mum, Dad with his new wife Kathy and my brothers, but neither Jackie's mum and dad nor any of her family were there. Instead, she just had her two best friends attending. My bosses even gave me £100 so that I could have a honeymoon and we decided to go to Salisbury, but the guy at the hotel didn't want to give us a room at first because he said the pair of us didn't look old enough to be married!

On the morning of our registry office wedding Eugene spent all the time he could trying to talk me out of it. He was even muttering dark warnings in my ear about the evils of getting hitched as we were about to take our vows. Despite his efforts we went through with the ceremony and on that January day my life suddenly took a very different direction.

2. KID GLOVES

WITH THE HONEYMOON OVER WE DECIDED TO LET JACKIE'S PARENTS IN ON our secret and told them we'd got married. When she eventually made contact her mum told Jackie she'd better come home. When she dropped the bombshell about us being married it didn't go down too well.

I never found out what her mother said, but I know the reaction wasn't exactly a happy one. On the positive side at least the call had broken the ice, even if Jackie's parents and her family would have preferred to break my neck at the time.

We decided that we couldn't carry on living in our Highbury hovel we shared with Vincent, who was about to begin an apprenticeship as a hairdresser. There was a furniture shop near us who had a great offer going at the time, where they would find you a rented flat if you bought stuff from them. We ended up moving to a place in Ealing, west London, because of this and in comparison to the old flat it felt like a mansion. It wasn't long after the move that Jackie announced she was pregnant. It was a bit of a shock but great news as far as I was concerned and I started to get really excited about the prospect of becoming a father.

NO BALONEY

I was still boxing as an amateur but had started to go to a gym above The Duke of Wellington pub in north London to train, and at the back of my mind was the thought that it might be a good idea for me to consider turning professional. I had a good job and the money wasn't bad, but with the prospect of another mouth to feed it seemed to make sense that I should maybe start to get paid for swapping blows instead of doing it for nothing, and follow in the footsteps of Jackie's brothers. Steve was already a professional and Tony was just about to join the paid ranks as well.

At the time they were the latest in a line of fighters from south London who used to have a very good local following. There was a light-welterweight called Alan Salter, from Peckham, who used to sell a lot of tickets for his fights. He was a bit of a local hero with us and after narrowly missing out in a points loss to Joey Singleton at the Albert Hall, he got a chance to put matters right in a re-match for the British title at Wembley. We all made the trip to cheer him on and were very confident that he'd head back across the River Thames with the title, but Singleton showed his class and stopped Salter in the ninth round.

The Duke of Wellington gym used to have a lot of good boxers training there at various weights, but the star of the show was John Conteh, who at the time was the world light-heavyweight champion. Conteh seemed to have it all. He was young, good looking and had the sort of skill and punching power that should have made him one of the all-time greats. But as so often happens in boxing, conflicts within his own camp eventually led to him going his own way. Although he'll always be remembered as a tremendous fighter there's no doubt in my mind that he could have achieved a lot more than he did. Conteh always looked terrific in the gym and was a real hard worker with George Francis, his trainer, barking out encouragement as they went through their routines.

There was another young fighter called Lee Graham who was usually up there at the same time and I used to be fascinated by the difference in their preparation. It was like comparing Manchester United and Hartlepool. Conteh was looked after and pampered while little Graham pretty much had to fend for himself. Conteh was at the top of his game, while Graham was in there hoping that one day he could make it big and things would be the same for him.

KID GLOVES

A trainer in the gym called Johnny Phillips told me there would be plenty of managers who might be prepared to take me on if I wanted to turn professional, but he also pointed out some of the pitfalls that could be waiting for me.

'See how Conteh gets treated?' said Johnny. 'That's because he brings in a lot of money for the people around him. You can see how the others get treated, and they have to be ready to fight at the drop of a hat if they're needed for shows.'

Then Johnny told me how much some of those boxers could expect to get paid the next time they stepped into the ring for a competitive contest, and said there wasn't much money at my weight. Even dripping wet I knew I was never more than 8 st.

Johnny said it might be best for me to stay amateur and told me his father ran the Civil Service boxing club. He thought it would be a good idea for me to go over there and see how I liked it. I only had a couple of fights for the Civil Service outfit before moving on to the Westminster and Victoria club. I soon got into the swing of things and began to enjoy my boxing, although I was by no means an exceptional talent and my approach left a bit to be desired.

I'm not exactly proud to admit that I was once disqualified for biting an opponent during a contest. Of course, this was long before Mike Tyson's infamous ear-biting incident with Evander Holyfield during their world heavyweight title fight in 1997. My moment came in a grubby little London hall. The referee, Reg Davis, saw the whole sorry episode and had no other option but to disqualify me. To be honest, it wasn't the only time I was disqualified: it happened on two other occasions for various reasons and was probably down to a lack of discipline on my part.

I was still enjoying my job and Jackie was looking forward to becoming a mum, although when the day eventually arrived, the whole thing wasn't quite as ordered as we'd hoped. In fact, it turned out to be a real panic because I didn't drive at the time and we had to get a neighbour to take us to the hospital.

Word soon got around that Jackie was there and somehow about 15 friends and family suddenly descended on the hospital to give me some support. It was nice of them really, although I could probably have done without my mates dressing me up in surgical gear and parading me through the hallway looking like a mad doctor about to perform a major operation. Jackie didn't hang around when it came to delivering our daughter, and baby Emma was born fit and healthy in the early evening of 14 February 1976, at Queen Charlotte's Hospital in west London.

It was a great experience for me and pretty emotional as I held little baby Emma up to the window to let her see the great wide world that was waiting for her outside. I kissed mum and baby, and told Jackie to get some sleep as I promised to see them the next morning. I then promptly disappeared for three days while I partied with my mates. It wasn't the best or most responsible of things to do, but I was a happy man and I wanted to celebrate.

I eventually turned up at the hospital feeling very sheepish and ready to apologise for going missing. When I got there I found one of my boxing clubmates, Guy Williamson, at the bedside clutching a huge pink toy elephant. Guy was a lovely friendly giant of a man. He was a huge heavyweight who must have weighed about 18 st. and after I'd gone on the missing list since Emma's birth, a lot of the other mums started to think he must be the father.

Because we had no car, Emma's first taste of London life came by way of a ride on the tube, and when we got home Jackie spoke to her parents, who had been told they had a granddaughter. They said they wanted to see us and that it was time to bury the hatchet. I started to wonder whether they meant it literally but we met and the cold war between us slowly started to thaw.

With Emma's arrival we decided it was time to take our first steps on the property ladder, so we searched around and found a maisonette in Leytonstone for £7,500. It was quite a lot of money for us at the time, but it felt good to have somewhere we actually owned and could call home. I'd changed my job and was working as an assistant catering manager for an American bank in Stratford, just a few minutes from the new flat.

I was also really keen to keep my boxing going and one day I saw an advertisement in the trade paper, *Boxing News*, for young boxers who wanted to be champions. I wrote away for more information and found out the man behind it was an old Jewish fighter called Benny Caplan. He was desperate to fulfil his dream of finding a young kid and nurturing him towards greatness in the ring. The trouble was he found me instead.

He was a bit of a perfectionist and although I trained hard and seriously under him for a while, I found his regime a bit claustrophobic. He wanted me to live like a champion, but it soon became apparent that things were not going to work out and he would have to look elsewhere for his dream pupil.

On the home front things were pretty good with Emma steadily growing and spending a lot of time with me. I used to take her everywhere, and she would often come to work with me, sitting in the corner and playing away happily. I suppose we were a fairly normal family, but our quiet and cosy existence changed dramatically one warm spring evening in May 1977.

I'd had my usual sort of day at work and wanted to make sure I was home in time to watch football on the TV, because Liverpool were due to take on Mönchengladbach in the European Cup final. On paper it looked like being an exciting game, but little did I know as I walked towards my house that I was going to be in for excitement of a completely different kind as soon as I put the key in the lock.

Perhaps I should have known something was up, because our road seemed incredibly quiet, and when I went into the corner shop for a paper and some chocolate the woman behind the counter, who was normally very talkative and friendly, seemed a little cold and apprehensive towards me.

Our home was only a few hundred yards from the shop and I was looking forward to putting my feet up, relaxing in front of the TV and having a cup of tea. When I got there I was a bit surprised to see the curtains were pulled because it was still light, and as soon as I opened my front door all hell broke loose. I was jumped on by two burly guys, who I quickly found out were policemen, and they wrestled me to the floor. I was so frightened and surprised that I didn't really put up any resistance and they were soon reading me my rights.

'Eugene Maloney,' said one of them, 'you're under arrest.'

I didn't really hear the rest of it because by that time my mind was in a daze after what had happened in the few seconds since I'd stepped through the door. They said they were from the regional crime squad and it was clear this was all very heavy stuff. Although I'd heard them call me Eugene, for some reason I never once tried to tell them that I was his older brother Frank. The reason may sound strange, but it was simply that, as kids, we were always brought up not to tell tales.

Perhaps it was fear or the fact that things had happened so quickly, but for whatever reason I just sat there stunned as they bundled me into a police car. I did ask where Jackie and Emma were and they said both of them had been taken to the police station in Leytonstone and were being looked after.

I was unceremoniously thrown in a cell while I waited to be questioned and saw that I had to share it with a gruesome-looking black guy who towered over me. I was scared stiff and when he asked me what I was in for, I blurted out a complete lie.

'I've murdered a copper,' I said.

The guy's face turned from black to grey and he jumped up pretty quickly to let me lie down on the rotten old bed that was propped up in the corner. The crazy thing was I was never actually questioned, just left to stew in the cell all night. A policeman did come along at one stage and I managed to find out that Emma had gone to her grandparents, while Jackie had been allowed to go just after midnight. I was worried about what had happened, but at the same time knew the police had made a terrible mistake.

I later found out that while all this was happening to me, my brother had telephoned my mother to find out what was going on. When she told him I'd been arrested Eugene simply said not to worry, because the police would have to release me as soon as they discovered their mistake. In the meantime, he was going to leg it over to Spain and stay there for as long as he could.

Sure enough, the next morning the police had to let me go, but there were no apologies, just a warning that they knew Eugene had been staying in my home and that they would come after me if they could link me with him.

When I eventually got home, the place was an absolute mess because the police had pulled it apart and not bothered to clear things up, even though they'd got the wrong guy and made a mistake. They even dug our garden up and the sight of armed men running around the place was enough to send the old lady who lived next door scurrying under her bed for safety.

It wasn't the last time Eugene and I were involved in a case of mistaken identity and many years later he came running into my office one day asking me to hide him because he had the police after him. Apparently he'd got into an argument with a traffic warden and had started to push the guy around. The warden spotted a copper further down the road and ran to get his assistance. My brother quickly realised he could be in trouble and dived through the door and into my office. When the policeman turned up with the warden I was carted off to the station for questioning, but as soon as we got there and I started to talk the traffic warden realised he'd made a mistake. Unlike Eugene, I didn't have a gap between two of my front teeth. They had to let me go after realising the warden had made a mistake and they'd got the wrong man.

The police finally got their man for that 1977 incident when they tracked down Eugene and charged him with three offences. He was found not guilty on two of the charges, but wasn't so lucky with the third and spent around 16 months behind bars.

Eugene ended up in prison on the Isle of Wight and towards the end of his sentence, to prepare him for his release, the authorities granted a weekend home leave. It was seen as a way of trying to help someone who has been inside adjust to life on the outside once more. Needless to say my brother had slightly different ideas, and he saw it as the perfect opportunity to get to know a girl he had been writing to while he'd been behind bars.

I knew nothing about this and when Eugene suggested that Jackie, Emma and I pop over to see him and his girlfriend, Mary, on the Saturday afternoon of his 48-hour pass I thought we were in for an innocent family get together.

As soon as we arrived my brother told Jackie and Mary that he and I were going out for a few hours to meet some mates of his and have a few drinks. I still thought nothing more of it, and we told the girls to book a babysitter for the evening so that when we got back we could all go out for a meal. But as soon as we were outside Eugene asked me whether my house was empty and then said we were going to east London to meet a couple of girls.

NO BALONEY

There are certain women who seem to get turned on by the idea of having a relationship with a prisoner, even if it is only through writing letters. Eugene explained that quite a lot of his correspondence with this woman had been pretty saucy and he'd not only arranged to see this particular girl, but also suggested she bring along a friend for me.

'I've arranged to meet them in this pub in Leytonstone, we can go there and have a look and if we don't like them we can leave,' he told me.

I might have been a married man with a little daughter, but the thought of going along to have a couple of drinks and a bit of a flirt with these girls just seemed like a bit of fun. I thought they would probably be a bit strange and not too attractive. We duly arrived at the Green Man pub in Leytonstone High Street, but there was no sign of the two women. Eugene seemed to get restless and decided he'd go and see a couple of people he knew who lived close by. He left me behind just in case the girls turned up, and I was happy to sit quietly in the bar and sip my drink.

Not long after he'd left the pub two girls did turn up, and both of them looked very attractive. I wasn't sure it was them, but I didn't have to wait too long because they came straight over and asked if I was Eugene Maloney. The fact that I wasn't didn't seem to put them off too much and once I'd explained I was his brother they seemed more than happy to keep chatting while we waited for him.

When Eugene eventually phoned the pub to see how things were going, I told him the girls were really nice and he certainly wouldn't be disappointed when he saw them. I could almost hear my brother dribbling down the phone with excitement. He suggested I took them back to my house and waited for him.

From the moment we got back it was clear the two of them had other things on their minds, and it wasn't long before Eugene's penfriend decided that actions spoke louder than words. She knelt down in front of me and started playing with my trousers while her mate stuck her tongue in my ear. I couldn't believe what was happening, but I was determined to enjoy it. I soon found myself stark naked and tied to the bed by my hands and feet, as the two of them started to live out some of the fantasies they must have described to Eugene in the letters.

KID GLOVES

When the doorbell suddenly rang I was in no position to answer it and I began to panic. Luckily I soon heard my brother's voice shouting to let him in. Eugene has never been the sort of person who is lost for words, but I can honestly say the sight that greeted him that day left him speechless. There I was, tied face down on a bed with one of my new-found lady friends giving my arse an almighty slap!

It didn't take Eugene long to join in the action, with the two girls determined to make sure his first taste of freedom after all those months inside was going to be something he would not forget.

Time certainly flies when you're enjoying yourself and we woke up in the early hours of the morning realising Jackie and Mary weren't going to be too pleased at being left waiting. We jumped in a mini cab and headed back to south London to face the music, knowing we had to try and come up with some kind of excuse. Finally Eugene said he had one.

'Hit me in the face,' he said as we stepped out of the car.

'What?' I asked.

'You hit me and then I'll whack you. We can rip each other's shirts, roll around for a bit and then tell them we were in a fight and had to make a statement to the police about it.'

The whole thing sounded totally crazy, but when you're in a hole it's amazing what you'll do to get out of it. We carried out our little plan and Eugene got a really sympathetic reception from Mary, but I wasn't so lucky with Jackie. She flew into a rage, called me a bastard among other things and then whacked me on the side of the head with a saucepan.

'I don't know what you've been up to,' she screamed. 'All I know is it wasn't anything good.'

I'd passed my driving test at about the fifth or sixth attempt and was determined to make the most of my new found mobility. I was working at the American Bank in their catering department and tried to think of ways to make some extra money, so I decided to add a few more quid to the family coffers by branching out a bit and starting a home gardening business.

I press-ganged my dad and an Irish neighbour called Paddy Doyle into helping me with my little venture. The idea was to place adverts in the local papers asking if people wanted their gardens sorted out for them. We ended up having more jobs than we could handle and it didn't last too long. Dad and Paddy were always the ones doing the work. I usually played my part by sweet-talking the lady of the house and sipping tea with her in the kitchen, while the other two toiled away outside quietly cursing me under their breath.

The garden venture came to an end one day after we had a job at a large house in Chigwell cutting the grass while the woman who'd hired us went out shopping. By this time Dad and Paddy had got a bit fed up with me drinking tea in kitchens and they insisted on me getting my hands dirty by using a Rotavator to churn up the ground. Unfortunately I managed to get a bit carried away with my new toy and ended up cutting right through the woman's prized rose bushes.

Dad and Paddy were horrified because they knew the woman was about to return to the house, but I told them not to worry, and instead got them to rip the rest of the roses out. When the lady of the house returned I ran over and told her the truth, or rather, my version of it.

'I'm terribly sorry, madam,' I said. 'I've got some bad news for you. I'm afraid your roses were badly infested with green fly. If we hadn't done something you would have had a terrible problem with the rest of your garden.'

She was so pleased with my swift action, we actually ended up getting a bonus for being so professional.

Although I enjoyed my job with the bank, I was feeling a bit restless and began looking for a change. My former boss at Somerset House had become responsible for catering at the DHSS offices at the Elephant and Castle and when he offered me a job I didn't need much persuading to move back to south London. We put our flat in Leytonstone up for sale and made a very decent profit, selling the place for £18,000 in what was probably my first real money-making venture.

I was still boxing and decided to enter the senior ABA Championships at flyweight, managing to get through to the divisional stages on a bye and soon found myself in the London finals. I took a half day off work for the morning weigh-in having spent some time drying out, which is the crazy process of eating and drinking very little in order to make the weight limit.

KID GLOVES

When I got to the offices I found our dessert cook was missing and that meant me filling in for her. I've always had a bit of a sweet tooth and having cooked so much food I was incredibly hungry after all the drying out I'd done. I just couldn't resist the sight of some baked apple and custard I had prepared earlier in the day and tucked in.

To my horror, when I stepped on the scales later in the afternoon, I was three quarters of a pound over the weight. The ABA officials refused to allow me to try and skip the excess off and my chance of glory came to an early end.

While I was changing jobs and using my green fingers, Jackie's mum and dad decided to turn their hands to the licensed trade and took over as landlords of a now extinct pub called The Duke of Wellington in Deptford, which was one of the roughest areas in south London. I was getting itchy feet again and was bored with the mundane day-to-day running of a restaurant.

Soon after taking over, Jackie's parents asked us if we wanted to run the pub for them and the two of us jumped at the chance. It was near another one owned by a famous local character called Harry Hayward. His place actually used to have a corner in it which was built like a cell. It was called 'Harry's Room' and he'd kitted it out to remind him of one of the cells he'd spent time in while he'd been inside.

He was the sort of guy you didn't mess around with but happily for us Harry took a liking to me and one day he came into our pub, closed all the doors behind him and announced to the local lads inside that if anyone took liberties they would have to answer to him. He told them all to treat Jackie and me with respect, and thankfully we never really had any trouble after those few helpful words from Harry. There were some real nutcases who used to come in for a drink, and one of their favourite games was to take their shirts off in the bar and stand in front of the dart board so they could throw darts at each other's backs!

We also had a live-in barman called Bill Alderman and having him there gave us the freedom to go out. One night we came back at around 10.30 to find all the pub blinds drawn and the bar empty as we walked in. Suddenly we heard the voice of our barman crying out for help. I turned around to see him dangling from a wall about 8 ft in the air with his jacket hitched to a hook.

'What happened?' I asked.

'Those crazy bastards,' he yelled. 'They came in here, hung me up on the wall and then started helping themselves to the drinks. They paid for everything and there's a pile of money on the bar, but they left me hanging up here while they did it.'

Having characters like that in the pub meant life was never dull. There seemed to be a lot of guys who were into things like the 'Rag and Bone' trade, or dealing in scrap metal. They'd work all morning but think nothing of going in the pub afterwards and drinking away what money they'd made. There seemed to be an awful lot of pubs in Deptford at that time, and they were well used. If you had a drink in every one you passed on the way to our pub, you'd have ended up drunk, but the area has changed a lot since then, and so many of the old places have gone.

Most of the time in the pub it was a bit crazy, but at least it was good natured stuff with nobody getting upset and everyone having a laugh about the antics. Although it wasn't always the case and unfortunately there were some blacker moments, like the occasion I was told that I might end up behind bars for a very long time following a suspected murder.

I was upstairs one evening when there was a bit of a commotion in the bar. Apparently there was a fight between a cousin of Jackie's called Johnny Darke, his sidekick and a black guy who was a local character and was drinking in the bar at the time. When I came down it was all over and things were calm again so I thought no more of it.

The next morning I was out for my usual run around the streets and when I got to Deptford Creek Bridge I suddenly saw a body being dragged out of the water by the police. I stood there transfixed and couldn't believe my eyes – it was the black guy who'd been in the pub the night before.

I remember being physically unable to run any further and walked back to the pub in a bit of a daze. When I got there I told Jackie what I'd seen and she was as shocked as I was. After getting myself together I decided to carry on as normal and went off to the gym for my usual training stint, but I couldn't train because my mind was racing. Not long after arriving I got a call to say the police were at the pub and wanted to talk to me.

I made an appointment to see them and had to go to Greenwich police station. As soon as I went into the place I got a bad feeling about what was going to happen. They showed me to an interview room and a very aggressive detective started to verbally lay into me, demanding I tell him exactly what had happened the previous night in the pub, and claiming that if I didn't I was likely to be charged as an accessory to murder.

I had the distinct impression they were trying to put words into my mouth and began to feel very uncomfortable about the whole situation. I stared blankly at him but felt panic in the pit of my stomach when he started to thump the table and shout at me. It soon became really frightening, and I don't mind admitting I broke down and cried, because I honestly thought they were going to charge me for something I knew nothing about. I felt helpless and the situation got the better of me as the detective insisted I could be locked up for a very long time.

It started to feel like a nightmare. The detective was then joined by another copper, but instead of ranting and raving this one tried to use a softly-softly approach. It was the old B-movie good guy, bad guy routine and they were taking it in turns to crack little old me as if I was some kind of hardened villain.

It was all a bit over the top and the whole thing was ridiculous. I kept telling both of them I wasn't actually in the bar and that I hadn't even seen the fight. Eventually they let me go, but seemed upset that they couldn't get anything more from me. The simple truth was that I didn't know anything, no matter how aggressive they were.

Johnny Darke and an accomplice were later arrested and charged with murder. We were told that we had to appear as witnesses at Lambeth Magistrates' Court for the committal proceedings, and when I was questioned on the stand I could only repeat the fact that I'd been upstairs and not seen any of the trouble in the bar. It became clear the case was going against the prosecution and the charges against Darke were eventually dismissed. The police weren't too pleased about the result, and outside the court the aggressive detective who'd questioned me came over and had a few choice words to say.

Darke actually came to a sticky end himself, when he was killed at the Raneleigh Yacht Club in west London in an incident with an actor called Johnny Bindon in November 1978. It was a big story at the time which made front page news. Bindon, who was alleged to have been on very friendly terms with Princess Margaret at one time and whose party trick was balancing pint glasses on his dick, had to stand trial at the Old Bailey but was acquitted of murder.

I enjoyed being in charge of the pub and the lifestyle. The place was full of characters, many of whom earned a living by 'ducking and diving' and sailing close to the wind. They would get into all sorts of things and some of them were not always on the right side of the law. Although I was completely innocent when it came to the grilling I was given in the Johnny Darke case, I can now own up to my one and only experience of being involved in a robbery.

Some of the chaps in the pub 'asked' me if I would help them out with a job they had planned. It wasn't exactly my scene and I've never been cut out for a life of crime, but when those kind of guys asked a favour, it was best to go along with them. I was told it was a simple job with no great risk and the reason they wanted me in on it was because of my size.

They needed to get into a building and the best way was through a small window. It was pretty basic stuff and we weren't quite in the Great Train Robbers' league, but it was my first and last taste of a life of crime. All I had to do was get inside and then unlock a door for the others. We got away with loads of coins, most of which found their way into cigarette and slot machines of pubs in the area for the next few weeks.

I didn't like having to disappoint my regulars but had to say no to some of the boys on another occasion when they wanted to keep drinking in the bar following a Millwall game. I put my foot down and told them that we would be closing the doors at about 11.30 and weren't going to stay open after that.

Needless to say it didn't go down too well and later on that night, when Jackie and I were in bed, we heard banging and kicking noises coming from the door downstairs. Ever since the fight incident with

Darke, Jackie had been scared and had never quite recovered, so you can just imagine her reaction when all the noise started.

It was left to me to try and play the macho bit as I slipped on my dressing gown and grabbed a big stick. I made my way downstairs shouting at the top of my voice and switched all the lights on to try and scare off anyone who might be lurking around. When I got to the bar and peered towards the door I could see a huge shadow through the frosted glass and then heard a strange grunting noise.

I finally got brave enough to open the door and found myself staring into the face of a pony! It had been tied to the door with a note attached which read, 'All I wanted was a drink.' I couldn't help laughing, but Jackie had trouble seeing the funny side of it and told me she'd had enough.

It wasn't her scene at all and Jackie's mum and dad decided to sell up and buy another pub in Sussex, while we moved back to our home in Orpington and I took a job at Bromley College as their catering manager.

In September 1977, Jackie's brother Tony was offered a contest in Copenhagen against Denmark's Jorgen Hansen, who a month earlier had lost his European welterweight title on a 13th round disqualification against a German called Jorg Eipel. The idea of his management was to get Hansen back in action as soon as they could and Tony was chosen as the ideal man for the job. I travelled on the ferry with Jackie's dad, Lenny, a couple of days before the fight was due to take place. We all wanted to get as much action as we could in a place like Copenhagen, which was well known for its nightlife, and almost as soon as we'd arrived it was decided we ought to go out and test the water by visiting a club.

It was basically a small cinema showing porn films, with stairs leading up to a brothel. Somehow I was elected as the guinea pig and given the task of climbing the smelly old steps to discover what delights awaited me at the top.

From the moment I put my foot on the first step I felt it wasn't a good idea and when I found myself in a dimly lit room with nothing but a dirty and soiled mattress on the floor, all my worst fears were confirmed. As if that weren't enough, more was to follow when a young girl came in wearing nothing but ankle socks, a T-shirt and a pair of knickers which she quickly dropped to the floor.

Her T-shirt and socks followed and she was soon stark naked on the mattress telling me to 'Get on with it quickly.' There was no way I was going to get on with anything other than making a smart exit. I started to go out of the door and at the same time demanded the money back I'd paid to get myself into the room in the first place.

It was clear refunds were not an option in this particular establishment, so I took the matter into my own hands by going back downstairs, jumping over the counter and grabbing a handful of money. I knew what I'd done wouldn't go down too well with the owners, but I managed to run through the main doors and out into the safety of the streets despite being chased by several large Danish bouncers.

Two days later Tony lost his fight against Hansen on points over eight rounds and we left the next day. It wasn't the best overnight crossing with the rough sea tossing the ship around, leaving me gripping my bed and throwing up for most of the trip. Luckily things got calmer in the morning and Tony and I decided we would make up for lost time after going on deck and meeting a couple of girls from Derby, who had been to Denmark as part of a Co-op outing. It wasn't long before I was sharing a cabin with one of them and things got pretty passionate. When I finally raised my head to look out of the porthole, I got a shock when all I could see was a wall instead of the sea.

Obviously I hadn't been the only one concentrating on my docking technique, and the ferry was by this time very securely moored to the quayside. I said thanks and goodbye to my new-found lady friend and jumped onto dry land just in time to see Lenny's car in the distance. After making a mad dash to get to it, I was surprised to find that Tony was nowhere to be seen. I couldn't really tell his dad what we'd both been up to, particularly as I happened to be married to his daughter at the time, so I kept silent as an angry Hudson senior decided to drive off without waiting for his son.

Although I'd drifted away from my training with Benny, I was still very much into boxing and used to go to the gym regularly with

Eugene to be trained by Billy Kingwell at the Trinity club near the Elephant and Castle. I had a couple of fights for them before Billy got me involved in training some of the youngsters there.

It was something I enjoyed and eventually I passed an Amateur Boxing Association training course which allowed me to become a trainer at the club while being paid by the local council. The money came in handy for the two nights a week that I was there, but I also used to work as a mini-cab driver on Thursday, Friday and Saturday nights to bring in a bit more cash. It was knackering at times, but we needed the money.

There were also a few added perks which went with the job when some of the female customers didn't have enough money for the fare, and instead offered another form of payment that was always gratefully accepted by the drivers. It might not have paid the rent but it left you with a grin on your face and certainly managed to break up the long nights.

The matchmaker at Trinity was an older guy who had reached the stage where he wanted to slow down a bit, so I started to do some of the matching and managed to involve a couple of local businessmen in the club by getting them to join the committee. It all became very enjoyable for me and it was something I got a lot of satisfaction from.

I liked organising things and we used to run shows at a place called the Radical Working Men's Club near the Old Kent Road. One of the most successful I was involved in was a clash between Joe Christle from Ireland and a young south London heavyweight called Frank Bruno. It was the only time Bruno lost as an amateur and the fight cost me around £100 to make, plus all the Guinness Joe could drink.

Bruno made a return appearance for me some time later beating fellow south Londoner Trevor Currie. I also matched Eugene against Duke McKenzie, who later went on to become a world champion at three different weights. Duke didn't do too well early on in that fight, but eventually showed his class and stopped my brother with a terrific shot in the third and final round.

By this time I wasn't really boxing any more but was heavily into training and matchmaking. Eugene was still very active and used to love having a fight in the ring. One night we travelled to a club called

Foley, near Surbiton in Surrey, for a bout which saw Eugene in with a local character who had huge support from the audience. They cheered every shot he threw and booed whenever Eugene had any success.

The hostility didn't bother my brother but when he won the decision, all hell broke lose with Billy, Eugene, my dad and me having to fight our way from the ring. We hit out at anyone and anything that stood in front of us so that we could get to the changing room. When we finally got there exhausted but happy to be safe, Billy came out with one of his typical little comments.

'Fuck me, Frank,' he said, 'I think you threw more punches getting back here than you ever used to in the ring!'

Not long after that contest I was approached by another local club called Hollington, who wanted me to go there as assistant matchmaker to a man named Tommy Condon. I was also given the chance to train the kids with two other guys called Barry Francis and Terry Edwards.

The club had its base at Camberwell Green and was a successful little outfit. It was well run and while I was there we became the first ever amateur club to put on a charity show at the Elephant and Castle Leisure Centre, which was in aid of a policeman called Frank O'Neill who had been stabbed. The show was also the first ever boxing event staged at the venue, and in more recent years I have promoted professional shows there and so has Eugene. Being involved all those years ago helped teach me the fundamentals of promoting, and it was a lesson that came in very handy later in my life.

One of the other clubs Hollington used to do a lot of work with was South Norwood, and I got to know a guy called Keiron Murphy who ran a pub and was also one of their trainers. One day he phoned me and said he was thinking of jacking it in to move into the professional side of the sport.

'I'm fed up with the amateurs,' he told me. 'I've met a guy called Frank Warren and I'm going to work as the manager in his organisation. Frank's the promoter and we'd like you to be our trainer.'

3. LET'S BE FRANK

I'D NEVER HEARD OF FRANK WARREN BEFORE KEIRON'S CALL. HE SUGGESTED we should all meet and run through some plans Frank had about taking on the big boys of professional boxing. People like Mickey Duff, Terry Lawless and Mike Barrett.

We met in a nightclub at the Barbican in the City of London and I later found out Warren had some involvement in the place along with former Arsenal captain and Millwall assistant manager Frank McLintock. The first thing I noticed about Frank Warren was how young he was and how friendly he seemed. He looked like a young businessman who would be more at home in the City than in a smoke-filled town hall watching boxing. But it soon became clear he was very ambitious and serious about his plans to break into the sport.

After the introductions and some small talk Frank surprised me when he said he'd already promoted some very well run and successful shows, and then told me how he planned to apply to be licensed by the British Boxing Board of Control. You couldn't help but be impressed by Frank. He had the sort of drive and enthusiasm that made you feel he would succeed. He said he wasn't going to be put off, no matter how difficult some of the cosy boxing establishment might try to make it for him. Frank's plan was to challenge them on their own ground by getting a British Boxing Board of Control (BBBC) licence.

I left the meeting feeling pretty pleased and excited by the plans we had, and not too long after that we were able to set everything in motion when I got my trainer's licence. Once that happened we were off and running, with Frank as the promoter and Keiron as the manager in the new set-up. We didn't exactly have a big stable of boxers, but we had a good fighter called Gary Knight, and Eugene decided he might as well start to get paid for doing something he enjoyed anyway.

Slowly but surely we began to build on the number of fighters we had, and Frank managed to pull off our biggest signing at the time when the much sought-after Liverpool flyweight Keith Wallace agreed to fight for us, rather than some of the big boys.

I'd given up my job at Bromley College, sold our house in Orpington and we'd started living with Vince and his wife in Strood, Kent. I also decided to open a greengrocery business in Blackfriars, because I thought it would be more convenient for me in my new trainer's role. I seemed to be working non-stop, either in the shop or the gym, and there was also a lot of travel involved as I went up and down the country to different shows with fighters.

Quite often I'd do a trip that would involve driving for about four hours after working all day at the shop, then drive back after the contest before going straight on to Spitalfields market to pick up stuff for the greengrocers.

The whole thing had an effect on me physically and I would often go without sleep for 24 hours. Frank thought it would end in tears if I didn't stop, and suggested I should think about taking on a pub. He claimed the lifestyle would fit more easily into what I wanted to do on the boxing front. The more I thought about it the more I liked the idea, and having already had a bit of a taste of pub life when we looked after Jackie's dad's place in Deptford, we both decided we'd like to give it a go on our own.

We didn't have to wait very long for an opportunity to come along, and were soon the proud licensees of The Castle pub in Aldgate, east

London. To be honest, it was a run-down mess when we took it over, but that part of the City was beginning to take off and we saw it as a great opportunity for both of us. It seemed our luck was beginning to change because while we were living with my brother we had applied for a housing association flat in Forest Hill, and just a couple of weeks after going into the pub we got a letter telling us we had a brand new home to look forward to.

After signing Wallace, it was decided he should come down from Liverpool and stay at my pub along with another fighter called Jimmy Duncan who came with his wife and baby. It was an exciting time for me and we were all enjoying the fact that each day we genuinely felt as though we were making progress.

The next boxer we tried to sign was Terry Marsh, who was an outstanding amateur and a local East End boy, who at the time was still in the Marines. We weren't the only ones interested in his signature and we heard that people like Duff and Barrett were also keen to get hold of Marsh.

When he eventually agreed to sign with us in September 1981, we felt we'd pulled off something of a coup. It was a great moment for Frank, and Terry eventually became Warren's first world champion when he took the IBF light-welterweight title in 1987. But to most people their relationship will be remembered for the fact that Marsh was the person acquitted of shooting Frank when he was gunned down before a boxing show at Barking in November 1989.

My brother made his professional debut for us on 12 October 1981 at the Bloomsbury Crest Hotel in London. He beat a guy called Steve Reilly, from Newport, on points over six rounds in a bantamweight contest, and while there was cause for celebration after the bout because of his debut win, there was also a bit of drama beforehand.

Eugene sold over £3,500 worth of tickets leading up to the fight, which was an awful lot of money in those days, especially for the size of the promotion. But my brother also loved gambling and by the time of the weigh-in on the afternoon of the fight, he'd managed to blow all of the ticket money that was owed to Frank as the promoter. I'm still not sure to this day how he did it, but my father spent the last few hours before the bout frantically scrambling around trying to raise enough cash to cover the amount Eugene had lost on his gambling spree. It turned out all right in the end and the victory over Reilly was swiftly followed by another a little over two weeks later against Robert Hepburn in Acton. Although it was a good start to his career, two winning fights certainly didn't make Eugene a world beater.

Eugene's love of gambling never left him and years later after a spell in prison on remand, he decided he wanted to continue his boxing career. We staged the show at a place called Pickett's Lock in Edmonton, north London, and it featured a Puerto Rican known as 'The Baby Face Assassin', who unfortunately took the nickname a little too seriously and was eventually sent to prison in the United States for attacking gays in Miami.

Eugene was paid £1,500 on the night to fight a journeyman boxer from Wales named Miguel Matthews, but on his way to the ring my brother happened to spot a bookmaker friend of mine in the audience. Eugene caught his eye and asked what his odds were for the fight against Matthews.

'Evens,' said the bookie.

Without batting an eye Eugene laid £1,000 on himself and continued his walk to the ring. He'd trained really hard over a period of about five weeks to get down from 12 st. to 9, and by the fourth round he was beginning to feel the strain of having to make the weight in such a short space of time. In one of the clinches Matthews stood back claiming he'd been bitten as Eugene jumped in and landed some blows. The exchange seemed to give my brother fresh hope and when the final bell rang an exhausted Eugene turned to the referee hoping to get the nod and with it the extra little earner he had coming from the bookie. But although the ref raised my brother's hand, he also did the same with Miguel's, as he called it a draw leaving my brother a financial loser thanks to his bet.

Eugene might not have been punished for the biting incident against Matthews but some years earlier he was disqualified during a hastily arranged contest in Belfast. My brother and I were celebrating my 29th birthday when the phone rang and he was offered a fight against Hugh Russell in Northern Ireland at very short notice. The contest was scheduled for 27 January and we made the trip to Belfast knowing it was going to be tough against the classy Irishman who had won a bronze medal at the 1980 Olympics.

The reason Eugene had taken the fight was because of the amount of money on offer – £350. He knew that he didn't have the kind of skills Hugh had, but for a good purse he was prepared to give it a go. Eugene also managed to have a bet on himself but it was soon obvious on the night that he didn't have a hope against Russell when it came to winning within the rules, so after getting bashed about and outclassed in the fourth round my brother finally decided enough was enough and head-butted his opponent, opening a cut on his eye. The referee stopped the contest and I told Eugene to stick up his hands claiming victory, but not surprisingly he was disqualified, though he still got his purse money and we decided to drown our sorrows with a drink back at the hotel.

At this time in Northern Ireland, Belfast wasn't exactly the safest of places to be, and we were staying in the Europa Hotel which had the reputation of being the most bombed in Europe. After a few drinks I left Eugene in the bar and wandered back to our room, but when I woke up the next morning my brother's bed hadn't been slept in and he was nowhere to be seen. I ran around the hotel looking for him and actually began to think he could have been kidnapped. With a name like Maloney and a few drinks inside him, Belfast was probably not the best place for him and I began to think Eugene could have got into all sorts of trouble.

After searching for about half an hour I eventually found him propped up on a toilet seat in the Gents. He was fine, but had slept there all night, having got lost on his way back to our room following a few hours spent with a chambermaid he'd pulled! A few weeks later, Eugene was actually offered a re-match with Russell at the Café Royal in London.

'Leave off,' said my brother when he got the call. 'It's bad enough getting beat up by him in Belfast, but I'm not going to have it happen in front of my mates in London.'

Like Wallace and Duncan, Terry Marsh moved to London after his time in the Marines and his girlfriend Jacqui came with him to work in my pub as a barmaid. Keiron had taken a bit of a back seat in proceedings, and later drifted away from the whole thing but not before I got a visit from the police over a petrol bomb incident at his pub.

They came to question me and wanted to know exactly where I was when Keiron's place had the device chucked through the window. After spending a few minutes with me they obviously realised I had nothing to do with it and I never actually found out if anyone was ever arrested or charged with doing it.

It didn't take long before my pub began to get used for a lot more than just drinking beer. Frank closed his club in the Barbican and moved his offices into The Castle. We also did a bit of decorating and with the help of some local firemen from the station across the road, converted the large bar room on the first floor into a gym with a ring and all the facilities to train boxers.

Keith Wallace was a great little fighter who had boxed for his country as an amateur and won an ABA title. He had bags of ability and was an exciting prospect, so naturally we wanted to make sure that he learned the game as a professional. That meant bringing him along with the right sort of matches that would build his record and at the same time be useful to him in terms of gaining experience.

Ernie Fossey was our matchmaker and he also taught me a lot in the gym. Ernie was a great boxing man and was known as one of the best in the business. He continued to work for Warren until his sad death last year, and I know Frank still misses not having him around. Keith was due to fight at Hornsey Town Hall which was becoming one of our regular venues. As so often happens with contests, his opponent dropped out at the last minute leaving Ernie scrambling around for someone to put in his place.

Wallace was our star attraction and Eugene was also due to fight on the show. I was told about the problem with Wallace's opponent, and asked if I could put Eugene in as the replacement. It's the kind of thing that happens all the time, and as a promoter you obviously want to make sure the show goes on and that a star like Wallace hopefully gets another win under his belt.

But this was different as far as I was concerned, because in terms of ring ability Keith and my brother were miles apart. Eugene would never give less than 100 per cent as soon as he stepped between the ropes, but I also knew he simply didn't have the skill or ability of

Wallace. As a street fighter Eugene could hold his own with anyone, but that doesn't mean you're going to be a good professional boxer.

There was no way I wanted to stand there and see my brother bashed up in the ring by a fighter who was recognised as a real class act. It was agreed that Eugene wouldn't get in the ring with Wallace but it was a difficult moment for me as someone who was not only his trainer but also his brother.

My marriage was going through a bit of a rocky period at the time because of my busy lifestyle. I was so involved with all of the boxing business that other things took a bit of a backseat. Jackie started to go out on her own more and I suddenly began to get a bit suspicious about just what she might be up to. One night she told me she was going out to see a friend and I decided to follow her. The friend turned out to be someone who had connections in the boxing world.

When I got back to The Castle and asked her where she'd been, things very quickly got heated and it developed into a major row. Jackie told me how selfish I'd been, paying more attention to boxing than I did to her and neglecting our marriage. She wanted some time on her own. The whole thing came as a real shock when I heard how upset she was, and I was also angry because suddenly my world was crumbling around me.

'You can go and do what the fuck you like,' I told her, 'but Emma's staying with me.'

My mother moved in to help me cope with it all but I was really cut up about the situation. As if things weren't bad enough, I was soon hit by another bombshell that set my life on a different course.

Anyone who has seen pictures of Frank Warren's houses in recent years will know that the kid from the backstreets of north London didn't do too badly for himself. A few years ago I went to lunch with Frank at his place in Hertfordshire to discuss a world title fight for one of my boxers named David Starie and thought I was walking into a stately home. But back in those days during the early '80s, when he was still trying to get into the boxing big-time, he had a more modest residence in the shape of an Islington flat.

Not long after the bust-up with Jackie I went to visit Frank because I felt as though I was beginning to get frozen out of the picture. Vic Andreetti had come into the organisation as a trainer and was a forceful character. To be truthful, I was carrying on as little more than the bucket boy when it came to training fighters. Warren told me it would be better all round if I dropped out and let Vic take over. I was devastated, but Frank claimed that maybe when things sorted themselves out the situation would change. He wanted to move the fighters out of the gym, but said it was up to me whether I let those living at the pub continue with the arrangement. As I left he told me not to worry and claimed the new arrangement might only last for a short time.

As things turned out it was to be something like 17 years before I worked closely with him again, and during that time we became two of the biggest boxing rivals on the British scene.

4. SMALL HALLS, BIG AMBITIONS

FROM THE MOMENT OF THAT MEETING WITH FRANK WARREN TWO THINGS very quickly started to happen in my life. I began to drift away from the boxing scene and my level of partying reached new heights. To put it bluntly, my life went out of control.

Keith Wallace and Jimmy Duncan were still living at the pub and they helped quite a bit when the split with Jackie came. Eventually Keith moved out and went to stay with Mick Williamson who was working for Warren at the time, but who later became a great cuts man for me and also a friend when I branched out on my own.

The split with Jackie hit me hard and in many ways I suppose my pride took a big knock as well, even though I was no angel. The truth was that we'd probably got married too young and in my own immature way I only ever saw the flirtations I had with other girls as a bit of fun.

When Jackie walked out I was devastated, but at the same time I felt the need to prove I could still pull women. I went through a stage where I must have tried to date every barmaid who worked for me, and at the same time partied almost constantly, with Eugene as a willing accomplice. It was almost like being a kid in a sweet shop for me, only instead of chocolate bars I was always trying to get the wrapping off the girls who worked in the pub.

We sometimes ran stag nights at The Castle and one of the girls who took part also worked for Cynthia Payne, the notorious Madame from Streatham who hit the headlines for running a brothel where clients used luncheon vouchers in exchange for sex. The idea was that you bought as many as you wanted and then handed them over without giving the girls actual cash.

I got invited to go there by the stag night girl and took along a friend just to find out what the place was like. Madame Cyn greeted us at the door and explained the kind of things that were on offer, only for my friend to ask if there was a TV in the place. 'I've heard it all now,' she said, obviously thinking he wanted to use it for some weird sex game. The fact was he'd had a bet on a race and wanted to know the outcome. We ended up making a quick exit to the pub so that he could find out if he'd won, but not before having a look around the house and seeing some very famous faces in some very unusual situations.

The pub was actually doing well, although that was no thanks to me because I wasn't really taking responsibility for any of the day-to-day business. Luckily my mother made sure everything ran smoothly, while I dedicated myself to getting drunk and trying to have a good time.

My mother and father both had a go at me. They let me know I was on a self-destruct course, and said I couldn't go on like it for too much longer. They also hit a real nerve by pointing out I still had Emma to care for, and said it wasn't very nice for my little daughter to see her dad in such a state.

Emma was so important to me, and I could see that what my parents told me was right, even though it didn't feel particularly good to have to admit it to myself. During this period I attended a school parents' evening and came face to face with Jackie. The atmosphere between us was frosty to say the least, but when we left the school she asked if she could come to the pub and talk to me. She felt we had a lot of things to sort out. I agreed, but when the day arrived we didn't really have a discussion, it was more like a verbal war. Jackie stormed out crying and I was left standing there with tears in my eyes as well.

She had moved into the flat in Forest Hill and not long after, I phoned her to see if we could meet. She claimed she was busy and suggested we talk later, but instead of waiting I decided to take things into my own hands and drove to the flat. I soon found myself knocking at the front door only to be greeted by a startled Jackie.

'You can't come in now,' she insisted, but I just ignored her and walked in. I asked if she had someone with her and went to both bedrooms to have a look, but found nothing. I carried on looking around with Jackie following me and finally got to the bathroom. When I opened the door, standing inside was the wide-eyed figure of the guy I'd seen when I followed her home that night.

He wasn't exactly Mr Atlas but he was certainly bigger than me, and when I saw him I snapped. It was like a time bomb going off in my head. The rage built up and I flew at him like a complete lunatic. To say I came off worse would be an understatement. All Jackie could do was look on in horror. It was probably quite spectacular while it lasted, but later in my career as a promoter I would have sacked anyone who made such a one-sided match. I'm afraid size did matter. He didn't knock me out, but I was well behind on points and finished up bloody and bruised – any referee would have stopped it.

I remember sitting in the kitchen afterwards with Jackie asking me repeatedly why I'd gone there. My face was a mess and she tried her best to clean me up. We sat and talked for ages before finally deciding that maybe we should give our marriage another try. Jackie explained that she was still in love with me but that I'd totally neglected her. The other guy just happened to be there at the right time and in the right place as a friend and someone she turned to for a shoulder to cry on. Looking back I have to admit she may have been right. Even to this day I know I can be hell to live with because of my work.

We started to sort out our differences and Jackie decided to move back into the pub. It was a little strange at first and we both lived under a kind of uneasy peace. A few months passed and I suddenly came to the conclusion that although I'd won my personal battle to get Jackie back, I'd started to relax and take the whole relationship for granted. I wanted us to be together, but the idea of being one big happy family was no longer as important to me as I thought it would be.

I began to take things for granted and started to think more about what I wanted than how Jackie was feeling. One evening I'd decided to go out with some other publicans to a boxing dinner and was wearing a brand new white dinner jacket for the occasion. Jackie was busily serving customers in the pub and I went behind the bar to get some cash from the till. 'Don't work too hard darling,' I said to her, sticking the cash into my pocket. But before I could say anything else she'd managed to throw a full pint of Guinness at me and my nice white jacket. It's not easy to try and maintain your dignity at moments like that, but I did the best I could and calmly walked out of the door with the rest of the guys who were going to the boxing.

I think I was beginning to feel restless again but things changed for me one day when my father came to see me with a friend of his to ask my advice on some boxing matters. It turned out the friend's daughter had a boyfriend who was a boxer keen on turning professional. He was an amateur with the Robert Browning club in Walworth and had a good local following. My dad and his mate wanted to pick my brains about who I'd recommend as a possible manager.

We were talking the whole thing through when my father suggested I should take out a manager's licence and look after the kid myself. My first instinct was to say no, but as we talked some more my dad's friend said he thought it would be a great idea, and deep down I could feel myself getting excited about the prospect.

I decided to go for it and in 1983 I got my manager's licence from the British Boxing Board of Control. The decision to apply for it was probably one of the best things I ever did in my life. It began a journey from places like Dulwich Baths to the big casinos of Las Vegas in the space of less than ten years, and from handling fighters for six-round contests to taking care of the heavyweight champion of the world.

Richie Edwards was the name of that first fighter and he combined his daytime job as a dustman with his boxing career. He remains one of the nicest guys you could ever wish to meet, but only had four fights as a professional before calling it a day, winning three and drawing the other. I loved every minute of it and Richie holds a special place in my memory because of it.

Getting involved with boxing again had exactly the sort of effect you might expect. I was quickly bitten by the bug once more and started to look for young up-and-coming fighters that I could manage. I also formed a partnership with a boyhood friend named Vince Heckman, who'd boxed on the same amateur circuit as me when we were both kids.

We started a promotional company called Maloney and Heckman, making my pub our headquarters. It was the first time it had been used for anything to do with boxing since my days with Frank Warren, and during my time out of the sport the gym had been converted into a pizza restaurant and function room.

It meant that I had to train Richie at my old haunt, the Thomas à Becket, but the place had good memories for me because I used to love hanging out there and listening to stories from boxing men like Danny Holland and Benny Caplan. I'd also watched with fascination as professional British boxers such as Mark Rowe and Jimmy Revie trained there, as well as the Mexican Carlos Palomino, when he took the world welterweight title from our own John H. Stracey in 1976.

We signed local fighters like Paul Gadney from Woolwich and Wayne Weekes from Downham, as well as some others from north London who'd been recommended to us. We knew we weren't signing world beaters, but they were decent kids and the two of us loved every minute of it.

We called a press conference at The Castle to launch the company, and in an effort to make sure we got decent publicity I managed to persuade Stracey to act as our general manager and spokesman. It was funny, because although we'd come from nowhere and had no big name fighters attached to our stable, we still managed to get the national press to turn up. It was all down to the fact that we had John there and he was still a sporting 'name' because of his ring achievements.

We staged a number of shows in south London at places like the Lewisham and Greenwich Theatres, as well as the Crofton Park Leisure Centre. I have to admit that when I first heard my name announced as the promoter of a show, it gave me a real buzz. It's a great feeling to be staging your own show, and apart from the boost it gives to your ego, there's also a feeling of excitement and anticipation that's hard to describe. On many of those early shows I knew I wouldn't be making any money. In fact, I knew for certain that I'd be losing money. When you added up the figures it often became apparent that there was a loss of a few thousand pounds, but somehow it didn't seem to matter and I found myself quickly looking forward to staging the next promotion. The guy who used to act as my whip, which is the person who makes sure a promotion runs to schedule, was someone called Ernie Draper. He knows his job inside out and back then I was hardly paying him anything for a night's work. He suggested once that it might be a good idea if I stumped up for a taxi for him, but I quickly told him if he needed transport he could get on a bus, because there was no way I could afford to pay for anything else.

At times it could be very frustrating and it was always hard work, but when I look back I realise what a great experience it was. We made mistakes and the shows weren't always a success, but there's no better way of cutting your teeth in the boxing business than staging local shows with unknown fighters. Vince and I worked well together, but eventually parted company and he promoted on his own for a while, before teaming up with me once again some time later.

Before the split with him we signed boxers who not too many people had heard of, like the brilliantly named Rudi Valentino from Plumstead. I also had my first venture into the heavyweight division with a fighter called Danny Moul. Danny was my first attempt at getting success with the big guys and I thought at the time he might just have the ability to make a bit of a name for himself on the domestic front. He stood 6 ft 5 in. tall, was good looking and had beaten Gary Mason as an amateur. Mason had gone on to make a splash as a professional under Terry Lawless and at the time was considered to be one of the best prospects around.

Moul was not the normal sort of fighter. He was well-spoken, immaculately dressed, worked in the City and played football at semi-professional level. His career was launched at Lewisham Theatre under the Maloney–Heckman banner, but it was hardly a great start. He lost on points over six rounds against a fighter from

Clapham named Barry Ellis, and went on to quickly show he wasn't really cut out for greatness with a fairly mixed and short-lived career. After a couple of defeats and a couple of wins he had what was to be his last fight when he took on Novak Radanovic at Greenwich, and the contest might have ended in another defeat if Danny hadn't been 'stung' into action by me.

As the contest wore on he was clearly getting tired, but at least I could see he was winning. At the end of the third round he came back to his corner and slumped onto the stool claiming he was exhausted and didn't want to go on. I decided it was time for actions to speak louder than words and got a hat pin which I promptly stuck into his arse. It had the desired effect and Radanovic retired in the next round.

Although the pub was taking money it was also taking the strain of subsidising what I was doing in boxing. I had a meeting with my accountant and he told me I was in a hole. By the time I'd sorted out my finances, I was left with a debt of around £100,000.

Jackie and I had left our flat in Forest Hill and bought a two-bedroom cottage in Maidstone, Kent, which we often used at weekends. With all that was going on I began to feel a bit stale and jaded. We left The Castle and thought that by moving to a new pub and selling the place in Maidstone it would help to get me out of the financial hole I was in.

So the Maloney and Heckman promotional business was closed down and I moved for a trial period to The Rising Sun in Stamford-Le-Hope, Essex. I was only there for about six or seven months before a disagreement with the brewery led to us leaving, but during that time we were very happy. I did have a little bit of bother with some local hooligans one night, but after contacting a few mates from south London and asking them to pay a visit, the ringleaders were quickly sorted out leaving us to get on with the business of making the move a success.

While we had the pub, Eugene once again found himself in trouble with the police. This time the charges were a bit heavy when he was held in connection with being involved in an armed robbery. The family sweated on the result of the trial and I was called as a witness at the Old Bailey, together with John H. Stracey.

Eugene was finally found not guilty, but not before spending several months on remand in prison. Once the verdict was given there was relief all round and we decided to throw a party for him at our pub. I shot off with my dad to make sure everything was in place for his homecoming, leaving a friend to drive my brother to Essex. On the way Eugene spotted a building society branch and told the guy to pull over.

'Stay here but make sure you keep the engine running,' my brother said.

He then ran across the road and through the doors of the building society leaving his driver sweating at the thought of what might be going on. After a couple of minutes my friend saw Eugene dash out of the doors again, dodge through traffic and jump into the car.

'Quick, let's get away,' shouted Eugene. 'Get the car going!'

By now the poor guy was fumbling all over the place as he wondered what the hell my brother had been doing. Eugene may have just been found not guilty, but my mate knew he was driving someone whose past had hardly been whiter than white.

'What have you just done?' he asked.

'Let's just say I've made a quick withdrawal and we'd better get the fuck out of here,' barked Eugene.

My mate immediately thought he'd been an accomplice to some horrible crime and in his panic stalled the car only to see my brother burst into laughter. 'I hope you didn't think I was trying to rob the place!' said Eugene. But my mate couldn't see the funny side of it, having been turned into a nervous wreck by the whole episode!

When I lost my battle with the brewery, I had to move out of The Rising Sun and I found myself unemployed for a few months while they tried to find a pub for me. I spent my time commuting between my mother's home in London and Jackie's parents in East Sussex, where she was staying with Emma. Our search for a pub ended when we got the chance to take over a run-down place with potential in Kent called The Crayford Arms.

The move came along about the same time as I was approached by Mike Barrett and Mickey Duff to become their matchmaker for some shows at York Hall in Bethnal Green. I had a meeting with them in their Wardour Street offices and found Barrett to be a real gentleman.

Duff was just as everybody had told me. He seemed to have a habit of talking through you, almost as if you weren't around. I also remember him having a chair in his office which was very low to the ground, while he sat high behind his desk. I've been told that it could have been a ploy to make visitors feel inferior, but it certainly never worked with me. When you're 5 ft 3 in. tall you get used to looking up most of the time anyway. After I got to know Mickey better my lack of height used to provide him with a line he loved using about me being superstitious. 'He never walks under a black cat!' Duff would joke.

I made quite a few matches for them and thought I was doing well. The trade paper, *Boxing News*, seemed to agree when they commented on some of the contests I'd put together, but things nearly came to an abrupt end the night I managed to get a 'house' fighter named Brian Nickels beaten by my own boxer Wayne Weekes, in March 1987.

The fight was submitted to Mickey and approved by him at a specified weight, but at the Lonsdale gym on the day of the contest, Nickels was over the agreed limit. Duff couldn't believe it when I insisted Brian take the weight off. He claimed that as matchmaker my loyalties should be with the 'home' fighter, but I pointed out that Weekes was managed by me and told them that either Nickels took the weight off or we didn't have a fight.

On the night it was Weekes who got the victory with a fifth round stoppage and we celebrated as if we'd won a world title, because it had come against a very good prospect on his home territory.

When I left the ring I was attacked by supporters of Nickels and needed a security escort. As if that wasn't enough, up in the dressing-room Mickey, together with his long-time associate Jarvis Astaire, verbally had a go at me. Duff told me he wanted to see me in his office the next morning and said it was the last time I'd ever work for them.

I went to see him and he sat me down before trying to explain the ways of the boxing world. He said that you made matches 80–20, or at worst 70–30 in favour of the home fighter and it wasn't the job of the matchmaker to get the home fighter beaten. In fact, you did everything you possibly could to make sure your man had a legal advantage.

NO BALONEY

It was a valuable lesson to learn but my own philosophy has always been to build a boxer's record as well as I can, and then test him to see if he can really fight. Another lesson I've come to learn is that it takes just as much time and effort to look after a bad fighter as it does a good one, so you might as well find out about the bad ones as soon as you can.

5. THE COCKNEY KING

NOT LONG AFTER ALL OF THIS I MET A CHARACTER WHO I ALWAYS THOUGHT had ambitions to be Britain's answer to Don King. His name was Ambrose Mendy.

I'd been learning my trade as a promoter and manager but I was still a long way from hitting the big time. As I promoted at small halls in London I'd got to know quite a few local boxing reporters, and one of them was a guy named Jon Robinson. He worked for an east London paper called the *Hackney Gazette* and covered quite a few of my shows. Jon was a big bloke and at one time he'd earned the title of Britain's 'heaviest man'. As well as writing for the *Gazette* he also had a flower shop in Bethnal Green, and I got a call from him one day to say he had a couple of people he wanted me to meet. When I turned up at his shop Jon introduced me to an elegant black guy who looked very smooth and confident.

'Frank,' said Robinson, 'this is Ambrose Mendy.'

Ambrose looked as though he'd just stepped out of the pages of *Vogue* magazine. He was really well groomed, wore an expensive suit and carried a Louis Vuitton briefcase. He quickly began turning on the sort of charm I later came to recognise as his trademark. There was a bit of small talk before Jon got down to the reason he'd arranged the meeting. He claimed Ambrose was bursting with ideas and desperately wanted to get into boxing promotion. But I soon found out he might have a bit of a problem doing it on his own, because he had a criminal record.

'I was in prison, Frank,' Ambrose admitted, and as we were talking Robinson sprang a bit of a surprise by introducing the other man who'd been invited to the meeting – Terry Marsh, who by this time was no longer fighting and wanted to get into promoting instead.

Jon said he'd brought the three of us together because he felt we could all help each other, and make more of an impact when it came to trying to promote bigger shows. Ambrose clearly seemed to like the idea of the three of us working together and suggested Terry and I continue the meeting with him at his office on the south side of Tower Bridge. It was above some shops and didn't look particularly grand, except for the little plaque at the entrance which claimed Mendy was 'The Trade Development Counsellor for Guinea Bissau'. I didn't know how or why it was there, and although it was a strange thing to find stuck on the wall in that part of south London, I never really thought too much about it as we went through the door.

Inside the furnishings were plush, and it was clear some money had been spent on getting everything to look stylish. The company Mendy had was called the World Sports Corporation, and he saw boxing promotion as something he could be successful at. He had big ideas and one thing I quickly learned about Ambrose was that he refused to think small. He was a natural ideas man, even if some of his ideas could be a bit outlandish at times.

He suggested Terry and I take out a joint promotional licence, saying he would fund the operation and that we could all work out of his offices. As Ambrose went about selling the whole idea it was impossible not to get caught up in the excitement of the plan. Ever since I'd got back into boxing I wanted to make my mark and have a go at breaking into the big time. The more I thought about it, the more I began to believe teaming up with Mendy would help me do that.

It wasn't long before we were up and running as a new promotional organisation, and we started having fun from the first day. I loved the whole thing and threw myself into it like a maniac. I still had the pub in Crayford but boxing provided the real excitement for me. I loved going to the office every day and planning what we'd be doing, but as a result I think both my pub and then my home life began to suffer.

Our first major promotion, on 17 February 1988, took place at York Hall where I'd worked so many times before promoting shows. The difference on this occasion was the class of fighter we were promoting – former world heavyweight champion Tim Witherspoon. 'Terrible' Tim had first come to prominence with the British public 19 months earlier, when he came over as the reigning champion to defend his WBA world title against Frank Bruno at Wembley stadium on a summer's night in July 1986. Witherspoon, like a lot of American heavyweights, had a history of drug problems outside the ring. He was a lively character and an excellent fighter who eventually overwhelmed Bruno in the 11th round.

We put Witherspoon in with a pretty awful Mexican called Mauricio Villegas who was built more like a Sumo wrestler than a boxer. The whole evening was really about staging an 'event' rather than the normal kind of contest. Villegas made his way to the ring with the song 'Speedy Gonzales' thumping out over the PA system, while Witherspoon had the crowd roaring as he started his walk to the ring by standing on the stage at the back of the hall and milking the applause.

It was over the top but the atmosphere was tremendous and the crowd loved every minute of it. In many ways Ambrose just took the entrance a bit further, after Frank Warren had started to hype things up at his shows. Mendy also arranged for a bunch of black guys dressed in Crombie overcoats, wearing leather gloves and sunglasses to act as security on the night. I got a few comments from people who said it looked a bit 'heavy' for a boxing show, but it was all part of the atmosphere Ambrose decided he wanted.

Witherspoon played his part, entertaining the crowd as he recorded an easy ninth-round win. He might not have been a world-beater at the time, but he was still a class performer and the fans loved him. What the punters didn't know about was the drama out of the ring on the night, with the British Boxing Board of Control giving Tim more problems than the Mexican ever had.

NO BALONEY

After getting back to his dressing-room Witherspoon was asked to give a urine sample for a drugs test which normally only took place after a title fight, but perhaps Tim's reputation had something to do with the request. Usually these things are pretty matter-of-fact affairs, with the boxer going into the toilet and coming out with a sample. But on this occasion Tim went in and didn't come out! All that was found was a small open window in his dressing-room. It soon became clear Witherspoon had done a runner to avoid taking the test. I think they later found him in a West End club, but I don't know if he ever did take the test.

It was all good fun and the work was genuinely exciting because there was never a dull moment. It was also around this time that I made my first trip to the USA, when we combined business with pleasure and attended the International Boxing Federation convention in Miami.

As well as the flower shop and his local paper interests, Robinson also became the European representative of the IBF. He invited us to the 1988 convention and although it meant having to pay for our own fares, Ambrose thought it would be a good thing to do because it was a way of letting people know who we were. I loved it all, not only because it was my first trip to the States, but also because it gave me the chance to mingle with some of the really big players on the world boxing scene, including boxing historian Hank Kaplan, who helped me over the years that followed and is still a friend.

I was a bit star-struck and just enjoyed being able to have pictures taken with some of the household names who were there, including my first ever meeting with Don King. I would never have believed that just a few years later I would be dealing face to face with him as we negotiated what was then the biggest ever purse for a British heavyweight boxer.

After the convention we decided to make the most of our trip and went on to Las Vegas, a place I was to become very familiar with over the next few years. I'd taken Jackie with me and she enjoyed the trip even though a lot of it was spent introducing ourselves to people and making the sort of boxing contacts everyone in the sport needs.

Don't ask me how, but while we were there the idea of taking the legendary Roberto Duran to England started to become a real possibility. With the help of Hank Kaplan, I eventually managed to track down a representative of Duran's and a plan was put in place to bring him to the UK as part of a tour that would involve exhibitions around the country. It's incredible to think we managed to pull the whole thing off because although Duran was 37 years old, he was a massive name in the sport. In fact, just seven months after coming to Britain he managed to open another remarkable chapter in his life by taking the WBC world middleweight title from Iran Barkley. Duran is one of boxing's all-time greats and before beating Barkley he'd already won world titles at lightweight, welterweight and light-middleweight.

The Panamanian had learned to fight in order to survive, so it was a bit strange to see him looking perfectly at home walking around leafy Orpington in Kent. But that's where he stayed for the two weeks he was in this country while he did the exhibition tour we'd arranged. We had a great time with him and Roberto seemed to love every minute of it. His English wasn't great but I soon realised he understood things pretty well, especially when it came to ordering champagne! The great man loved the stuff and couldn't seem to get enough of it.

Eugene was a big fan of Duran. He was happy to help out and at the same time made sure everything went smoothly. The two of them seemed to hit it off straightaway and my brother quickly found a way to earn some money for himself, as he took Duran to various pubs he knew, putting in unscheduled appearances. It worked well for both men because Eugene always made sure Roberto was paid in kind by getting the publican to give his famous guest bottles of champagne. Duran was happy enough to get a taste of his favourite tipple and my brother was delighted to get some extra cash for arranging the whole thing.

Apart from the exhibitions, Duran was more than happy to socialise into the early hours and seemed to have just as much energy out of the ring as he had in it. One night we took him to a club in the Old Kent Road and the champagne soon began to flow. We were all having a good time when suddenly some idiot wandered over and decided to try and pick a fight with Duran.

Roberto didn't even realise what had happened, but my brother and another guy called Alan Matthews who was helping out on security certainly did. They leapt into action and pretty soon it was like a scene out of some Wild West movie, with punches being thrown and tables crashing over. The amazing thing was that Duran seemed completely oblivious to it and just sat there drinking champagne.

When the dust had settled we decided it would be better to get him out of the club in case it all flared up again. Eugene and Alan hustled Duran to the car but just as they opened the door for him Roberto ran back inside because he'd remembered leaving half a bottle of champagne on the table! He was always known as a hungry fighter, but he also showed what a thirsty one he was on that trip.

To be fair to him, Duran didn't come over to fight. It was purely a personal appearance tour with some exhibition fighting thrown in as part of it. He may have enjoyed his drinking and clubbing, but whatever he'd done the night before, Roberto was always up the next morning to go running. The tour was a big success and I really enjoyed the whole two weeks. Duran obviously had a good time as well because whenever I see him he always jokes about the trip and asks how Eugene is getting on.

We signed quite a few fighters and put shows on all over the place including the one I mentioned earlier involving my brother at Pickett's Lock. Within a fairly short period of time we became serious promoters, and maybe the biggest factor in helping us achieve more success came when Ambrose became Nigel Benn's adviser.

Benn had made a big name for himself since turning professional after winning the ABA middleweight title in 1986. He'd been skilfully brought along by Frank Warren and built up a big following. But Benn and Warren parted company after Nigel failed to appear on a big open-air show at Luton in June 1988, and the 'Dark Destroyer', as he was known, teamed up with Ambrose appearing on shows we were promoting.

One of the most memorable and spectacular was his contest with a Jamaican called Anthony Logan at the Albert Hall in October of that year. There was a great atmosphere and Terry Marsh and I co-promoted the show with Mike Barrett. I walked Nigel to the ring from his dressing-room and the tension and feel of the whole place on the night made the hairs on the back of my neck stand on end. The fight itself was short and dramatic, with Logan hurting Benn and virtually knocking him out before Nigel pulled things around in spectacular fashion to stop his man in the second. When Benn went down I felt the blood drain from my face, because for an instant I had the feeling that having got my foot on the ladder, any hopes I had of climbing to the top in boxing might end there and then with defeat for Nigel. It was a spectacular win for Benn, a ferocious puncher and a tremendous performer in the ring, whose fights were guaranteed to produce an exciting atmosphere.

At the end of the Duran tour Roberto had an exhibition bout with Britain's Errol Christie in London. Ambrose brought along two women from a marketing company to see the show and have a chat about some possible business opportunities. They were both quite posh girls and I had fun flirting with them. One of them, whose name was Pamela, seemed to be keen on taking things further and a bit later telephoned to ask if she could take me out to dinner. I was more than happy to see her again and we had a nice meal before heading back to her place in Wandsworth. As soon as we got there she asked if I wanted to smoke some dope, but I said I never touched the stuff and instead stuck to drinking wine.

It was getting late and I knew I had to drive all the way back to Crayford, so I thanked her for the meal and said I was going. She suddenly disappeared into the bathroom and after about ten minutes emerged wearing only black underwear and stockings. It didn't take me long to forget all about the journey home and I ended up staying for another two hours after she led me into her bedroom and closed the door.

As far as I was concerned it was a bit of fun and I never expected to hear from her again, but the next day a dozen red roses turned up at the office with a love note from her attached to them. She telephoned to say she'd like to discuss some possible business with me at her office and asked if we could meet. When I turned up I told her I needed to use the phone and she suggested I make myself at home at her desk. Midway through my call she suddenly disappeared under the table and the next thing I knew, my trousers were round my ankles and her head was in my lap. The guy on the other end of the phone must have wondered what the hell was going on, and I quickly realised it wasn't going to be just another day at the office.

But things began to change quickly and my new lady friend turned out to be more than a little bit possessive. In the end she made Glenn Close in the movie, *Fatal Attraction*, look like a Girl Guide. The whole thing got a bit heavy and on one occasion she turned up outside my pub in a fur coat and asked to speak to me in her car. When I got in the passenger seat she undid the coat and had nothing on underneath other than a pair of stockings. It gave a whole new meaning to the expression 'All fur coat and no knickers' as she threatened to expose herself in the bar of my pub if I didn't do what she wanted.

After a lot more hassle I managed to break free of her clutches, but during the time I was seeing her, I popped over to have a chat with Jasmine, the girl who was with Pamela on the night they'd come to the Duran exhibition. She was quite tall and very attractive, but I only really went there for a chat and we were getting on well when the buzzer to her flat sounded. She went to the hall and asked who it was before coming back into the room to tell me.

It turned out to be an already well known British boxer who later went on to become a world champion. I didn't have a clue that she was seeing this particular fighter at the time, but I thought it might be best if I did what she suggested, so I hopped into the cupboard. I thought I'd only be there for a couple of minutes while she got rid of him, but two hours later I was still trapped. The two of them quickly got at it as I crouched there sweating buckets. I wasn't able to see anything, but what I heard left very little to the imagination. Let's just say I think she tested the boxer's fitness and powers of recovery far more than most of his opponents ever did during his ring career.

By now Nigel Benn was a bigger star than ever with Ambrose always on the look-out for a marketing angle, but even he was surprised at the unwitting helping hand he was given by the London *Evening Standard* newspaper one day as we were preparing to take Clinton Mackenzie to Birmingham for a British light-welterweight title fight.

On the way up there Ambrose decided he would buy a copy of the paper and almost fell out of his seat when he opened it to see a story about a man who was wanted by the police. There was a photofit picture with it and to our amazement it was the spitting image of Benn. The guy in the photofit was apparently a wanted gunman and mugger who'd shot at a cyclist in Battersea Park.

After getting over the initial shock, Ambrose quickly saw the potential of it all and the publicity we could get. He even helped to set up a stunt which involved having someone trying to make a citizen's arrest while Nigel was out running during preparation for a forthcoming fight with Mike Chilambe at the Albert Hall. The incident was reported to have resulted in Benn bruising his knuckles and having treatment in order to make sure he could go ahead with the contest. It was incredible, and the Mendy publicity machine went into overdrive as it set out to milk the whole incident. He even threatened legal action at one point and in the end got an apology from both the police and the newspaper for what had happened.

The last and biggest promotion I was involved in, while working with Ambrose, was the Nigel Benn–Michael Watson contest, which was shown live on TV in America and staged in a big-top tent in Finsbury Park, north London, on a May evening in 1989.

It was a terrific event and involved a lot of planning and hard work in order to get the thing put together, but I remember the build-up to the show for different reasons as well. Although the fight took place in May, the idea for the contest and the negotiations started months earlier. I seemed to spend most of my time in the office at the World Sports Corporation and it was while I was at my desk one morning in February that I took a call which was to change the course of my life. It came from Las Vegas and was made by a photographer named Lawrence Lustig, who was out there covering Lloyd Honeyghan's world welterweight title fight with Marlon Starling. I picked the telephone receiver up and was surprised to hear Lawrence's voice on the other end of the line.

'Frank, you're not going to believe this,' he said. 'You know how you want to be a big player in boxing? Well, what if you could sign a heavyweight who could win the world title, and that heavyweight was British?'

6. IT'S GOOD TO TALK

THERE'S NO DOUBT HEAVYWEIGHTS HAVE ALWAYS FASCINATED ME AND WHEN
I first became a boxing manager, it was my dream to one day have
some real success in the division, but I have to admit that nothing
had prepared me for the situation I found myself in that morning.

I'd been surprised to hear Lawrence on the other end of the line
and my first thought was that he must have been on the booze with
the rest of the press in Vegas and got pissed. But Lustig reminded me
he didn't drink and insisted he was deadly serious. He told me the
fighter's name was Lennox Lewis. He'd been born in the East End of
London before going to live in Canada at the age of 12, and had won
the super-heavyweight gold medal for them at the Seoul Olympics
the previous autumn.

Lustig and his reporter colleague from the *Daily Star*, Ken
Gorman, weren't only in Vegas for the Honeyghan fight, they were
also there to cover Frank Bruno's attempt to take the world
heavyweight title from Mike Tyson later that same month. The place
was buzzing with fight people and Lawrence had recognised Lewis
when they were both in Caesar's Palace Hotel. He'd found out that
Lennox was there with a young Chicago lawyer called John

Hornewer who was advising him, and the pair were listening to offers from different managers and promoters.

Suddenly I realised the phone-call wasn't a 'wind-up' and knew Lawrence was letting me know about a potential golden opportunity. I was desperate to talk to Lewis and his attorney, but I wasn't sure he'd want to talk to someone like me. After all, he was in the States talking to the likes of Don King and Bob Arum, while I was a struggling British promoter and manager.

Gorman and Lustig suggested I should try to put some sort of package together, before speaking again at roughly the same time the next day. When I got off the phone my head was spinning. The whole thing seemed too good to be true, especially the bit about Lennox being born in London. I knew I needed to make sure Lewis and Hornewer took me seriously when I got to speak to them, but the problem was finding a way to finance any deal. I was going to be dealing with the current Olympic super-heavyweight champion and some of the biggest players in world boxing were falling over themselves trying to sign him.

The good thing was that Lawrence and Ken seemed to be singing my praises to Lennox and Hornewer. So when the call came through from Lustig's room at the Flamingo Hilton on the Saturday morning, I was ready to let this 24-year-old West Ham-born kid know that coming home to England and having me as his manager was a serious option.

After talking to Lennox and Hornewer I was even more excited, but talk is cheap and I was well aware that the next move was to make sure I followed up the conversation with some action. I spent hours on the phone trying to track Hornewer down about a week later, and lost count of the number of times I rang.

I finally spoke to John and suggested that both he and Lennox should come to London and discuss things further. I felt that if I could get to see them face to face I would have a better chance of convincing them England would be the ideal place to launch Lewis's professional career. Hornewer was happy to make the trip as long as air travel and accommodation were taken care of, and he also wanted me to provide security.

The travel and hotels were no problem but the overall cost of financing any long-term deal with Lewis certainly was, because at the time of that call I had no backers to prop up the grand plans I had swirling around in my head.

I was encouraged by Ambrose to think big and sometime before the Lewis idea came up, he had introduced me to the former Chelsea, Arsenal and QPR footballer John Hollins, as well as another guy named Charles Meaden. They were part of an organisation called Olympic Gold, which was attached to the Levitt Group, a highly successful financial advisory company specialising in insurance and pensions. It was claimed the company was worth around £150 million and its head, Roger Levitt, had set up the Olympic Gold sports division in an effort to compete with IMG, a giant sports agency run by American Mark McCormack.

Ambrose had made contact with Meaden, Hollins and someone else called Jonathan Barnett who later went on to become a successful football agent. They seemed keen to get into boxing and it became clear that if it was going to happen, the Levitt Group would be happier dealing with me. I think perhaps Mendy's criminal past could have been something of a stumbling block to him ever being involved with such a company, but Ambrose understood that better than anyone and wanted me to make the running with them.

He seemed happy for us to be involved with them, knowing they had the sort of financial muscle we could do with, especially as we were trying to put together a fight between Benn and Watson. It was clear that if I was going to have any hope of signing Lennox I would need some big money behind me to match my equally big ideas.

With that in mind I put together a proposal and business plan for Meaden emphasising that if the Levitt Group backed it and were prepared to finance the sort of contract Lewis wanted, they could open their own bank if he became world heavyweight champion because the rewards would be so enormous.

I found Meaden easy to get on with even though we came from very different backgrounds. He was an old Harrovian with great contacts in the City and had boxed when he was at school, but wasn't really into the professional game. Charles was about the same age as me, bald except for a few strands of hair around the side of his head and constantly smoked cigarettes. He seemed keen to add a boxing wing to their expanding sporting interests, and they saw me as the man to run it for them.

I eventually signed a deal with the Levitt Group after Charles agreed they would be willing to back my idea of signing Lewis, and they also wanted me to bring along all the boxers I was looking after. It meant me breaking up with Ambrose, but I believe he thought it could benefit both of us in the long run and I think he saw a possible commercial role for himself with Lewis in the future. But although he'd been instrumental in introducing me to Olympic Gold, Mendy was to have nothing to do with the actual signing of Lewis.

Joining the Levitt organisation turned out to be a great deal for me at the time: I got a £25,000-per-year management consultancy fee, a percentage from all the fighters I signed to the Group, a brand new white Mercedes as a company car, mobile phone and my own offices with a secretary in Great Portland Street.

Air tickets and accommodation at the Churchill Hotel in London were arranged for Lennox and Hornewer, who were both due to arrive at Heathrow on the morning of 8 March. Lennox was coming in from Canada, while Hornewer was flying from Chicago. I was really excited as I stood there waiting for him to arrive. Jonathan Barnett was with me and I'd also arranged the security they'd insisted on for the duration of their stay.

I had no problem spotting Lennox even though Terminal Three was as busy as it always is. He stood head and shoulders above everyone else, and when he made his way over to us we introduced ourselves as he stuck out a massive hand for me to shake.

It may sound silly but that first glimpse of him made me feel as though I'd met someone who was going to be very special. He just had a kind of assured air about him and seemed like a born winner. All I could remember thinking was that somehow I had to make sure I put the right deal together and pulled the whole thing off. It seemed to be fate that he hadn't signed with anyone and I felt that maybe I was the one who was waiting out there for him. I'd already been told that Lennox had spoken to Don King, American promoters Main Events, Stan Hoffman from the Houston Boxing Association, Manny Steward and Mickey Duff. But I felt from the moment I met Lewis we clicked.

IT'S GOOD TO TALK

I knew it could be my chance to break into the big time, but my more immediate problem was telling him and Hornewer that I wouldn't be around for a day or so. I had to fly off to Belfast that evening because I was acting as an agent for Anthony Logan, the fighter who'd almost caused an upset against Benn.

Neither of them seemed to mind and John told me that he'd arranged to go to the Albert Hall to watch Duke McKenzie in a defence of his IBF flyweight title against Tony de Luca. Although Hornewer was a lawyer he also liked taking fight pictures as a freelance photographer. I was surprised by Hornewer when I first saw him because he looked so young. He was quite short and had a fresh face that made him look more like a schoolboy. He actually reminded me of the puppet called Joe 90 in the kids' TV series.

He was very sure of himself and I'm afraid I didn't warm to him, but at the same time he was there to represent Lennox and I knew I would have to do business with him. He was 28 years old and was doing a masters degree in business studies. He'd been given permission by his university to accompany Lennox around the States and use the negotiation of his contract as part of the practical side of his studies.

Hornewer first met Lennox after negotiating a couple of contracts for the Canadian fighter Matthew Hilton, and had been called in by the Mallett Group, a management company who had plans to handle the career of Lewis. He got on well with Lewis and offered to act for him without a contract as they tried to get the best deal they could following the Olympic success.

While John said he had plans to go to the fight, Lennox told me he was going to meet up with his brother Dennis who lived in Harlesden. All I wanted to do was make sure everything went smoothly and I said goodbye knowing they were in safe hands with Alan Matthews and his sidekick Brian, the guys I'd brought in to act as minders.

It was hard for me to concentrate on anything other than Lennox Lewis at that moment and although I went off to Belfast, I couldn't wait to get the first plane back to London the next morning. I went straight to the Churchill Hotel and later in the Levitt Group offices we began a meeting aimed at trying to find out exactly what sort of package Hornewer and Lewis were looking for. I was joined in the discussions by Charles and Jonathan, as well as a finance guy from the company. Things went well, but once again I had to break away from the meeting because I was scheduled to see Mickey Duff for talks about the proposed contest between his fighter Michael Watson and Benn, for Nigel's Commonwealth middleweight title.

The meeting with Mickey was held at the offices of Mendy's lawyer, Henri Brandman. When we got there Duff refused to take part in any negotiations that involved Ambrose because Mendy was not licensed by the British Boxing Board of Control. Far from this being a stumbling block, Ambrose was quite happy to stay outside, while I sat in on the meeting trying to thrash out a deal.

He desperately wanted the fight to take place and was prepared to do whatever he had to for the deal to go through. He also wanted to get the backing of the Levitt Group to finance the whole thing. I kept popping out of the meeting to let Ambrose know how things were going and Duff was his usual bombastic self when it came to trying to strike a deal.

He was often very loud when shouting about some point or other, but everyone has their own way of negotiating and that was how Mickey liked doing things. Brandman suggested we continue the meeting over dinner at the Phoenix Apollo in Stratford, a restaurant that at the time was quite a popular place with some page three girls and minor East End celebrities.

I'd already arranged to meet Lennox and John at Brandman's offices before taking them to have an Indian meal. When we left, the two of them were sitting outside in a car waiting for me along with Alan the minder. The sight of them clearly surprised Duff who quickly realised I was trying to sign Lewis. I told Alan to take them back to my pub in Crayford so that Jackie could sort the meal out and said I'd join them later.

We called a taxi with Brandman, Duff and I travelling separately to Ambrose, who followed on in his own car. When we were in the cab Mickey turned to me with a grin on his face. 'So you're trying to sign Lennox Lewis?' he asked. 'You must be joking. You won't get much joy there!'

I told him I thought I had just as much chance as he did and settled back into my seat content in the knowledge that I probably had a lot more going for me than he thought, simply because of the money I had available from the Levitt Group.

Mickey gave a virtuoso performance at the Apollo that night. He was still negotiating hard with me, while once again Ambrose was content to sit it out in the hope that the fight could be made. At one point Benn's trainer, Brian Lynch, joined us and I got the distinct impression that both he and Ambrose were content to let Mickey have his way, because they were so totally convinced Nigel would beat Watson.

Duff was a very cute operator who had spent a lifetime in boxing and knew every trick in the book. I'm sure he'd used a similar routine in other negotiations down the years. When he stood up and started shouting you got the feeling there was no need for any kind of cabaret in the restaurant. Mickey was providing it all and seemed to enjoy every minute because he had a captive audience.

I never did make it to the Indian restaurant for the meal with Lennox, but he didn't seem to mind and the next day I spent my time shuffling between Brandman's office and Levitt's in Great Portland Street. The Benn–Watson deal started looking good with the clinching factor for Duff being the knowledge that his fighter's money would be safe because the promotion was being backed by the Levitt organisation.

The negotiations with Lennox and Hornewer had a good feel to them and we pretty soon began agreeing on some of the more vital points. It was apparent to me that Lennox was like a toy to the people at Levitt, and they just wanted to add him to the list of other sporting personalities they already had on their books.

The whole organisation was like nothing I'd ever seen or experienced before, it was all so over-the-top. The office furniture must have cost a fortune, the men all liked to wear expensive suits and the whole place seemed awash with money. There was never any question of worrying when it came to spending, and they splashed the cash as if money was no object at all. The only people I came into contact with who seemed to know what they were doing and appeared to be normal were Charles Meaden and John Hollins.

I quickly got the impression that whatever Lennox asked for he would get, and I doubt that Hornewer realised I was his biggest ally during all the talks, because nobody wanted the deal to go through more than me. I'd talked to John throughout the negotiations and had a pretty good idea of exactly what other people were prepared to offer him. It meant we would have to come up with a fairly spectacular deal, and although a lot of progress was made, Lennox and Hornewer flew back across the Atlantic without a final agreement being struck.

Some time later on a Friday evening I was sitting in my office and suddenly felt a lot of activity around me. People were making themselves busy; tidying things up, putting stuff away in drawers and there seemed to be a general buzz of excitement around the place. I began to wonder what was going on, and was told by someone that Roger Levitt was on the floor.

I got ready to meet him for the very first time and it was as if we were about to receive a royal visit. It wasn't long before Levitt was standing right in front of me. He was sharp featured, with slicked-back black hair, a Groucho Marx moustache and a massive cigar that seemed to go on for ever hanging from his mouth. He was dressed in an immaculate dark suit, set off by a bow tie, and had a navy blue coat draped over his shoulders. To top the whole thing off a bright red silk scarf dangled from his neck.

'Who are you?' he said.

'I'm Frank Maloney,' I told him. 'Who are you?'

'I'm Roger Levitt,' he replied. 'You're supposed to be the man who's running my boxing for me and getting me this heavyweight who's going to be world champion one day.'

I explained we were still negotiating and proceedings had come to a halt because a couple of his guys were messing things up. I told him that because of it we might end up losing out on a fantastic opportunity. It clearly was not what he wanted to hear.

'I've heard you're good,' he said. 'Now prove it and get that signature on the contract at all costs. I don't care what it takes, just get him. If it means jumping on a plane tonight, do it.'

I got the feeling there was a lot of showmanship in the way he'd told me to go after Lewis, but at the same time I also realised I'd been given the green light to write a blank cheque. It was the chance to realise my dream of signing the man I believed would be a future world heavyweight champion.

Pretty soon after my brief conversation with Levitt I was on the phone to Hornewer making arrangements to meet him and Lennox in New York. John was keen to talk again and also suggested we meet some American trainers who might work with Lennox in the future.

I was pretty confident I could come back with a deal because I'd already gone over some of the finer details with Hornewer and now had the go-ahead from Levitt himself to sort the whole thing out and come back with the job done.

I flew to New York determined to come home as the manager of Lewis, and as I sat in my business-class seat, I had a little chuckle to myself at the way things had changed for me. Not too long before that trip my only real experience of world travel had been a package holiday in Spain. Now I was jetting off to New York in an attempt to clinch one of the biggest deals in boxing.

It was my first taste of the Big Apple and I was in awe of the place, but as a kid from the streets of south London, I could identify with it in many ways. From the moment I touched down there was something about it I loved. I'd booked a hotel on 42nd Street because I knew that trainer Angelo Dundee was in town for a fight and was staying there, but Lennox and John didn't like the place and instead moved to a suite at the Marriott.

Lennox, Hornewer and I met with Dundee who did a great sales pitch, saying what a good move it would be for Lennox to sign with me and begin his career in England. It was all good stuff as far as I was concerned and coming from a man who had trained the great Muhammad Ali, it gave my cause a lot of credibility.

But after the meeting John claimed Dundee would not be the right trainer for Lennox and then said Stan Hoffman, an American boxing manager who was working with an organisation called the Houston Boxing Association, had recommended a guy who could do the job. It was obvious at this point that Hornewer was paying quite a lot of attention to what Hoffman was saying, and I wasn't going to start rocking the boat.

The good thing was that we seemed to have an agreement and it was decided Hornewer and Lennox would fly to England in April for the formal signing of the contract. It was a brilliant feeling to know the whole thing was actually going to happen, but I knew there was going to be a lot of work ahead and it wasn't going to be easy.

It was agreed he would fly in on Sunday, 23 April 1989, to put pen to paper, 12 weeks after that call from Lawrence Lustig. During that time I'd lost 16 lb in weight. I'd been chasing around and not eating properly, snacking on things like ice-cream and puddings to keep me going.

When the day finally came for me to pick Lennox up at the airport I felt like a kid on Christmas morning. I was up at 6 a.m. and took Emma with me. I drove like a lunatic and managed to get to Heathrow in about 40 minutes. Not surprisingly, I was there with plenty of time to spare and met Lennox at Terminal Four as he came through the arrivals gate, before driving him to Terminal Three where we picked up Jonathan Barnett who was waiting for Hornewer to arrive from Chicago. Once I had everybody in the car I relaxed a little.

Everything was very informal and friendly as I dropped them off at their hotel, The Black Prince in Bexley. I gave them a chance to unpack before picking them up again later that afternoon for a typical Sunday lunch back at my pub, prepared by my mum. Lennox really seemed to enjoy it and the locals who were in The Crayford Arms at the time gave him a great reception.

It was quite an emotional time for me and I knew my life was about to change dramatically. I wanted Jackie to share in it as well, so I insisted that she come to the press conference and be part of the whole experience.

We shot over to their hotel and had breakfast with Lennox and Hornewer on the Monday morning before heading for London to meet the press, but before doing that we made a trip to West Ham United football club for a photo shoot and interview session with the two men who had first alerted me to the possibility of signing Lennox.

Lawrence Lustig and Ken Gorman met us at the stadium, getting Lennox to blow bubbles for a shot outside the club that had been his local team when he lived in London. West Ham's theme song is 'I'm forever blowing bubbles' and Lennox was happy to pose and answer questions as the Lewis publicity bandwagon began to roll.

Most people who know me now would probably never recognise

the nervous and uneasy figure who sat at the top table in the Press Centre that day, as the media were introduced to the man who was setting out to make British boxing history. I dried up during all the questioning and didn't really feel comfortable with the whole new experience. I'd always been chirpy and confident at press conferences, but I had never been involved in anything as big.

The Levitt Group had really pushed the boat out and there was plenty of food and drink for everyone. It was an important day for them as well, because it signalled their entrance on to the big sporting stage. Lennox was very good and Hornewer seemed to lap up every moment of it. He clearly liked the idea of being centre stage and I suspect most people in that room would probably have thought he was about to become the manager of Lewis and not me.

After the press conference we all went back to my office where the contract was actually signed. From that moment on I stopped being called Frank Maloney and instead started to be introduced as 'Frank Maloney – manager of Lennox Lewis'. It was a great feeling for me, but I didn't have too much time to dwell on things because that same evening I had a couple of fighters on a dinner show in Nottingham. Lennox and John came with me and enjoyed the night. It was a good end to a fantastic day for me and on the way home we stopped off at one of the motorway service stations at three in the morning, where we all got stuck into some dubious looking burgers and chips.

Lennox was relaxed and unassuming. He enjoyed joking around and although I didn't know him that well I quickly began to warm to him. He was a big likeable guy with bags of talent and a determination to succeed. As far as I was concerned that night just reaffirmed what I'd thought when we first met. Lennox Lewis was going to climb to the top of the boxing tree, and I wanted to be there with him every step of the way.

Only a few hours earlier he'd signed a deal that was probably unheard of for a boxer. It gave him tremendous security and assured him of some very decent money even before he'd thrown his first punch as a professional. The contract meant Lennox would get a signing-on fee of around £150,000, the use of a house in Crayford, a Mercedes, living expenses of £500 a week, and a place for his mother Violet on the Levitt Group's payroll.

NO BALONEY

The boxing revenues were split 70 per cent for Lennox with 30 per cent going to the company, but that would also cover training expenses and pay the salaries of the training team. The company provided £750,000 in health and life insurance policies and made provision for education and training when Lennox retired. A sum was also set aside to cover any outstanding debts in Canada.

It also meant that I became the manager of a potential world heavyweight champion, but despite what a lot of people thought at the time I was not about to get the sort of 25 per cent cut many may have believed. I actually got a much smaller percentage, but I certainly had no complaints about it and was just pleased to finally get the deal done.

I knew Lennox and I were at the beginning of an exciting journey and life for both of us was never going to be quite the same again.

7. ROGER AND OUT

THERE WASN'T TOO MUCH TIME FOR SLEEP FOLLOWING THE LATE NIGHT RIDE
home from Nottingham, because the next day we had to hop on a
plane for New York and another press conference, this time with the
media from the States.

If my last stay in a New York hotel had been nothing to write
home about while negotiating the Lennox deal with Hornewer, this
time the circumstances were very different. I was suddenly in the lap
of luxury with a magnificent room at the Plaza. I'd never seen
anything like it before in my life and my first reaction was to get on
the phone to Jackie and a few others back home and tell them about
it because it was such a novelty at the time.

The press conference the next day had been arranged by Hoffman. It
was my first experience of the New York boxing writers, and the main
thing they had in common was their cynicism. There was no doubt a
few of them thought the idea of this unknown little Brit managing an
Olympic super-heavyweight gold medal-winner was a joke. They just
couldn't believe someone like me had pulled the deal off.

They were used to dealing with the likes of Don King and hearing
stories about how boxers were ripped off by managers and

promoters, but the whole thing about my relationship with Lennox was that I saw myself there in the role of someone who was going to help him to the top. He was calling the shots but I was more than happy to be there to advise and guide him. I was under no illusions. It was me working for him, not the other way around.

As well as the press conference I also got to meet John Davenport, the trainer Hoffman had recommended to Hornewer as the ideal man to help Lennox. I think Hornewer thought Hoffman was the right person to help out in America because of his knowledge and contacts in the business there.

Davenport appeared to be a nice enough guy, even if he looked as if a smile might crack his face and he seemed to carry the worries of the world on his shoulders. He was a stocky black guy and the day I first met him he wore a dark top, a baseball cap and had a little, grey, goatee beard. His appearance didn't change too much during the time I knew him, and his background as an American ex-marine helped to give him the look of a drill-sergeant.

I could relate to some of the stories he told me as the little guy fighting against the more established names in the sport, because that was exactly what I was doing. I told him we'd fly him over to England and get a contract sorted out that would safeguard his interests. I also told him we wanted everything to go well and be professionally run in preparation for Lennox's first fight, which had been provisionally pencilled in to take place at the Royal Albert Hall on 27 June.

The whole operation was beginning to come together and I was enjoying every minute of it. The next day we were off once more, this time to a press conference in Canada where Lennox was already a hero after winning his gold medal for the country in Seoul.

Being introduced as his manager was a bit of a thrill for me and I got a nice feeling about the way things were going. As well as his friends and girlfriend at the time, Marcia, I also met Lennox's mother, Violet, for the first time and immediately warmed to her. She was then and is now a very kind person whom I've always got on well with. Just like any other mum, she wanted the best for her son and was also keen to see the sort of people who would be steering his career.

The press conference went well and I began to feel more at home with the media. It was also good for me to spend a decent amount of time with Lennox so early on in our relationship, and it gave me an insight into the sort of character he was.

The one thing I noticed right away was just how well organised he was in everything he did. He was meticulous about the way he looked after himself. His clothes were always sorted out in a neat and tidy fashion and he ironed things. Lennox told me that being on the road so much as an amateur had taught him how to look after himself. I was impressed, particularly as I'm a complete disaster with things like that.

I also got the impression that at times Lennox seemed just as overwhelmed by the whole experience as I was. We were both being catapulted into a new way of life and things were never going to be the same for either one of us again. I realised I couldn't afford to fail. If I did I knew that would be the end of me in big-time boxing. Nobody would take me seriously.

It worried me that a lot of the people I would be working with, like Hornewer and Davenport, had been thrust on me and that I had no real knowledge of them at all. For me to succeed with Lennox I realised I would need to get some people around me whom I knew and trusted.

I slept for most of the journey back to London, having left Lennox to clear up some personal business in Canada and was happy to be heading home after a manic seven days in which we'd held press conferences in London, New York and Toronto to publicise the start of Lewis's professional career.

Apart from getting a taste of a new kind of boxing world the trip also came at a useful time, because it got me out of having to help Jackie with all the packing involved in moving to our new house. My main objective at the time was making sure everything went smoothly for the professional debut of Lennox.

I arranged for Davenport to fly in and spend a long weekend sorting out the details of his contract with Jonathan Barnett. It was all straightforward, and needless to say John ended up getting a pretty good deal, with the Levitt Group again showing they were happy to throw the cash around including the use of a house and car.

If Davenport's first trip was uneventful the former military man from New Jersey certainly didn't have it so easy when he tried to enter the country on some later occasions. First he was stopped over an incident involving his baggage and sent back, and then he was turned away at Heathrow because he didn't have the right documentation. When Barnett heard about this he came up with the brilliant idea of telling John to get on another plane and fly into Gatwick. His previous refusal must have flashed up like a beacon on the immigration officer's computer and Davenport was marched away and sent back to the States once more.

The third incident came as John was flying in to start preparations for Lennox's first pro fight and it happened on the morning of the long-awaited clash between Benn and Watson. There was a mix-up over work permits and poor old Davenport was sent packing again.

I suppose if I'd been in his shoes I would have been steaming as well, but I couldn't help seeing the funny side of it. There he was, the man who never smiled and seemed to dislike all things British, being stopped from coming in to the country three times! It was all finally sorted out, but Davenport was furious and didn't like being reminded of the incident.

Although I was working full-time for the Levitt Group I was still involved in the Benn–Watson promotion. By this time my relationship with Ambrose had soured and he'd accused me of deserting him. The Levitt Group were underwriting the promotion, so it was my job as their boxing man to keep an eye on things. I'd been in at the beginning when the Benn fight was first set up and, as I've said, it was me who negotiated with Duff as Mendy left me to it. Ambrose seemed to like cultivating a certain image, but the truth is that, as well as his criminal past when I met him, he's repeatedly found himself inside over the years that have followed, on a variety of charges.

I always felt that he tried to appear smooth and sophisticated in public, but Frank Warren once told me about the time Mendy turned up at a restaurant just as Frank was helping himself to some nibbles at the bar. Ambrose thought he'd join him and stuck his hand into the bowl in front of him. Unfortunately, what he thought were nuts turned out to be coffee beans, but instead of admitting his mistake

Mendy just carried on crunching them as if nothing was wrong. He also seemed to have a problem with the coffee at the end of the meal, when he ordered a cappuccino but asked the waiter to make his black.

The fact of the matter was that I'd moved on and Ambrose resented it. In simple terms it was a career move for me and an opportunity I couldn't pass up. The people at Olympic Gold wanted to deal with me and not him because they said I was the right man to run their boxing operation.

The fight between Benn and Watson was a massive event staged on a very warm May Sunday evening in a big-top tent at Finsbury Park. Despite the fact that it was such a huge occasion, I couldn't get that worked up about it all. In many ways, it was really Ambrose's little baby, and he saw it as the perfect way to further the career of Nigel who was unbeaten in 22 fights.

As the day of the fight drew closer the promotion was rarely out of the headlines and the weigh-in was just the sort of chaotic affair you might expect. Benn went off after it and had a new hairstyle with extensions put in, and then the whole arrangement was pulled back so tightly that it seemed to stretch the skin on his forehead.

Duff showed all his experience in the way he handled things and often had Ambrose tied up in knots. He even threatened to take Watson out of the ring on the night if they were kept waiting too long. Years later when Paul Ingle fought Naseem Hamed, I actually went a step further and marched Paul out of the ring after Naz made us stand there for too long.

There was an amazing atmosphere in the tent and as the preliminary bouts were going on word reached me that Ambrose had lost his temper with a finance guy from the Levitt organisation called Colin Myers and lashed out at him. It was obvious Mendy was hyped up and had gone over the top, and I nearly came to blows with him as well after a massive row in a portakabin which was being used as an office. It was all over the fact that I was firmly part of the Levitt Group and he felt I'd betrayed him. He clearly felt like the man on the outside looking in, and reacted badly.

I walked out of the room and made my way to the ringside for the big fight. Watson looked very cool while Benn's shining outfit would have looked more at home in a West End show. From round one you could tell it was going to be a tough fight for Nigel because unlike some of his other opponents, Watson showed no signs at all of being intimidated by the Dark Destroyer's reputation.

While Nigel tried to unload his bombs, using up energy all the time, Michael covered up well and picked his punches, hardly wasting a shot. It didn't help Nigel's cause too much to have a corner that seemed to be at a loss as to how to deal with the situation. At one point Ambrose leaned over my shoulder asking if I could help sort things out, but Brian Lynch was the man in charge and he was the one who had to take control.

By the sixth Nigel looked a beaten fighter and had nothing left. A sharp jab from Watson put Benn on his backside and took the Commonwealth title away from him. It was a sad night for Nigel and a disaster for Ambrose, who had such big plans for his fighter.

After the contest Lynch claimed Benn had abandoned a game plan they had, but in the end the defeat by Watson was something of a turning point for Nigel. He went back to the drawing board, with Ambrose taking him to America, and he eventually became a world champion. But the greatest success in his career came later when he joined forces with Warren once again.

Frank couldn't resist having a dig at Ambrose following the result of the fight. In the days leading up to the contest Mendy had started issuing press releases with different themes on them as the big day approached. One was headed 'Bad,' the next, 'It's bad,' and he followed that with 'So bad' and 'Who's bad?' When Benn lost Warren faxed Mendy with a simple message, 'Too bad!'

Lennox watched from ringside as Watson beat Benn, and because of all the problems with Davenport's work permit, we decided to use a camp in the States. Lewis was to be based at Stan Hoffman's place in the Catskills.

I was getting used to the ways of the world in the Levitt organisation. The whole place had a slightly unreal feel to it, with most people there more concerned with image than substance. For the most part I enjoyed it, even though so many of the people I came into contact with seemed to have lost touch with reality. They were so far up their own arses they hardly ever saw daylight. Everyone had a massive ego and I never saw anyone doing too much work, although they all seemed to have the ability to look busy. It was like a giant playground with some big financial perks thrown in. A lot of the guys in the Group used to have a league table for all the girls they'd slept with from the office, and the women did the same for the men.

As for Levitt himself, it was probably easier to get an audience with the Pope than seeing him on a regular basis. He was always telling people how clever they were as he pandered to their egos, and they would lap it up and never said a word against him. He was a great absorber of knowledge and overnight he became a boxing expert – or so he thought.

I believe Levitt tried to intimidate people all the time and never expected to have his views questioned. I remember once having a meeting in the boardroom and disagreeing with something he said. I quickly felt a sharp kick from under the table, as someone whispered to me to let Roger have his own way. He thought he could buy anyone, and gave Lennox just about everything he wanted to join the company. To Roger it was just another acquisition. He often talked about how he wanted to own the heavyweight championship of the world and his beloved Arsenal Football Club.

Roger once told me in front of Charles Meaden that there was a bit of a problem with Hornewer, and said he was going to hang John out of the window by his ankles. Levitt eventually met with Hornewer, and Roger did a bit of shouting and ranting. He also knocked over a bottle of expensive red wine, which he did on a number of other occasions and seemed to be a way of trying to intimidate people, but by the end of the meeting, rather than being hung out of the window, John actually found himself being given a substantial annual sum, which staggered me. It was possibly Roger's way of trying to keep some control, but the way he went about it was puzzling.

On the boxing front I had to make sure the team was in place for Lewis's debut. It soon became clear Davenport was one of those perfectly balanced people you sometimes have the misfortune to meet – he had a chip on each shoulder. I don't quite know why but it was obvious John had no time for the British, which was a bit unfortunate, given the fact that we were setting out to make sure this country got its first world heavyweight champion of the century. But despite Davenport's attitude, things were coming together well and I felt excited about Lennox's first fight.

With the training camp for the Albert Hall fight fixed up in America I headed off for the IBF convention in Jamaica at the end of May 1989. I'd been told to take Jackie along with me and we travelled to the Caribbean with Jonathan Barnett, who seemed keen to attend the meeting and no doubt try to make some new contacts in a sport he really knew little about at the time.

Everything started well and I was looking forward to talking to all the boxing people and meeting some of the characters who were going to be there. Ambrose and Nigel also made the trip and Mendy got upset with me once again as we waited to be taken on an organised riverboat trip on our second night there. It was a shame but I wasn't about to lose any sleep over it, although the next day I did get some news that stopped me in my tracks and gave me more of an insight into the sort of character I was dealing with in John Hornewer.

While I was in Jamaica he'd faxed the office in London claiming Lennox was unhappy with certain things that were happening. When I found out I immediately got on the phone and told Hornewer in no uncertain terms what I thought. At one point I think he must have believed I was threatening him, because a little while later I got a call from Charles Meaden asking me what had gone on. I told him that I wasn't happy with Hornewer and what he was up to. I was Lennox's manager not John and it seemed a lot had been going on that I knew nothing about.

Jackie could see I was upset by all this and suggested the best way to deal with it was by hopping on a plane to New York and going to see Lennox face to face. If he had any problems or concerns, then he could tell me and I would make sure they were sorted out.

When we got to the camp in the Catskill Mountains everything seemed fine and Lennox looked relaxed and happy. It made me wonder why I'd flown there in the first place. My first impression was that it seemed a good camp. The mood was very good, with Lennox training and sharing a big house with several other fighters. This was also the first time I met Harold Knight who was later to become Lewis's assistant trainer.

ROGER AND OUT

After my little chat with him when I was in Jamaica, I'd told Hornewer that if he had any more problems he should contact me first rather than play the power game with the people back in London.

If I'm honest I have to say this was the start of what was often a stormy relationship with Hornewer. To put it bluntly, I soon made up my mind that I didn't like him. He just wasn't the sort of character I could ever really get on with. It was never going to be easy working with him, but I had to for quite some time until Lennox finally put an end to Hornewer's involvement in the Lewis set-up.

When I asked Lennox about the faxes he said he didn't know exactly what was in them. It seemed strange to me that he hadn't picked up the phone and told me if he was upset with certain things. After all, I was his manager and that was what I was there for. It was probably the first time I had experience of a certain side to Lennox that was to become familiar over the years.

For all his courage and ability in the ring I very soon realised he didn't like personal confrontations out of it. That doesn't mean to say he gives in and can't be bothered, but quite often he would rather go through a third party instead of meeting the problem head-on and confronting the individual.

After the fax business with Hornewer, there were quite a few occasions where I came to hear that Lennox was not happy with certain things. Sometimes it involved me, sometimes it concerned other people. But I never really heard it from Lennox's mouth, or when he did speak to me, he would manage to hedge around the major issue. I often used to come away not knowing exactly how he felt. It can be frustrating and also lead to unnecessary rumours and unrest, particularly within the close confines of something like a training camp. But it never interfered with his success, and maybe it's been a way for him to detach himself from things and concentrate on the job in hand.

The Albert Hall show was billed as 'The Birth of a Champion' with Lennox making his professional bow against Al Malcolm from Birmingham. Lennox arrived in the country eight days before the fight and we had a press conference for the show which got a lot of publicity. As the days went by during the build-up to the contest I got more and more nervous, and it was a pattern I repeated over the years, often going without real food for days before a big fight.

Lennox at 16 st. 7 lb was 16 lb heavier than Malcolm and proved to be too strong and powerful on the night, stopping his first professional opponent in the second round. Lewis looked the part, but there was a lot of work to be done. The priority was to get regular fights that would help him gain experience and move him towards world level at the right speed. I had a great feeling of relief when the contest was over and after celebrating at my pub in Crayford, I fell into bed exhausted at about three in the morning and slept like a baby for the first time in three weeks.

With no disrespect to Malcolm, Lennox had hardly broken sweat in beating him and just over three weeks later Lewis was in action again when we travelled to Atlantic City for a fight with American Bruce Johnson from Ohio on a show promoted by Don King. It was an easy contest for Lennox against the 13 st. 10 lb Johnson who was stopped in the second round, but the real point of the exercise was to get Lewis on a top-line American bill and his fight at the Convention Hall on 21 July was part of the undercard for the Mike Tyson v Carl 'The Truth' Williams world title clash.

Lennox's purse for that fight was just $1,000 and it was arranged by Stan Hoffman. A little less than four years later Lewis made the first defence of his WBC world heavyweight title in the States when he beat Tony Tucker in Las Vegas and, thanks to King, he walked away with a cool $9 million purse.

Levitt turned up with some friends to witness the second fight of 'his heavyweight' and then jetted out again. It became quite a funny spectacle to see him and his guests at shows. He would troop in with his huge cigar and dark overcoat to sit at ringside and watch the contest, but never struck me as someone who really had a feeling for boxing.

When I got back to England after the Johnson fight I was still on a bit of a high and decided to take Jackie out for a meal. What should have been a relaxed evening turned into a bit of a shock for me. Jackie got upset and once again claimed she was being left out and pushed to one side as I went after my dream of managing a world heavyweight champion. It was clear things were no longer the same for either of us.

If cracks were beginning to show in my relationship with Jackie, my professional life seemed to be going from strength to strength. The careful planning of Lennox's career meant he was to have another four fights during 1989, the last of which helped make those cracks with Jackie even wider.

We followed the fight with Johnson with another learning contest against Andy Gerrard from Wales at Crystal Palace in London. It brought a fourth round win for Lewis, and he then went on to gain a first round victory over Steve Garber in Hull which had no TV coverage. It was all part of a plan we hatched to take Lennox on a tour of Britain so that the public could get to know him. It was partly a PR exercise, but also the chance for him to pick up ring experience.

The Hull show was memorable for the way the whole thing had to be held up at one point because Levitt was late arriving after flying up from London in a private plane, and it cost him around £2,000 an hour to keep the airport open so that he could fly off after the fight.

It was back to the Royal Albert Hall on Bonfire Night as Lennox disposed of the much lighter Melvin Epps when the New Yorker was disqualified in the second round. To round off the year it was decided Lennox would make an appearance in the town that had become home to him after leaving Britain for Canada. We arranged a contest at the Kitchener Auditorium in Ontario against a journeyman fighter from Kansas named Greg Gorrell. John Hornewer and I negotiated a purse of $10,000 for Lennox and the fight took place just a week before Christmas, on 18 December. But it was the build-up to the fight that I will never forget and the fact that it almost led to me walking out on Jackie.

Getting away from Britain and my domestic situation was good for me at the time. I still felt under a lot of pressure as Lennox's manager and I couldn't help thinking I was being tested to see if I was really up to the job. I always accepted it would be like that but it still didn't make it any easier to cope with. As far as I was concerned, I was trying to prove myself after taking a big leap up the boxing scale. It was a bit of a battle for me on all fronts and I felt I had to look over my shoulder a lot of the time at people from within the Levitt Group as well as at people like Hornewer, who was clearly still determined to play a central role in the career of Lewis even though I was his manager.

More than anything else I think I wanted to gain the respect of people in boxing for what I was doing and the way I was going about the job. There were always grand schemes being dreamed up by people in the Group, but I just kept my head down and concentrated on what I thought I was good at – being a boxing manager.

It was good to be part of the training camp for the Gorrell fight and over the years I have always enjoyed that side of being a manager. Being in camp actually helped me to relax and although the main reason for being there was to prepare Lennox for his fight, there was also time for the rest of us to have a few laughs at night when the serious work had been done.

Although it was freezing in the mornings, we all used to go out running because Davenport insisted it was a good idea. We were dressed like a bunch of SAS soldiers and must have looked a bit scary to some of the locals, because on one occasion we were stopped by the police who seemed to think we were burglars.

The whole training team had been kitted out in some very nice white tracksuits to use for leisure wear with Lennox's name printed on the back of them. It certainly made us stand out in a crowd and the reaction of the local people whenever they saw us was very friendly. That friendliness reached a new level one evening when I was out in the town having a game of pool with one of the sparring partners. While we were playing, a good-looking blonde girl came over to me and started chatting. She told me her name was Barbara and that she'd seen us all on TV. I immediately felt comfortable with her and after dinner later that night a combination of the arctic conditions and a bit of hot passion saw the two of us end up in bed together.

It was actually a lot more romantic than it sounds and I felt I'd found a girl who was prepared to listen and understand some of the things that had been such a problem for Jackie. The sex was great and exciting, but there was more to it than that. I suddenly began to realise I was falling for her in a big way. I even told Lennox what had happened and he said I was getting a real taste of Canada – the weather might be cold, but the girls were really hot!

Lennox did what was expected of him in the ring by beating Gorrell in the fifth round, and the day after the contest I flew back to England knowing that in the short period since I'd known her, I'd fallen for Barbara. I talked to her a lot on the phone when I got back and the fact that my life with Jackie was in a terrible state only made me want to be with Barbara more. That year probably produced the worst Christmas of my life with the atmosphere between Jackie and me very brittle.

I was desperate to see Barbara again and the day before New Year's Eve I made the decision to fly to Canada. I went to the office and told my new secretary, Sophie Caffell, to say she didn't know where I was if anyone asked. It was difficult for her but Sophie proved to be totally loyal and trustworthy in the years that followed. She was actually hired by the company to keep an eye on me but turned out to be just the sort of person I needed at the Levitt Group.

I flew off to Canada determined to get myself away from Jackie and put some space between us. When I did phone home she wanted to know where I was, claiming that she and Emma, who was 13 at the time, would drive to see me so we could all spend New Year together. She obviously had no way of knowing that I was thousands of miles away in Canada. It wasn't easy for me because although my relationship with Jackie had turned sour, I began to feel guilty about leaving Emma behind.

Barbara was a breath of fresh air for me at the time. When I eventually flew home I knew I had some tough decisions to make about my crumbling marriage. I wasn't sure whether Barbara was just an ego trip for me, but I did know she offered something that was missing from my relationship with Jackie. I decided it was time for me to move out of the pub and leave my wife.

I went to Canada again on the pretence of having a look at some marketing opportunities with someone from the Levitt Group, but it was Barbara I really wanted to see. Despite calls from Jackie while I was there I decided I wasn't going back to her. Instead, I asked Barbara to live in England. When I told Sophie what I was going to do she thought I was mad, but I'd made up my mind and I wasn't about to change it. I actually went to Canada and brought Barbara back with me. I had to laugh. When I was a kid I was happy to come back from a trip with a stick of rock, this time I was bringing home a 5 ft 7 in. blonde!

The whole thing was crazy and instead of taking pressure off me, I only succeeded in heaping a whole lot more on to my shoulders by having Barbara around. My mum was away at the time and so we stayed at her flat, but it certainly wasn't the ideal situation. I was seeing Jackie and Barbara at the same time, even though I never really meant it to happen that way.

On top of all this I was sorting out Lennox's next fight which was to be against Noel Quarless at York Hall on 31 January. The fight produced the right outcome with Lewis getting a second round win in front of an enthusiastic East End crowd. I saw Jackie at the show and agreed to meet her for dinner a couple of days later, even though I'd said that I thought our marriage was over.

When I turned up for the meal it didn't take me long to realise my wife was trying to seduce me. She looked very sexy and tried to throw as much wine down my throat as she could. The situation with her and Barbara was getting out of hand and I needed to make some decisions. I'd behaved like a rat towards both of them, and the only person I was really pleasing and looking after was myself.

Barbara and I decided it was time to cool things and she went back to Canada. The idea was that she would only be going to visit family and friends, but as I said goodbye to her at Gatwick I think we both knew our brief affair was over.

Despite all my grand plans to end my marriage I took the easy option and slowly drifted back into life with Jackie as I prepared for Lennox's eighth fight of his professional career, which literally turned out to be a non-event.

It was due to take place at Crystal Palace with Lennox meeting an African boxer who went by the name of Proud Kilimanjaro in a contest that was set to go out live on satellite TV. But with just 20 minutes to go before the main event was due to take place, the whole thing was called off.

The reason for the cancellation was the fact that Kilimanjaro would not produce a certificate giving evidence that he was not HIV positive. He also refused to release results of a blood test he had taken, which was mandatory for any foreign boxer appearing in Britain. It wasn't until the night of the show that we found out the test was positive and the Boxing Board had no alternative other than to call it off.

Once that decision had been made, there was a frantic search to see if we could get a replacement in time to face Lennox. We had Welshman Chris Jacobs lined up and Levitt was prepared to hire a helicopter to fly him to London, but strong winds had closed the airports in Cardiff and Swansea. Jacobs even tried to drive to London, only to find the bad weather had forced the Severn Bridge to be closed.

It wasn't an easy situation because the crowd had come to see Lennox in action and when a statement was read out saying the bout had been cancelled there were quite a few boos. It was understandable, but Lennox rescued the night by climbing into the ring and saying that anyone who fancied replacing Kilimanjaro was welcome to step through the ropes. Needless to say, nobody took him up on the offer, but it helped to calm things down.

After all that had happened with the Kilimanjaro show we wanted the next fight to go well and not produce any hitches. But for lots of different reasons the opponent for this particular contest seemed to change about a dozen times. The whole experience eventually helped to teach me a valuable lesson about the fighter I was hoping to guide to a world heavyweight title.

In the end Lennox fought an American from Ohio named Calvin Jones at the Gateshead Leisure Centre on 22 March, and the biggest memory for me was the way he got so upset with me for all the chopping and changing that had gone on in trying to find an opponent. He was in a really bad mood going up on the train for the fight and it quickly made me realise that I could never afford to let something like that happen again. It was clear Lennox wanted everything well planned and in place when it came to his career and it was my job to make sure that happened.

The good thing was that he produced his best performance since becoming a professional. He knocked Jones out with a terrific shot in the first round and looked sensational. I told him after the fight if I'd made him mad, I'd better try doing it every time. It was meant as a joke, but I could see just how serious he was about making sure there were no further cock-ups that would upset him.

He maintained his busy schedule with first round wins against

Zambian Mike Simuwelu and Argentinian Jorge Descola. Things were going to plan with Lennox getting good exposure and at the same time learning his trade. He got more of a work-out in his next contest after Descola, at the City Hall in Sheffield against an Irish-American called Dan Murphy. Lennox had to go looking for Murphy, which was good experience at that stage in his professional development, and it turned out to be his longest fight to date before two big right hands from Lewis forced the referee to stop the contest in the sixth round. Murphy had a guy in his corner who was a real fight character. He was an American known as 'The Mouse'. As a fighter he claimed to have had more than 500 contests in the States and he was known to have even had more than one fight on the same night! At one point in the Murphy contest Dan got cut and there were some calls for the fight to be stopped, but The Mouse wasn't having any of it. 'Never let it be said that one of The Mouse's fighters is scared of a drop of blood,' he said with a loud voice as he stood in his man's corner.

It was Lennox's 11th fight and we were moving towards getting him into position to challenge for a title. After wins in the summer against Puerto Rican Ossie Ocasio on points over eight rounds in London, and a second round victory against Mike Acey in Canada, Lewis got the chance to fight Frenchman Jean Chanet for his European heavyweight championship.

The Chanet fight was staged on 31 October at Crystal Palace and it was the last fight we did as part of a promotional partnership with Barry Hearn, which began with the Simuwelu contest. Hearn had approached me some time earlier about the possibility of working together, and I'd agreed because not only was it a good way of sharing some of the financial burden, it was also a way of getting TV exposure on a regular basis. Barry was also the only person who had bothered to contact me directly.

There were other people in boxing at that time who obviously wanted to get in on the action as far as Lennox Lewis was concerned, but they never spoke to me. Instead, they went along to see Levitt and the suggestion from them was that they could help Lennox's career, but that he'd be better off without me.

Lennox was in a different class to Chanet, who was the 36-year-old son of a fairground wrestler. He was well paid for the fight against

Lennox, but never seriously looked like winning, and in only his 14th fight as a professional, Lewis gained his first major title with a sixth-round stoppage. In the press conference afterwards Davenport was asked by Colin Hart from *The Sun* what he thought of the performance, and the trainer said it was between him and Lennox. Harty told Davenport in no uncertain fashion that if he wasn't going to answer any questions he should go and stand at the back of the room. It was typical of Harty and typical of Davenport, although some time later the two actually spent about three hours just talking boxing with each other.

The Chanet fight lost money as a promotion but the win meant we were well and truly on our way. Everything looked rosy as Lennox got the chance to really put his name on the boxing map with a clash against another unbeaten British heavyweight, Gary Mason, who was managed by Mickey Duff. The fight was a mandatory defence for Mason and while Lewis was a relative novice in the professional ring and his new European title was also on the line, Gary had been around for some time and had built up an impressive unbeaten record of 34 wins. He not only held the British title, but was also world ranked which meant that a win for Lennox would really make people sit up and take notice.

Mason was a big favourite with most people as soon as the fight was talked about, but as far as I was concerned it would count for nothing because Lennox had all the class. Mickey must have obviously felt differently and seemed to think it was a good fight for Gary to take. It appeared as though everything was going to plan as 1990 drew to a close, but instead of having a merry Christmas and looking forward to a happy New Year, my world was thrown into turmoil with the spectacular crash of the Levitt Group.

Although I never felt particularly comfortable with a lot of the people at the company and the way so many of them went about their work, the one thing I did believe was that somehow or other Levitt had managed to create a massive organisation that was financially as solid as a rock. How wrong I was. You can imagine what a shock it was to discover the Group was about to go into administration. One minute I was part of an organisation that was supposed to be worth around £150 million, and the next I was sitting in my office while the police and liquidators roamed the building putting virtually everything in boxes.

I honestly couldn't believe what was going on at first, even though there had been some rumours that all was not well with the company. Charles Meaden filled me in on what was going on and it basically boiled down to the fact that the Levitt Group was all about show and had no real substance. We continued to go into the office during the days that followed, and on one occasion after being questioned by the police, Roger came over to see me. 'You've got nothing to be worried about, Frank,' he told me. 'This will all be sorted out and everything will be back to normal.'

The salesman in him never stopped operating and he was still trying to flog me the idea that it was just a minor hiccup. Normal service would soon be resumed. The sheer front of the man was amazing to witness at times. Particularly when you think he went on to face more than 60 fraud charges.

Not long after Roger's little pep talk one of the police officers asked me just how valuable the European Championship belt was that Levitt had on display in his office. They were pretty surprised when I said it was probably worth no more than £200 top whack. Apparently the master salesman had told them it was worth around £100,000 and they'd immediately put a guard on it because they thought it was a valuable asset!

The collapse of the group was not only a blow to my boxing hopes it was also a financial blow to everyone who worked in the organisation. It certainly made things tense for a lot of the people who were working with me as we tried to get on with the business of looking after Lennox Lewis without being paid a penny.

I was at home one morning when Davenport, along with his assistant trainer Harold Knight and John Hornewer, paid me a visit. I invited them in and could see that Davenport looked agitated and even more miserable than usual. It almost seemed as though there was steam coming out of his ears from under the baseball cap he was wearing, and he started to mutter something which included having his usual pop at the British.

The next thing I knew he launched himself at me and we were rolling around the floor fighting. He had a big ring on one of his fingers and as he pinned my neck to the floor with one hand, he started to gouge the ring into my face just below an eye. A mixture of aggression and fear took over and it was all I could do to get a hand up towards him and poke two fingers into his eyes. It had the desired effect and he sprang back giving me enough time to get up off the floor as Harold jumped in to make sure the two of us broke it up.

After they'd left I was convinced that Davenport had been wound up by someone. He was never the happiest of individuals and was obviously under a bit of stress because of the Levitt collapse, but something must have been said to get him that worked up. He ended up having to go to hospital to have his injuries looked at and I was quite heavily marked around the eyes.

I found out later he thought the attack on me was going to cost him his job as trainer, because he was convinced I would go in and spill the beans. But that has never been my style and although I didn't take kindly to him trying to beat me up in my own home, there was no way I was going to run around telling everyone what had happened.

We must have looked a right sight in the office a couple of days later. There was no doubt we'd both been in a fight, and I suppose it didn't take too much for people to realise something had gone on between us. The funny thing was I probably got more respect from Davenport for that than for anything else I ever did during the time I worked with him. He actually made a point of coming to see me.

'Frank, you're a man,' he said.

'Why?' I asked.

'Because you never said a damn word about the fight,' he added, and just to emphasise the point he shook me by the hand, instead of my throat.

The administrators started spending more time with me because they wanted to know all about Lennox's contract. They asked how much it might cost to fund the whole operation if someone was interested in taking over the contract. The fact that Lewis was a genuine talent capable of going all the way to the top obviously made him quite an attractive proposition.

It was clear I needed to start talking to potential new backers. Lennox was signed to Frank Maloney Promotions and Management and I was also his manager under the terms of the British Boxing

Board of Control contract we'd signed, so it made sense that I would be the one to start negotiating.

One of the first people I had contact with was the football agent, Jon Smith, whom we were going to meet in New York, but he was only prepared to pay for Lennox's ticket if a deal was done. I also met with Jarvis Astaire at the White House Hotel in London, and I found out later that Mickey Duff had a meeting with Hornewer. Millionaire David Sullivan, who is the current owner of *Sport* newspapers and co-owner of Birmingham City, also expressed an interest and I met with him at his home, but when he found out about some of the finer details involved which Levitt had agreed to, he decided not to go ahead.

It was all looking very uncertain and we still had the problem of trying to set up a training camp for Lennox as he prepared for the Mason fight. The whole boxing operation at this time was being funded by a loan that Colin Myers had managed to get from the bank and by my own credit card.

Things were pretty tight for everyone and I knew Christmas wasn't exactly going to be a great time for me. Levitt called me one day and asked to see me at his house because he wanted to know what was happening and how things were going. He was his usual upbeat self when he opened the door but I think he could see the strain was beginning to show on me. There was no doubt I was in a depression, but at the same time I was determined that it wasn't all going to end.

After I had been talking to Levitt for a while he suddenly went over to a briefcase and opened it to reveal neatly stacked piles of £50 notes. The case was full and I could only guess at just how much was in there. Roger peeled off ten notes and gave them to me.

'You take this for Christmas, Frank,' he said. 'Buy your daughter a nice present, get some food and look after yourself. And don't worry.'

The £500 was certainly handy, because the only other cash I had coming in that Christmas was from the purse money of one of my fighters, Ian Honeywood, who fought and lost a British lightweight title fight against Carl Crook in Preston. It was a nice gesture by Roger and whatever else went on between us, I will always remember how grateful I was and how it helped me out.

The search was still on for a backer and Charles Meaden came up with the name of a very wealthy American he knew called David

Smith. I met him at his house in Belgravia and agreed to put a package together for him to look at. It seemed as though we might be making progress, and David asked me to fly out to his home in Beverly Hills for another meeting because it looked as though a deal could be done.

By this time Lennox was training in California for his fight against Mason. The place they were using was a ranch-style house with a gym in the grounds, owned by a guy named Jimmy Gambino. His main claim to fame seemed to be that he was involved in helping to choreograph the fight scenes in one of the *Rocky* movies. Jimmy ran a pretty tight ship, insisting his fighters eat red meat. He was also a religious man and would always say grace before our meals. He and Davenport never really hit it off and on one occasion following grace Gambino looked straight into the eyes of John who was sitting at the other end of the table and added that he wanted God to drive any evil spirits from his table. It was a clear reference to Davenport who got up and stormed out of the room.

When the second meeting was set up Hornewer joined me at Smith's house to talk about a possible deal. For the first time in weeks I thought I could actually see some light at the end of the tunnel, but just when I started to feel optimistic about the situation I was hit by a bombshell from within my own camp. Negotiations with Smith were going well and it really did seem as though he could be the man to rescue the situation. We talked about the sort of set-up that was in place, and then Hornewer chipped in with a comment that knocked the stuffing out of me.

He claimed that in any new deal I would not have such an active role to play and also that my percentage would be reduced. I would be kept on but it was clearly only going to be as a gesture.

I was in total shock and could actually feel the tears welling up in my eyes. Not only did I feel betrayed, but I'd also been humiliated in front of a relative stranger. I was too hurt to feel angry, but it just reinforced my view of Hornewer. I disliked him from the moment I first set eyes on him and had never trusted him, now he was really showing his true colours.

David asked to see me outside and when the door was closed he simply said, 'The deal's off.' It was almost a relief after what I'd just heard and he went on to tell me why he'd decided to pull out. 'Look,

Frank,' he said. 'You and me have pretty much negotiated a deal and now this young lawyer kid comes in and stabs you in the back. If they can do it to you after what you've done, they may try to do the same sort of thing to me further down the line after I've put my money in.'

When Hornewer and I got outside I told him I just couldn't believe what had gone on. He said it was what Lennox wanted, so I asked why Lewis had never said anything to me. It left me wondering whether it really was what Lennox wanted or whether it was Hornewer making a power play. As far as I was concerned that kind of thing said a lot about the sort of person Hornewer was.

From the very first day I'd met Lennox I'd been totally straight with him and worked my arse off to make sure his professional career was handled in the right way. I may have been part of the Levitt organisation, but there was no way either Lennox or Hornewer could ever question my loyalty. After what had gone on in the meeting I began to wonder how I was ever going to get a backer, and I realised my job was going to be made even harder with someone like John Hornewer lurking in the background.

I can honestly say I've never felt so low in my life and I actually contemplated topping myself. As well as all the problems I was having in my professional life, with debts on my credit card going through the roof as I tried to help finance the Lewis operation, my personal life was also suffering.

Jackie and I had decided it was time to finally end our marriage in the summer of 1990 and she was running the pub in Crayford with her new boyfriend, while I was living at our house not too far away. I'd started seeing a girl called Claire from the Levitt Group. We enjoyed each other's company and used to talk a lot, but one night when things got a bit more intimate I found that for the first time in my life I couldn't perform sexually. I was stressed out to the point where I wasn't even able to have sex and I began to wonder just what else could go wrong.

Driving home one night from London I just felt as though the world was caving in on me and that there was no escape from my problems. As I reached my turn-off on the motorway I suddenly found myself heading towards trees on the side of the road – for a split second I just felt like giving up and ending it all there and then by crashing into them.

ROGER AND OUT

If I'd have gone ahead and hit them there was no doubt I'd have been smashed to pieces. I genuinely felt suicidal but in the end a mixture of survival instinct and fear took over as I swerved to avoid the trees and cut right across a couple of lanes. By the time I got home I was shaking but after a phone call to my father I pulled myself round a bit and knew I had to do something to ease the pressure I was under. I found the number of a hypnotist in the local paper and going to see her helped to relax me, but the thing which really lifted my spirits was a conversation with Levitt.

I told Roger all about David Smith and what Hornewer had done. He didn't seem in the least surprised by the way John had acted, and said he thought he might have some people who would be interested in taking over the contract.

'And don't worry, Frank,' he told me. 'I'll make sure your position is protected, because you've always been loyal to me.'

After putting some figures together for Levitt to show to any prospective backer, I got a call from him one day asking if I could go along to a meeting. The guy Roger wanted me to see turned out to be Conrad Morris. He was a small, neatly dressed Jewish man, who apparently was wealthy enough to consider taking on some of the financial responsibility for Lennox's contract. I told Conrad that it wasn't going to be a cheap operation, but Roger said there was someone else he knew who might also be interested in getting involved and sharing in the financing of the project.

It was agreed that I would speak to the Administrators, KPMG Peat Marwick McLintock about buying the contract. The initial figure they put on it was £50,000, but it quickly dropped to £25,000 and after more discussions I was able to walk away having negotiated a payment of £18,000. Obviously it was their job to get the best possible price for any assets, but neither they nor the main creditors really knew anything about boxing, so it was better for them to get what they could as quickly as possible.

By then I knew the other backer Roger mentioned had decided he wanted to be part of the whole thing. He was a neighbour of Levitt's who'd made his money as an accountant specialising in liquidation cases, and was the man who would eventually play a much more public role in the operation. His name was Panos Eliades.

NO BALONEY

I was asked to go to a meeting at his offices in Bloomsbury Square and when I walked into the massive boardroom I could hardly believe my eyes. Standing at the top of a huge table was Levitt and right beside him was someone who looked just like him.

Panos, who apparently had stood bail for Roger when the police swooped on the Levitt organisation, was a fast-talking Greek Cypriot Londoner who was about my own age. He was dressed in an expensive-looking suit, with a brightly coloured tie and, just like Levitt, he had a cigar stuck between his fingers. He was short with dark hair and a moustache that made him look like a Mexican bandit from a poor western movie. Panos was very friendly right from the start and it was difficult to not get caught up by his enthusiasm. After looking over details of the contract and joking about how much it was all going to cost him he was happy enough to go ahead with the deal.

Roger explained it would be Panos and Conrad who would be putting up the money to finance the whole operation. Considering both of them knew nothing about boxing, it was a big gamble to take. Not only were they taking on the contract, but they had also agreed to pay money owing to the Lewis team following the collapse of the Levitt Group. It also worked out well for Lennox, because at the time of the collapse he was still owed £70,000 from his signing-on fee, and as part of the new deal Panos agreed to pay it.

For the first time in weeks I felt I could afford to relax a little bit. The whole experience had been a nightmare, and the only thing that kept me going was my determination to make sure all the hard work I'd already put in was not going to be wasted. I'd managed to find a new backer who was happy to let me run things. Panos was going to take on the same sort of role as Roger while Conrad Morris was clearly keen to stay very much in the background.

A new company was formed called Products of the Far East and registered in Jersey holding the main Lewis contract, with Panos, Morris and Levitt's family in the form of a trust, all holding shares.

Despite what had happened to him, Levitt was not about to let go of things completely. Instead, he officially became Lennox's commercial manager with the task of trying to get him sponsorship deals. As usual, Levitt the salesman began talking big from the very first day until it finally ended in tears for him 17 months later.

8. RAZOR SHARP

WITH THE MASON FIGHT IN PLACE I COULD FINALLY CONCENTRATE ON THE
preparations without worrying where the next penny was coming
from. Lennox had switched his training camp from California to
Bristol, after I'd received a telephone call saying the set-up in the
States just wasn't working. This had all happened before we'd found
a new backer, and once again it was my credit card that took a
pounding as I booked flights for everyone to return to England and
travel to Bristol.

The fight itself was a big event with a purse of more than
£250,000 split between the two boxers, and Mason was a hot
favourite to teach the young upstart a lesson. As the day drew closer
more and more of the press came out on Gary's side, claiming he
would have too much experience and that Lennox was being thrown
into the fight too early in his career.

But although it was going to be only his 15th professional contest,
there was never the slightest doubt in my mind that Lewis would
beat Mason. Lennox might have lacked professional experience, but
Mason's record had been padded out with some tried and tested
nobodies and when it came to quality, Lennox was streets ahead.

NO BALONEY

Remember, here was a boxer who had not yet reached his peak, but who had already shown his class and potential by winning an Olympic gold medal. Gary was a lovely guy, but with all due respect to him, Mason hadn't even managed to win a south-west London Divisional title and had been beaten by Danny Moul as an amateur.

On top of all that, Mason was going into the fight having recovered from retina surgery and, as distasteful as it might seem to some people, concentrating on hitting the damaged eye was a big part of our strategy. Davenport used to regularly make sure that there were two pieces of tape stuck on the headguards of Lennox's sparring partners, just above their right eye. For week after week Lewis would stick out his jab aiming at the tape so that it became second nature to him. The preparation for the contest was good and it was the first time that Lennox's boyhood friend, Courtney Shand, worked on the team, when he joined as Lewis's conditioner and would prove to be a valuable member of the set-up in the years that followed.

We had a final head-to-head press conference a couple of days before the contest at the Stakis Casino in Russell Square. We left there feeling pleased with ourselves, not just because of the fact that we all believed Lennox was going to beat Mason, but also because this was the day we had arranged to finally sign a contract with Lennox's new financial backer. We went straight from Stakis to see Panos Eliades, whose office was just five minutes away.

It was a real relief when we finally put pen to paper and I felt happier than I'd done for a long time, particularly as I got a £5,000 bonus for the way I'd managed to negotiate with Peat Marwick for the contract. But if I'd known what had gone on during the signing I might not have been so pleased. It was only later that Levitt told me Hornewer had tried to pull the same stroke with Panos as he'd done with David Smith, by asking that my role in the whole operation be reduced. In the end that never happened and I was led to believe that Levitt had actually helped make sure everything stayed the same as far as I was concerned.

With the contract in place and the fight looming it was full steam ahead for what was the biggest night in Lennox's career so far. Barry Hearn offered to let us have his stretch limo for the night so that Lennox could arrive at Wembley Arena in a bit of style, and we set off from Crayford eager to get the job done and prove a lot of people wrong.

The atmosphere was electric and Mason probably had more support with a lot of people seeing him as Britain's best hope to go all the way to a world title, but by the end of the night any dream Gary had of that happening was in tatters. Lennox went out and did exactly what we thought he would. He boxed Mason's ears off and just as Davenport had planned, Lewis's jabs had a devastating effect on Gary's eye. By the end of the sixth it looked as though the contest would be stopped. Mason's eye was swollen like a balloon but he bravely went out for the seventh and took more punishment before the referee Larry O'Connell finally called it off.

It was only after the fight that I realised I'd actually had quite a big bet on Lewis to win in the sixth round, but despite missing out on some extra cash I couldn't have been happier. Seeing him take the British title to add to his European crown and beat a world-ranked fighter was the icing on the cake, and for the first time I actually took my percentage from one of his fights. After all the problems and doubts of the last few months, I knew we were finally on our way, and the fact that it had been done against a Mickey Duff fighter made the victory even more sweet for me.

I'd had to suffer some stick from a lot of people in the boxing business who thought I would never amount to anything. There was also a lot of jealousy involved, but I knew that after beating Mason they were going to have to start eating their words. I couldn't help feeling satisfied as Lennox left the ring that night because I remembered one of Duff's comments when he'd said I was doing a Cecil B. De Mille in reverse. 'They're taking a star and turning him into an unknown,' he claimed.

After beating Mason it seemed to me the boot was on the other foot. Before the contest Gary had been unbeaten and on course for a possible world title fight. He was a star. After the contest he really had nowhere to go and, following a brief comeback, he finally retired as a fighter. If I'd been in their shoes I would have avoided Lennox like the plague, but it was their decision and from our point of view things couldn't have worked out better.

Levitt was at the fight but not in a particularly prominent position, while Panos hadn't even gone to the Arena. He hadn't actually told anyone about his involvement with Lewis and not even his wife, Angela, knew. Apparently he started getting excited as he watched the contest on BBC TV and she asked him why he was taking such an interest in a sport he knew nothing about, so Panos ended up telling her how he had invested a small amount of money in Lewis to help out Roger. From that night on boxing suddenly became a very big part of his life.

After the fight I celebrated with a party upstairs at a friend's pub in Aldgate called Cauthen's. I was determined to enjoy every minute of the win and I remember standing there drinking, asking people if they'd seen the look on Duff's face at the end of the fight. Victory had never tasted so sweet and although I couldn't actually remember how it happened, I found myself waking up in bed the next morning with a 19-year-old blonde who'd been more than happy to help me get into the party mood the night before.

We had a press conference for Lennox the next day and the whole team had a great feel to it. We were on our way and the future looked good. Suddenly Britain had a heavyweight who really was capable of going all the way to the top. And let's face it, everyone loves a winner.

A few days after the contest I found myself having to deal with the kind of hassle I could have done without. Having been on a high since the victory, an envelope stuffed through the letter box of my house in Crayford soon brought me down to earth with a bump.

It had been put there by Jackie with a note inside and a bunch of keys. She basically told me she wasn't going to be running the pub any more and had walked out on the place. As part of the agreement we had when we split up, Jackie had been looking after the business and I hadn't taken anything from it. I'd washed my hands of the whole thing. I'd been wound up in my own world and hadn't paid attention to what Jackie had been up to. As far as I was concerned our marriage was over. I had the house and my daughter living with me and she had the pub.

So it was all a bit of a shock to suddenly have the keys dumped on me. I went down there and found the till empty and a lot of the stock gone. In the safe there was a note saying, 'Good riddance'. After getting in touch with the brewery and the bank a couple of days later

I found out the full extent of what had been going on and soon realised the business was in debt.

If it had happened a few weeks earlier when I was still trying to find a backer for Lennox and didn't know where the next penny was coming from, I don't think I would have had second thoughts about killing myself in the car. It would have been the final straw.

With the help of my mum and her boyfriend John, we eventually turned what could have been a disaster into a real success. The debt was paid off and they ran the business for me as I used the pub for a base following Lennox's win. Jackie's walk-out really did signal the end for our marriage. We did get together for Emma's birthday a few years later when we all went out for a meal, but it ended badly with the two of us having a row and no doubt spoiling the evening for my daughter. We finally sorted out our divorce and put a formal end to the marriage, allowing both of us to get on with the rest of our lives.

Roger Levitt might have been facing the sort of charges that would worry most people sick, but there was no way you would ever have guessed it from the way he acted. He was still his old confident and brash self, willing to tell anyone who would listen just how many millions he was going to be making for Lennox in his new role as commercial manager.

He was also always letting everyone know he was completely innocent of any charges brought against him and that the whole thing was a complete misunderstanding. Levitt might have had a new title and Lennox a new backer, but you would never have believed anything had really changed. After the Mason fight we set up offices in Crawford Street, sharing them with a company that Conrad Morris had an interest in. And through a couple of guys who used to work in the Music and Entertainment section of the old Levitt Group we ended up having a meeting with the woman responsible for the voice of Lady Penelope in the puppet TV series *Thunderbirds*.

Strange as it may seem, she had some sort of contact in American TV, and we eventually got a call from Seth Abraham, the head of HBO cable network and one of the most powerful men in boxing at the time because of his company's financial involvement in staging big fights in the States. Seth was due to visit Britain for a pre-Wimbledon planning meeting because HBO were going to be televising the tennis championships, so Roger and I went along to a meeting with him at Harry's Bar in London to discuss details of a possible deal.

Abraham was a short, dapper New Yorker. He reminded me a bit of Woody Allen and was quite trendily dressed in expensive clothes. He was middle-aged and very talkative, with the air of someone who liked letting you know how important he was. He was the sort of guy who would have eaten himself if he'd been made of chocolate.

Throughout the meeting Seth jotted down details of any proposed deal on the back of a napkin and explained that if we were going to go forward with Lennox's career we needed exposure in America. He claimed this couldn't really be done without the aid of a top promoter in the States and suggested the names of Bob Arum at Top Rank who operated out of Las Vegas and Dan Duva at Main Events, who were based in New Jersey.

We actually came away with an agreement in principle, even though Roger rejected Abraham's original offer claiming we needed more money if we were going to go ahead and sign with HBO. Some time later we agreed a deal with HBO, but as part of it I insisted Lennox should fight in Britain as well as the States because I saw that as an important part of his career. We'd worked hard at getting him accepted by the British public, and after beating Mason his popularity was on a new high. As far as I was concerned it would have been stupid to just turn our backs on the very people who had supported us. Lennox was also the British champion and wanted to win a Lonsdale belt outright. He held the European title at the time and wanted to add the Commonwealth crown as well. That meant boxing in Britain, and so as part of the deal it was agreed that he would have fights in the UK as well as the USA.

There was no doubt Lennox was flavour of the month as far as TV and boxing people were concerned and the next stage was to meet and agree a contract with our new USA promoters. During the talks with Seth, it became clear his preference was for us to sign with Main Events. They already promoted Evander Holyfield, who was the undisputed heavyweight champion of the world and held the WBC, WBA and IBF belts, so it made a lot of sense to go with them if we were aiming to get a crack at him down the line.

RAZOR SHARP

I flew out to meet Dan Duva and immediately got on well with him. It was a relationship that flourished in the years that followed until his untimely death from a brain tumour in 1996. Dan was the most unlikely promoter you could imagine in so many ways. He certainly wasn't a brash extrovert like Don King, and was actually quite shy and retiring. But he was a clever man who was sincere and always delivered on his promises. When it came to negotiating and handling egos Dan was up there with the best of them.

Duva was a lawyer whose father Lou is something of a legend in the game, having trained and managed fighters for decades. Dan was short and stocky, with a serious face that rarely broke into a smile when he was talking business. I can honestly say I learned more about the fight game and the politics of the sport from Dan than from anyone else in my career. He was meticulous with contracts and was always thinking ahead when it came to fighters and promoting contests.

It was agreed that our first fight with Main Events would take place in the States at Caesar's Hotel and Casino in an outdoor arena at Lake Tahoe which was over 6,000 feet above sea level. The date was set for 12 July, four months after the Mason win, and we set up camp for Lennox in nearby Carson City which, like Lake Tahoe, was several thousand feet above sea level.

The opponent picked for the date was veteran former WBA world champion, Mike Weaver, who was 40 at the time of the fight, but had the kind of experience and ring know-how that was perfect for Lennox who still only had 15 professional fights under his belt.

Training and preparing for a fight like that in the States was a world away from so much of what I'd been used to in the past. I really enjoyed it although I also had to put up with being threatened by one of Lennox's old sparring partners when we decided to break camp one day and travel the short distance to Las Vegas to watch Mike Tyson's second fight with Donovan 'Razor' Ruddock. It was a tough fight for Tyson who eventually won on points over 12 rounds, but the contest helped to further establish Ruddock as one of the best heavyweights around.

After it was over Elijah Tillery, who had worked with us as one of Lewis's sparring partners in the past, spotted me and began making threats. He claimed he was owed money and that if I didn't sort it out, the next time he bumped into me he would be carrying a gun ready to shoot me. It certainly wasn't the sort of thing you expect on a night out watching some boxing and I promised I'd clear the whole thing up and send him any outstanding money when I got back to England. I don't know whether it was just an idle threat, but some of these guys are big enough and ugly enough to do some crazy things, so I wasn't about to take any chances.

Interest in Lennox from the media back home was getting bigger and I remember chatting with one well known British boxing writer before the fight. He joked that if Lewis won he'd be seen as a British fighter, but if he didn't he'd be the Canadian heavyweight who fought under a flag of convenience. It might have been meant as a joke, but it was exactly the sort of feeling we were battling with all the time.

In the end there was no real danger that Lennox would not win against the cagey Weaver. Lewis was disciplined and patient before stopping the American in the sixth round with a good right hand punch. By way of celebration Lennox treated everyone to dinner and also managed to get me drunk on Long Island Ice Teas. While he stayed sober, I had to be helped to my room.

The win was a job well done as far as we were concerned and I was beginning to enjoy life again. After retreating to my house for long periods during the dark days of the Levitt collapse and not bothering to go out and socialise, I was determined to make up for lost time.

Soon after we arrived back from the Weaver fight I went out for a night on the town with my mate David Byrne, who played for Millwall in their famous side that won promotion to the old First Division in 1988. Dave brought along a few of his footballing mates and we ended up in Stringfellows nightclub, drinking champagne and chatting up some girls.

The one I was interested in was a cute little blonde who had been dancing with a friend, and after some small talk and more champagne we exchanged telephone numbers. I sent her flowers a couple of days later before taking her out on a dinner date that ended in the early hours of the morning. She told me how she'd been married to someone in Dubai and had a young daughter from the relationship. We got on well and things developed pretty quickly, with Caroline soon becoming a permanent fixture in my life.

I used to enjoy going out with some of the footballers I knew and on one occasion Paul Gascoigne came to watch some boxing at the Albert Hall. Gazza decided we'd all go out for a drink and we ended up playing this mad game where each person had to invent a drink from various mixtures, then everyone in the party would sample it. I don't know how many I had but I got so drunk that I had to be put in a taxi, leaving Gazza and his mates to carry on.

It was nice to let off steam but my life still revolved around the career of Lennox Lewis. I'm not going to say it was all about work, but it was never far from my thoughts even when I was out socialising. There always seemed to be things to plan and deals to be done. After the win against Weaver, Lennox got the chance to fight in Britain once more and took on Glenn McCrory at the Albert Hall on 30 September. The fight produced a convincing second-round victory for Lewis, but although Glenn left the ring having taken some heavy shots, he could at least console himself with the fact that he'd managed to put a nice lump of money in his bank account thanks to Levitt's negotiating skills – or more precisely, the lack of them.

Before the fight was signed and sealed Roger and I met with Glenn in a hotel for what I thought was going to be some tough bargaining over how much McCrory would be paid as a challenger for Lennox's British and European title belts. Glenn, who had been world cruiserweight champion and is now a well-respected boxing commentator for Sky TV, could hardly believe his ears when, after asking for the crazy figure of £100,000, Levitt said, 'You've got it, son.' And that was that. No haggling, no negotiating, Levitt just agreed to pay Glenn exactly what he'd asked for. As if that was not bad enough, Levitt gave another example of his crazy way of doing deals when we met with Frank Warren a few months later to talk about Lennox fighting Derek Williams.

The idea was for Lewis to put his two belts on the line against Williams, who held the Commonwealth championship, making it a triple title fight. Once again the contest was due to take place at the Albert Hall but although Derek was managed by Mike Barrett, his promotional rights were down to Frank who worked with ITV. By this time Levitt had negotiated a TV deal with Sky, after having already taken some money up front from ITV when it looked as though they were going to be the company we would go with. When that all fell apart and we switched to Sky, it made matters very awkward for Roger because they naturally wanted to screen all of Lewis's fights.

I'd already managed to come to some kind of deal in principle with Warren over promotional rights when Levitt suddenly got involved. Frank seized the opportunity to get a much better purse for his fighter after Roger simply offered a lot more money without any real haggling.

'It was like taking sweets from a baby,' Frank told me. 'It's got to be one of the easiest deals I've ever done in my life.'

In between the McCrory and Williams fights Lennox had two other contests, both of them in America, and the second one proved to be the end of the line for trainer John Davenport. The first fight was in Atlanta, Georgia, on the undercard of Evander Holyfield's world title defence against Bert Cooper. Lewis's opponent was Tyrell Biggs, who had defeated Lennox in the 1984 quarter-finals of the Los Angeles Olympics.

Needless to say the outcome was a lot different in Atlanta, with Lewis stopping Biggs in the third round, as well as putting him down three times. At a party after the fight, Lennox looked happy and relaxed as he posed for photographs with his fans, knowing he'd just put in a convincing performance against Biggs.

Despite looking forward to a rest Lennox was persuaded to fight again in February 1992 after a personal telephone call from Seth Abraham, who told him that HBO wanted to stage a show they were going to call 'The Night of the Young Heavyweights' that was also going to feature Michael Moorer.

So Lennox travelled to Caesar's Palace in Las Vegas and chalked up another win on his record against the rugged and awkward Levi Billups. It was only the second time Lewis had been forced to go the distance, and the first time he'd been in a ten-round fight. Some of the post-fight comments in the press conference were a bit unflattering, but nothing really prepared us for the outburst that came from Davenport.

He'd never really liked England or the English and seemed to have a particular dislike for the British press. After the fight he claimed that some of the reporters wouldn't know a left hook from a fish hook, and also made a comment to the effect that when God made stupid people he had put them all in England.

The comments were hardly likely to win us friends in the media and the papers were full of it all back home. It was clear Davenport's personality was proving a problem, but more important than that was the fact that Lennox was becoming unhappy with the sergeant-major approach John seemed to take to work with him in the gym. It was clear Lennox had had enough and he decided to take matters into his own hands and sort the situation out with John. I know Davenport wasn't happy with what happened, and it was easy to understand why. But at the same time his personality seemed to be casting a shadow over the whole camp and when Lennox told me to expect a call from another trainer named Pepe Correa, I was eager to see what he was like.

Apparently, Lennox and Correa had met in a shoe shop in the States and after making contact Pepe later flew into London for talks and it was clear from the start that his personality was totally different to Davenport's. He talked a good fight when it came to selling himself as a trainer. Pepe was in his early fifties with a big moustache and glasses. He was quite a slender black guy, originally from Puerto Rico, who was based in Washington. It didn't take him long to start demonstrating how he wanted Lennox to move around the ring, and just how good he thought Lewis's jab was. Lennox also met with Pepe and the decision was made to take him on as replacement for Davenport. Little did we know at the time that we weren't really getting the sort of trainer Lennox needed.

He was given a salary of $100,000 a year, $25,000 up front, and paid 2.5 per cent net of any Lewis purse for a world title fight. The percentage was subject to Lennox actually winning the title fight.

Correa's first fight as Lennox's new trainer was the clash with Williams, who had Angelo Dundee in his corner on the night. But all of Angelo's experience and know-how couldn't help poor Derek, who was stopped in the third round after a big right hand had him in all sorts of trouble. The funny thing was that in the opening two rounds Lennox hadn't really got out of first gear, and there were some comments afterwards about Lewis almost holding back and keeping Williams in the fight. It was particularly ironic for a few of us who'd had a bet on Lennox winning in the third or fourth round, and there were some mutterings about what had gone on in the opening six minutes.

But the fact of the matter was that Lennox never really got into his rhythm during the opening two rounds, and when he came back to his corner Pepe told him to go out in the third and forget what they'd done in the gym. 'Just go and knock him out,' he said. It was an instruction that worked perfectly against Williams, but one that was to have disastrous effects in another fight more than two years later.

If Lennox's previous fight in America was to spell the end of the road for Davenport, his next on 11 August in Atlantic City against Mike Dixon saw the very public departure of another original member of the Lewis team – Roger Levitt.

Roger's role as commercial manager saw him come out with plenty of grand schemes and promises, but in real terms he delivered very little. I think Roger still saw himself as the man who was running the career of Lennox Lewis, even though he was preparing to face fraud charges following on from the collapse of the Levitt Group. Although he might have believed he was helping Lennox's career, it was Roger's involvement in the whole set-up during the summer of 1992 that cost Lewis a straight crack at the world heavyweight title.

Holyfield was the world champion but Lennox, Riddick Bowe and Razor Ruddock were the three top heavyweights behind him. The idea being talked about before the Dixon fight was for Lewis, Bowe or Ruddock to get a straight crack at the title against Holyfield, with the winner meeting the man who came out on top in the other fight involving the quartet. It was a simple idea that was guaranteed to produce three big fights.

Roger's brain immediately went into overdrive at the thought of Lennox possibly fighting for a world title. He'd once hoped he could celebrate his 40th birthday by seeing Lewis crowned king of the world at the huge indoor arena in New Orleans. But when he thought there might be a chance of Lennox fighting Holyfield, he tried to make sure it would take place at Arsenal's stadium in Highbury. We even went as far as having a meeting about the possibility with Arsenal's Ken Friar, who told us all about the time Henry Cooper had fought Muhammad Ali at the famous stadium in the 1960s.

But things changed after a meeting in New York with Dan Duva and the Main Events people. We talked through all the scenarios involving the four fighters and Dan promised to get back to us. After more discussions over a period of time it was decided that Bowe should be the man to go straight in with Holyfield, which meant Lennox taking on Ruddock for the right to face the winner and get a world title shot.

It was a massive fight for Lewis but I did wonder why it was Bowe, a man Lennox had defeated in the final of the Seoul Olympics to win a gold medal, who was going in with Holyfield. Some time later I found out that within 15 minutes of that first meeting in New York, Dan Duva had decided against the idea of Lennox fighting Holyfield straight away, and the reason was Roger Levitt.

'Frank,' Dan told me, 'it wasn't that we didn't trust you, and if it had been just you that we were dealing with we would have gone ahead with a Holyfield fight. But it was the fact that Roger Levitt was so heavily involved. If Lennox had won and Levitt had gone back to England with the title, we were afraid there might have been all sorts of problems for us. At least with Bowe's manager, Rock Newman, we knew we'd have more control because he's in America.'

Once things were put in place it was agreed that both Lennox and Ruddock would have warm-up fights. Ours was to be against Mike Dixon, while Ruddock took on Phil Jackson in June. It was during the build-up to Razor's fight against Jackson that I turned down the chance to swell my bank balance after an offer from Don King. I was in San Diego on business when the phone in my hotel room rang and the unmistakable voice of King boomed down the line.

'Frank Maloney, how are you, my little man?' asked King.

It was as if I was his bosom buddy, but the fact was I didn't really know him and the last time we'd met was when Levitt entertained him over breakfast at the St James's Club in London more than three years earlier. On that occasion it was more a meeting of egos rather than minds, with King and Levitt trying to outdo each other from the moment they entered the room.

NO BALONEY

I was surprised to get a call from him out of the blue, but I soon understood why he'd bothered to track me down in California. After Razor's two fights with Tyson, King had claimed he still had a tie-up with Ruddock's people. He was keen to make sure he was part of the promotion for the contest with Lennox, and it wasn't long before he was in full flow on the phone to me.

'Maloney,' he went on, 'I'm going to make sure you're the biggest name in boxing Britain has ever seen. People like me and you, we come from the same background, we're both from oppressed minorities. I'm black and you're Irish. They want to try and make sure they keep us down. They don't want us to succeed, but they can't stop us.'

He then went on to give me a lecture on, among other things, the potato famine in Ireland before getting back to what he'd really called me for.

'You can help steer things my way,' he added. 'You're the man who can help do that and if it happens I can make you rich. How does $1 million sound to you?'

I never actually answered his question but told him my loyalties were to Lennox and Main Events. After putting the phone down to King I spoke to Dan and told him exactly what had gone on. Lennox and I ended up going to watch Ruddock's fourth round win over Jackson in Cleveland with HBO and Main Events arranging the trip. We got pulled up into the ring after the contest, with King going into overdrive and screeching on about why he was the best promoter in the world. By the time I got back to my hotel room my ears were still ringing from his non-stop talk. But despite all that he said, when the fight with Ruddock was finally signed, Don was not part of the action.

While Razor had come through his warm-up contest unscathed, Lennox still had to take care of business both in and out of the ring in Atlantic City. First Dixon was despatched in the fourth round of a pretty one-sided fight, and then Levitt was sent packing shortly afterwards.

Lennox had obviously decided that enough was enough as far as Roger was concerned, and I think he got fed up with some of the things Levitt came out with. The bottom line was that Roger really wasn't delivering on the promises he'd made and that was something Lennox really didn't like. We had a meeting in Lennox's suite and I actually started feeling sorry for Levitt at one point. He was dressed in an expensive blue blazer, white shirt and jeans and seemed to be his normal confident self when he entered the room. But it didn't take long for him to realise this was one situation he was not going to be able to talk himself out of. Lewis had made his mind up, despite Roger almost pleading at one point.

When he finally realised there was no way out, Levitt asked if he could at least leave with dignity by telling the press he was stepping down as commercial manager because of the pressure of his court case and his mother's illness. The press were invited into the room and Roger made quite an emotional speech in which he claimed he would always be there to help and advise Lennox if he was needed.

If I thought that was going to be an end to things with Levitt, I couldn't have been more wrong. Once the build-up to the Ruddock fight got underway I had my biggest run-in with Levitt, when I ended up physically threatening him in our offices. We didn't actually come to blows but things got very heated, with Roger saying he wasn't scared of me because he'd had martial arts training. It was a ridiculous situation because although Roger had been sacked as Lewis's commercial manager he still came into the office on a regular basis. He'd done the deal with Earls Court in London to stage the Ruddock fight at the Arena on Halloween night, a deal where I thought we'd paid well over the top. He also managed to find some sponsorship to help with the cost of the contest which was going to see us pay Ruddock more than $2 million in order to secure home advantage.

It was during the lead-up to the fight that Lennox's brother Dennis and I phoned Panos to let him know we were concerned at what was happening. Roger had basically been carrying on as if he was still running the show and had given the impression that Panos was just minding the shop for him and using Levitt's money. But we got the full story from Panos, who told us that he and Conrad were the ones responsible for the finances and assured us things would change once the Ruddock fight was out of the way.

By this time it was clear that the promotion was going to lose money, and we were gambling on the fact that a win for Lewis would guarantee a world title fight. Although Main Events had started as Lennox's sole promoters in the USA, we had negotiated a new deal and were partners with them. It meant we shared in any profits, but also that we had to be able to fund any loss as well. We had a pre-fight meeting with Dan Duva in London and he offered to underwrite any loss the show might suffer, but wanted the exclusive rights to promote Lennox's next three fights.

'What do you think, Frank?' Panos asked me.

'Panos,' I said. 'I think Lennox wins this fight.'

Without too much hesitation Panos said we'd stay 50–50, which was a big gamble on his part because he stood to lose so much money if things went wrong, but Dan told him he'd made the right decision, and it was pretty clear as the fight drew closer that we were about to stage one of the biggest sporting events the country had seen for some time.

We booked the White House as the fight hotel and there was a real buzz around the place in the final few days before the contest. Ruddock arrived in town with a massive entourage and a couple of unsmiling security guards that we nicknamed 'the bookends'. They were as wide as they were tall and always tried to look menacing. From the moment Razor arrived you could tell how big the fight was and we got a lot of publicity. There was also a miners' dispute taking place at the time and we let the press know that Lennox was going to donate some tickets to them for nothing. We were actually given a couple of miner's lamps by them as a way of saying thankyou for our gesture.

Panos decided to host a dinner for everyone at his home a few days before the fight, but although Roger was not on the guest list, he still turned up with his wife and wandered around the place as if he was in charge of everything. I went along with Caroline who was with me after a sticky few months in which she'd gone off to Dubai. Our romance was back on, and that night we got an assurance from a rather large foreign woman at the party that Caroline and I would go on to get married and have two children together. The woman who told us this turned out to be employed by Panos to help look after the house and her daughter's name was Lydia. As well as being told I would marry Caroline, Lydia also claimed Panos and I would make a good partnership, and we would work well together in the future. I never paid too much attention to the whole thing at the time, but Panos told me later in the evening that Lydia and her mother could tell fortunes. It soon became clear he was interested in the spiritual world.

We had our final press conference at the White House the next day and Panos asked me to make sure I kept three seats empty right at the front of the room. The place was heaving with press, photographers and TV crews. It was an incredible scene and the atmosphere was electric. Just before we were due to get underway in walked Lydia, her mother and another woman. They sat in the seats Panos had asked me to keep empty and stared straight ahead at Ruddock and his entourage. It was impossible not to notice them from where I was and I asked Panos what was going on.

When he told me I wasn't sure if I'd heard him correctly. He said they were able to tell the future and could put some kind of spell on Ruddock. Panos also said that Lydia's mother should touch Lennox's glove before the fight. It sounded crazy, but I was too wound up in the fight to think much about it. Later in my relationship with Panos it became clear that he paid a lot of attention to what Lydia or her mother had to say, and would often consult them on where certain people should sit at ringside for Lennox's fights to help make sure he won. When Lennox's mother found out about things like this later on, she had Lydia and her mother barred from his dressing-room.

On the day of the fight I was a bundle of nerves. Because of American TV the contest wasn't due to start until about 1 a.m. and for most of the time I was in a daze. I'd decided to move Lennox out of the White House and into a hotel in Chelsea Harbour. The fight hotel was chaotic and I thought it was best to be away from it all. I went to visit him in his room about six hours before he was due to step into the ring and was amazed at how calm he was.

'Are you worried, Frank?' he asked me.

'It's a big fight, Lennox,' I said.

'You don't have to be worried. I'm going to do the job and win,' he insisted.

I looked at him and could see he was absolutely certain about what he was going to do, but it still didn't stop the butterflies in my stomach. I walked all the way from his hotel to the Arena in a world of my own. If a bomb had gone off in front of me I don't think I would have noticed, and when I got inside all I did for the next couple of hours was eat ice creams.

Razor arrived in England with a reputation as a big puncher. Even Tyson admitted being hit by Ruddock's right hand was like getting a kick from a mule. A lot of people thought Lennox might have bitten off more than he could chew, but despite my nervousness I honestly believed Lewis would be too good for him. If it all went wrong I knew I would probably get the blame for helping to steer him into such a big fight too soon after only 21 contests as a professional.

Ruddock was really hyped for the fight on the night, and I think I played a part in getting him even more wound up just before he entered the ring. As part of the rules it was agreed that a representative from each camp would visit the dressing-room of the other fighter to witness him getting gloved-up. When I went into Razor's dressing-room he already had his gloves on and was working out with his trainer. I immediately insisted that he take the gloves off and let me watch him do the whole thing again.

Ruddock went mad, screaming and shouting at the top of his voice, but I was determined to insist that he stuck to the rules, especially as I could see I was really getting under his skin with the request. Floyd Patterson, the former world heavyweight champion who was working in Ruddock's corner that night, told Razor he'd have to do as I asked and eventually the big Canadian agreed but not without letting me know exactly what he thought of my antics.

The Earls Court crowd that night managed to produce one of the best atmospheres for a big fight that I've ever known. The noise level and tension was amazing with the fans right behind Lennox. It was fantastic support and he didn't disappoint them.

Ruddock was decked once near the end of the first round and then twice in the second as Lennox put on the most devastating display of punching power produced by a British heavyweight for years. He was superb and when the fight was stopped I was catapulted over the ropes as the celebrations went wild. I could hardly speak when I was asked to give radio and TV interviews because I was too emotional.

Lennox had shown that he was truly world class and the win meant he was within touching distance of becoming heavyweight champion of the world.

There were two parties held after the fight. One was at a West End nightclub and the other was at the White House. I popped in at the nightclub but soon left because the heavy smoke and pungent smell it produced, which often seemed to be part of the after-fight scene, was a bit too much for me. It was probably also true that some of the people there and the things they got up to didn't really appeal to me. I headed for the White House ready to enjoy myself after what had been the greatest night of boxing I'd ever been involved in.

9. THE RICHEST PRIZE IN SPORT

THE CELEBRATIONS WENT ON LONG INTO THE EARLY HOURS OF THE MORNING following the win over Ruddock. Poor Razor didn't know what had hit him in the ring and as if that wasn't bad enough, he had to suffer more humiliation out of it.

Eugene had been brought in to drive Ruddock around during the build-up to the fight and it worked well because he was able to report back to us on anything useful he might have overheard while ferrying his passenger from place to place. But on the night of the fight my brother drove Lennox in a brand new Jaguar that he had, while Ruddock had somebody else driving him in a Mercedes. The only problem was that when Eugene went to collect his car after the fight to take Lennox back to the hotel, he discovered the Jag had been stolen. Without missing a beat, he went back into the Arena and found Ruddock's driver, telling him Lewis wanted to use the Mercedes instead. He swapped keys with the new man and drove off with Lennox, leaving poor old Razor without a car. In the end a bad night was made even worse as he had to bundle himself into a minivan for the lonely drive back to the White House.

When he got there Ruddock was greeted by a scene that looked like the terraces at Wembley after a Cup Final. The whole place seemed to be partying and everywhere you looked there were Lennox Lewis supporters. It was an amazing scene and it took me more than a week to come down from the 'high' I felt after the win. I also celebrated in another way by going out and buying an engagement ring for Caroline and deciding to set up home with her by getting a flat in Surbiton.

In the press conference which followed the fight, Panos had made his first real public appearance, when Dan Duva praised him for helping to make sure the contest actually happened. Everything looked rosy for us and we started thinking about the next stage which was meeting the winner of Holyfield's fight with Bowe. But the picture changed dramatically when the two fought in Las Vegas on 13 November. It proved to be an unlucky date for Evander and for Lennox.

Lewis and I travelled to the States to see the fight, with Lennox doing some work at ringside for HBO, while I helped out on the commentary for Sky. We went there hoping Holyfield would retain his titles because we knew that would make things easier for us, but it was Bowe who came out on top with a points win and from the moment his hand was raised in victory I knew we had problems.

Bowe's manager Rock Newman was not the easiest man to do business with. He was loud and brash with the ability to come out with the most outrageous statements and ideas when he was negotiating deals. One minute you'd think something had been achieved, and the next moment you found yourself back to square one. He looked like the actor Orson Welles and was a former car salesman and radio host. As soon as Bowe had beaten Holyfield I knew there was no way Newman was going to let him near Lewis. His fighter was the undisputed heavyweight champion of the world and that gave him an awful lot of bargaining power.

I knew there was no love lost between Lennox and Bowe but I wasn't prepared for what happened almost immediately after the Holyfield fight. From my commentary position I noticed that he had spotted Lennox at ringside and could see they were having a go at each other. Then as Bowe went to walk back to his dressing-room it started again and Lennox apparently threatened to knock him out. At the post-fight press conference, Newman invited us up to the top table and despite Lennox trying to congratulate Riddick, the new champion seemed determined to bad-mouth Lewis, claiming he had sisters who could 'whup' him. Then as we got up to leave he made a comment about the small ponytail Lennox had before calling him a 'faggot'. It wasn't a particularly dignified start to his reign, but it was a taste of things to come from Bowe and his manager.

Although we had a contract in place covering Lennox as the WBC mandatory contender, it didn't include the WBA and IBF titles. Had Holyfield won it would have been enough for us to go forward and fight him, but Newman and Bowe were a different proposition.

Lewis against Bowe was the fight everyone wanted to see but it soon became clear that Newman wanted to avoid the contest and concentrate on some easy defences. I started calling his fighter 'Chicken Bowe'. I even had some business cards printed with Riddick Bowe on one side and a boxer with a chicken's head on the other with the words Chicken Bowe printed on it, and handed them out to the press in America. I was even chased by Bowe himself on one occasion when we came face to face in a hotel lobby.

When we discovered he was coming to London in December 1992 I decided to give Bowe a welcome he'd remember. We found out which plane he would be coming in on and I employed two actors to dress up in chicken outfits and go to the airport to meet him and hand out more of the cards. They also turned up at his hotel and got escorted out when they tried to get into the lobby. It might sound childish, but it was all good fun and got us publicity. At a later date as negotiations rumbled on, I even called a press conference after returning from talks in America and told the media I'd brought someone with me. All eyes were on the door to the conference room, when I suddenly reached under the table and opened the lid to a box I'd arranged to have placed there. I stuck my hand in and pulled out a live chicken before releasing it into the room. It got lots of laughs and plenty of press the next day, but I was also warned I might have the RSPCA on my back after pulling the stunt!

Right from the start we tried to goad Bowe into agreeing to the fight, but it had no effect. During that visit to London he soon showed what contempt he had for the WBC title by dumping the belt into a dustbin while he was in town. It still meant that he held the WBA and

IBF championships, but it also ensured he wouldn't have the WBC on his case trying to make him defend against Lennox.

The WBC reacted by awarding their belt to Lennox so instead of the mega-fight we'd hoped for, he actually became a world champion while dressed in a dinner suit instead of a pair of boxing shorts. He was awarded the championship belt at a ceremony in January 1993 held at the Marriott Hotel in London's West End. But along with the WBC belt came an obligation to the organisation, or more precisely its president, Jose Sulaiman.

It pretty soon became clear that we weren't going to get the option of a voluntary defence against Alex Stewart, a fighter who was based in the States, but was actually born in Britain. Instead we were told we had to make a mandatory defence against number one contender Tony Tucker, who was a Don King fighter. Since Mike Tyson's loss against Buster Douglas in 1990 and his subsequent conviction on a rape charge, King had found himself on the outside looking in when it came to getting a piece of the world title. The heavyweight championship has long been considered the richest prize in sport, so you can understand how desperate Don was for Tucker to get a crack at Lewis.

Sulaiman is one of the major figures in the fight game because of his position as President of the WBC. Short and round, the little Mexican wields tremendous power and King has had a close working relationship with him for years. You only have to attend a WBC convention to see how powerful Sulaiman is within the sport, with so many people willing to suck up to him. I've seen plenty of people back down or fail to stand up to him over the years including our own British Boxing Board of Control. In theory the WBC is not just about Jose, but let's just say he's a very big part of it.

When the Lewis–Tucker fight was ordered to take place King did everything he could to make sure he came out of it a winner. Originally he wanted a 60–40 split in Lennox's favour, while we were looking for an 80–20 percentage split. In the end, after more pressure from King, there was a vote of the WBC's board of governors who decided it should be 75–25, and the fight eventually went to purse bids which were opened in Mexico City.

We knew the Tucker fight was going to be Lennox's first defence, but we also had to plan for the future, and despite Riddick's reluctance,

THE RICHEST PRIZE IN SPORT

Bowe versus Lewis was still the fight everyone wanted to see. It was also the biggest contest out there, and the winner would once again be the undisputed champion. Newman was certainly taking no chances with Bowe and his first defence was an easy one-round job against Mike Dokes in New York on 6 February. By this time it had been worked out that there could be a total of around $32 million available if Bowe and Lewis fought. The only problem was the little matter of how it should be divided up, and also the fact that we had to deal with Newman.

He came up with all sorts of proposals, one of which was offering just $3 million. Another was that both fighters would get $5 million with the winner getting an extra lump sum and the loser only getting training expenses in addition. But Newman seemed to think he would really scare us off by offering a winner-takes-all option, with the loser again getting next to nothing apart from his training expenses. Lennox pressed me on what I thought and I said it was a risk but that I believed he would beat Bowe, so we faxed Newman saying we accepted but never got a reply from him.

Meanwhile, the three purse bids for the Tucker fight had been opened. Our own company, Champion Enterprises, was one of the bidders, Main Events was another and then there was King. The envelopes were opened one by one, with King's the last to be unveiled. When it was, there was a kind of shocked silence around the room as we heard the figure – $12 million.

It meant that Lennox would earn a massive $9 million for his first title defence, which was a staggering amount. I just couldn't understand how King was going to make any money out of the fight, because the bid seemed well over the top to me. Ironically, when I telephoned Lennox to tell him, he was more concerned with the fact that he'd lost the chance to have the contest in London. The fight was eventually set for Las Vegas on 8 May. From the moment it was announced I think King wanted to try and impress Lennox and win him over. But once we'd signed the contract for the fight one of my main jobs was to make sure we only did what we had to.

Lennox had to publicise the contest and was contracted to do certain things like press conferences and TV appearances, but Dan Duva and I decided right from the start that there was no way he was going to be distracted from preparing for what was such a big fight.

NO BALONEY

One of the things we had to do was shoot a TV commercial for Showtime, the network which was going to be screening the contest in the States on a pay-per-view basis. They sent us tickets to fly over to New York on Concorde. So I jetted off with Lennox and Eugene, who was by this time acting as Lewis's personal security man. It was a bit of a change for the Maloney brothers, because only a few years earlier we'd have struggled to get a ticket for a flight to Spain.

It was all a new world for me but I knew I had to learn quickly and there was no better teacher than Dan Duva. He told me, 'Frank, there are two sorts of business in this sport. There's boxing business and then there's heavyweight boxing business. Right now you're at the top of the heap because you manage the heavyweight champion of the world, so make sure you enjoy it and use it properly.'

As usual it was good advice from Dan and I knew what he meant. When you're treated differently and there are a lot of people who suddenly want to be your friend, it also means you have more muscle when you're trying to get things and open doors that would otherwise be closed to you. It's easy to get carried away with it all and start to believe you've cracked it, but one of the things I've learned over the years is that if you become complacent there's always someone there who's ready to knock you off your perch.

In the middle of March Lennox left for the States to start his preparations for Tucker. Ollie Dunlap, a former American footballer who had been brought in by Pepe for the Ruddock contest as camp co-ordinator, had set things up on Hilton Head Island in South Carolina. It was a good place to train, with wide flat beaches perfect for early morning runs, and good gym facilities. I shuttled back and forth spending time in camp and in England as I tried to start planning ahead.

The chance of a contest with Bowe looked dead in the water at this time. It seemed clear that if he was ever going to get in the ring with Lennox it certainly wouldn't be for some time as Newman pursued the easy option route. We had to look elsewhere and that meant a possible meeting with someone closer to home, in the shape of Frank Bruno. Although big Frank had been battered in previous world title fights against Tim Witherspoon in 1986 and Mike Tyson three years later, he was being skilfully guided towards another crack at the crown by Duff. We knew if Bruno came through a contest against American Carl

THE RICHEST PRIZE IN SPORT

Williams in Birmingham in April and Lennox beat Tucker, the possibility of Britain's biggest ever fight might become a reality.

Training camps are never easy for fighters. They not only have to try and physically prepare for a contest, they also have to have the mental toughness to be away from home for weeks putting up with the same routine day in, day out. It gives you lots of time to think and you soon become detached from the rest of the world. It's all about what goes on in camp and the smallest of things can become a big problem.

We had a bit of trouble with Tony Tubbs who was in camp as a sparring partner. He didn't turn up for the usual morning run one day and was later found at a house in a pretty undesirable neighbourhood. It was clear from the state he was in that he wasn't going to be much good to us in terms of preparing for the fight. Tubbs had briefly held the WBA world heavyweight title, and it seemed crazy that he'd gone from that to not even being wanted as a sparring partner. It was sad, but I don't think there was really another option open to us in the circumstances.

It was obviously important that preparations for the Tucker fight were spot on. Britain had waited for an awful long time to have a world heavyweight champion, and there was no way Lennox or anyone else connected with him wanted to make any mistakes. We knew if we all did our jobs professionally and to the best of our abilities everything would work out well.

But in boxing, just as in any other sport, the thing that can really upset matters is an injury. So you can imagine how everyone felt when Lennox damaged his right hand during training. With less than three weeks to go before the fight we arranged for him to fly to see a specialist in New York who diagnosed a split in the extender tendon in the knuckle of his little finger. That was the bad news, but the good news was the doctor also said Lennox would be all right to go ahead with the fight.

Throughout the time Lennox was in camp I was still trying to juggle some of the other boxing business I was involved in. Although there was the little matter of a world heavyweight title fight in Las Vegas to prepare for, I was also planning rather smaller shows back home as well as looking after my other fighters.

NO BALONEY

Over the period of five days during late March and early April 1993, I had a show at York Hall with some of my boxers on it, was verbally assaulted by Don King at a press conference in London, and physically assaulted by Ambrose Mendy.

There was a bit of a disappointment for me on the York Hall show because a heavyweight, Warren Richards, whom I was hoping to guide towards a British title shot was beaten in an eliminator by Roger McKenzie. Just to add to my woes King decided to have a go at me less than 24 hours later at a press conference to publicise the Tucker fight. He actually managed to talk for 73 minutes, which even for Don was quite something, and a lot of the words that tumbled out of his mouth attacked me and my management of Lennox. It was a bit of a shock at first but I wasn't going to let it upset me. It was all good fun which helped to prepare me for what was to come a few weeks later in Las Vegas. They were words and they can't really hurt you.

The Mendy incident was slightly different. It happened a few days after the King onslaught when I went to a Sunday boxing show I was involved in at the Crofton Park Leisure Centre in south London. After the show there was a dispute with Mendy over the amount of money he was being paid for one of his fighters who had appeared on the promotion. I told him in no uncertain terms that I'd had enough of his antics and that Ambrose would have to find a new promoter. But just as I went to walk out of the door Mendy threw a punch at me and blood started to pour from my mouth. Luckily a few people jumped in before anything else could develop, but the incident left me with a cut lip and a sore tooth. It wasn't the nicest of things to happen to me, particularly as I had a meeting the next day with Mickey Duff to discuss terms for a possible Lewis–Bruno fight later in the year.

We were only in the early stages of discussions with Mickey and I knew from past experience that there was going to be a lot of hard bargaining before we reached any agreement, but I couldn't help smiling at his cheek when he started talking about a 60–40, or 65–35 split in the purse. Remember, Bruno was going to be the challenger and he would be getting a crack at the world title for the third time, so there was no way we were going to have him walk away with 35 or 40 percent of the money.

There was so much going on in my life at this stage both

professionally and personally, because I was also trying to sort out my divorce from Jackie. I was on the go non-stop, and although I was enjoying a lot of it I also found it very stressful. I suppose a lot of people in those circumstances might have turned to drink, but in my case I just gave in to my sweet tooth and started eating chocolate as if it were going out of fashion.

Despite his hand injury I was pleasantly surprised when I flew back to the training camp to find how well Lennox was coping. I watched him spar one day and he boxed brilliantly, but only really used his left hand. By this time Lennox had put in weeks of hard training and we were just about to embark on the hype part of the contest, which is part of the territory for any major world title fight. I'd agreed to fly back to England to do some TV work on Bruno's fight with Carl Williams. Frank duly won his fight with Williams on points and it was enough to keep him on track for a shot at Lennox, but he looked very wooden doing it.

King wanted us to set up in Vegas earlier than was normal and we ended up arriving in town about ten days before the actual contest. When I got there I was amazed at the suite I had. It was like nothing else I'd seen before and looked like something out of a movie set. It was actually bigger than the flat in Surbiton, and the sunken bath was big enough for me to have a swim in! It was the first time I had ever been involved in such a huge promotion and I soon started to realise that along with the headaches, there were also quite a few nice little perks that went with the job.

I soon settled into both life in the gambling capital of the world and the suite I'd been given. Although I was becoming reasonably well known because of my association with Lennox, the person who really made me famous that week was Don King. From the moment I set foot on the famous neon strip, until the day I flew back to England, King never stopped having a go at me whenever he got the opportunity.

A 'mental midget' and 'pugilistic pygmy' were just two of the phrases he used to try and undermine me and the job I was doing for Lennox. According to him I was a snake in the grass, a weasel and I was treacherous. He even had a letter printed and pushed under the doors of the media as well as our own camp four days before the fight. It was called 'The indiscretions of Frank Maloney. Vicious, Stupid or Both?' In the letter, which was addressed to Lennox, his family and genuine friends, he claimed Lewis was being held back by me. One of the lines in it was, 'You can't fly a multimillion dollar airplane properly when you are being guided by a ten cent control tower.' King was clearly hoping there would be a crash landing for me, but the beauty of it was that his $9 million purse actually helped us all take off in a big way.

I think he was pissed off with the fact that we'd only done as much as we were contractually obligated to do, but more than that was the fact that I think he wanted to discredit me and undermine my position with Lennox. Perhaps he also thought I would be intimidated by his tactics because I was the new boy on the block, but having Don King shouting at you is no worse than getting an earful from a disgruntled punter in East Street market, or a drunk in your pub. It didn't frighten or intimidate me.

Instead, all I did was stay calm and make sure I was my usual self. The fact that I did that for the entire time I was in Vegas seemed to wind King up even more, because he couldn't get any reaction from me, and Lennox made sure he ignored Don and just got on with his preparations.

Lennox didn't actually stay in the hotel; even though provision was made in the contract for him to have a suite, he preferred to stay in an apartment. Tucker was also there in another apartment and it was quite funny to see each camp post security guards on the door 24 hours a day. We were determined to make sure nothing interfered or upset our preparations, and we even used our own bottled water throughout the time we were in Vegas.

We actually had some T-shirts made with a cartoon of King on the front waving two little American flags and a quotation from Samuel Johnson underneath, 'Patriotism is the last refuge of a scoundrel.' King also spotted my mother in the lobby of the hotel one day and wanted to know how such a beautiful woman could have such a horrible son like me!

Although I was totally focused on the fight and had talked myself hoarse at the end of some days with all the media interviews, I did have time to enjoy the whole thing as well. I had one very drunken night where I ended up staggering around the lobby of the Mirage hotel in the early hours of the morning. I'd taken to wearing cut-off dungarees and a cap turned backwards on my head. I'd started doing it after seeing a picture of Mike Tyson dressed like that when he was with King, but I don't think Don ever saw the joke. On this particular night I'd let off a bit of steam by going out and having a few drinks with some of the press. I don't quite know how, but when I got back to the hotel I'd managed to replace my hat with a condom which was perched on top of my head as I stood at the bar chatting to some amused young American women. Apparently one of the press guys told me later someone had asked exactly who I was.

'That, my friend, is the manager of the world heavyweight champion,' said the pressman, and burst out laughing as the other guy just shook his head in amazement.

Despite the fact that I must have got to bed at about 5.30 a.m., I was up a few hours later ready to prepare for the weigh-in later that afternoon. There were hundreds of Brits in Vegas by this time and they really made their voices heard as they cheered Lennox when he stepped up to the scales, and then gave King a chorus of boos. They also chanted my name, which was a bit of a new experience for me. The fans were brilliant for that fight, as they were right through my time with Lennox. I always got on well with them and I think they could relate to me, because they knew I was no different to them in many ways. I just happened to be Lennox's manager.

On the morning of the contest I was my usual bundle of nerves. I think most people would find it hard to understand the pressure you go through, or the mental agony of it all. It's not like being a football manager, where you can lose a game and then put things right in a week's time by winning the next match. There just isn't the chance to put things right if you lose. You're at the top of the world during the build-up and then on the actual day of the fight, the enormity of it all really dawns on you. That morning my stomach was in knots, and I just wanted the whole thing to be over and Lennox to remain world champion.

When I got to his apartment later in the afternoon, the doctor was just about to give him a cortisone injection in his injured hand. I noticed there was tension in everyone's face including Lennox, but once again he showed how well he handles pre-fight nerves and he was still able to be relaxed and determined at the same time.

NO BALONEY

There was a good atmosphere in the dressing-room at the Thomas and Mack Centre with all of us going about our jobs in a very calm and professional way. I've always felt it's so important to do things right in the dressing-room just before a contest. If things go wrong, or routines are not the same, it can have an effect on a fighter. He's prepared long and hard for the big moment, so he doesn't want things going wrong, or the place feeling chaotic just before he steps into the ring. Pepe, assistant trainer Harold Knight and fitness conditioner Courtney Shand, were making sure everything was as it should be, and just before Lennox left the room we all huddled for a prayer, which became a regular thing before a fight.

Tucker was a big guy weighing 16 st. 11 lb which was the same as Lewis. Physically they were evenly matched. But despite the fact that the American's only loss had come on points in a world title fight with Tyson three years earlier, Lennox showed what a good boxer he was, decking the challenger a couple of times before emerging as a unanimous points winner.

I later found out that Tucker not only missed out on the world heavyweight championship, but to make his night even more miserable, he also lost out on getting a brand new black Mercedes 500SL car. My press officer Andy Ayling saw King show Tucker the car before the fight and, pointing to the gleaming Merc, he told the challenger, 'You knock this motherfucker out and the Benz is yours.' After the contest Andy couldn't help smiling as Don told his press officer to 'take the motherfucker back to the showroom'.

It was a special feeling to be in the ring as the verdict was announced. The last Englishman to hold the world title had been Bob Fitzsimmons at the end of the previous century, so it was incredible to be there as the manager of Lewis after he'd just defended the title for the first time, and done it on American soil. He'd put on a great performance and done it virtually one-handed. If Lennox had slipped up and been beaten he would have been a laughing stock and the Yanks would have been gloating. As it was, all you could hear in the Arena were the cheers and chants from the British fans. At last they had a real winner.

10. BEST OF BRITISH

I ENJOYED THE POST-FIGHT PRESS CONFERENCE. KING TRIED TO PUT A BRAVE face on things but there was no doubt in my mind that he had taken a huge gamble and lost.

As he left the podium that night I looked across at him and for the first time he actually looked old and drained, but I also knew it wouldn't be the last time our paths would cross. Whatever else you thought about King, there was no denying his ability to bounce back, but that night I knew both his pride and his pocket had taken a pounding.

Although I was delighted with the way things had gone, I just had a bottle of beer and two cups of hot chocolate at the after-fight party that had been organised. Just as I was about to leave a couple of people spotted me and said they had a present. It turned out to be a big troll doll that bore a striking resemblance to Don King. They'd even brushed his hair up so it looked like King's famous electric shock look, and he was dressed in a suit with an American flag in his hand. I loved it and wandered off to my room with Caroline, holding my new found friend under my arm.

We were all pleased with a job well done. The only sour note was created by Levitt. He may have been publicly out of the picture, but he still went to Vegas and, in his wisdom, decided to call a meeting with Panos and Conrad Morris to discuss bonuses and payments to the training team and me. Roger still felt he had a role to play in the whole thing, even though by this time Panos seemed to be doing no more than just tolerating him. Word spread that Roger had suggested that nobody would get a bonus and would just make do with their salaries. He also suggested I shouldn't get the percentage I was due unless Lennox was involved in a unification fight.

News of this grand plan soon got back to all of us, including my brother who had been in camp with Lennox for all those weeks, working as his security man. Eugene had even missed the birth of his baby daughter because he'd been with Lennox in Hilton Head, so you can imagine that he wasn't exactly pleased when he heard what had been suggested. Unfortunately for Roger, it wasn't long before Eugene got the opportunity to show just how unhappy he was.

Levitt was his usual confident self one day as he waited in the Mirage for one of its many elevators to take him up to his room. The trouble was that as the doors pinged open Roger found himself face-to-face with Eugene, and when my brother saw him the old red mist took over. Levitt was grabbed by the throat and pinned against a wall as he tried to call for help. Eugene told him that if he tried to screw him out of his money, it would be the last thing Roger ever did.

Luckily Panos arrived like the cavalry and calmed things down by telling everyone they would be paid and that nobody would be cheated out of any bonus money. Levitt was clearly shaken by the whole thing and actually tried to get Eugene sacked, but it was another one of Roger's suggestions that fell on deaf ears.

We stayed in Vegas to do more press conferences the day after the fight and then packed up and prepared to leave on the Monday. We were flying to Dallas first and were then due to get a connection to London. When I turned up at the airport, as well as all my bags I was carrying the doll I'd been given, and by pure coincidence King was on the same flight as us. It didn't take him long to notice the doll and soon everyone could hear his booming laughter.

'Look,' said Don. 'Maloney likes me so much he wants to take me home with him!'

He seemed to have got over the disappointment of losing the fight two days earlier, and was back to being the Don King everyone expects to see in public.

There was a lot of press interest when we eventually got back to England, with Lennox and me being asked to appear on quite a few radio and TV shows. I even appeared on the David Frost show holding my Don King doll, which seemed to go down well with the audience. We also had some time to unwind with a visit to Ascot for some racing. Eugene was a regular punter with a local bookmaker called John Humphreys, and he invited my brother, me and Lennox to his private box at the race course one day. The hospitality was tremendous and when it came to placing bets, there was a guy who came round and asked what you wanted on each race. Eugene was keen to have a bet on a particular horse and when the guy asked him how much he wanted to bet my brother said, 'I'll have two large ones,' which meant £2,000. He then went to ask Lennox if he wanted a bet. 'I'll have fifteen,' said Lewis, and then said, 'no, I'm feeling lucky, I'll have twenty.'

The guy taking the bets wasn't sure whether Lennox meant hundreds or thousands, but quickly found out that it only meant £20. He was clearly surprised that Lennox wasn't going to have more on the race, but as far as I was concerned it just showed how shrewd he was with his cash, and he certainly was not going to be the sort of sports star who blew his money on gambling. Just to top things off nicely, the horse won and Lennox was delighted. You got the impression that winning meant more to him than any money he'd had on the race.

I tried to catch up on things with Caroline as well, because I knew she'd been upset with the fact that I'd spent so much time away from home during the build-up to the Tucker fight.

But my life was still dominated by the career of Lennox Lewis and whatever else I did, there was always the task of making sure everything stayed on course. It wasn't just me, because there were a team of people involved, but as his manager I always felt I had a special responsibility – I'd done well out of the job and after four years I knew my life had changed dramatically. The good far outweighed the bad, but it meant I tended to have less time to myself.

NO BALONEY

Pretty soon after the Tucker fight Lennox flew to New York and had a successful operation on the hand he'd damaged while training in Hilton Head. It was also around this time that we began to plan for the future. Apart from the possibility of a contest with Bruno there were also other big fights on the horizon, one of which was against Tommy Morrison, a white American heavyweight who had lost just once in 37 contests. He was supposed to have been related to the movie star John Wayne, and had appeared in one of the *Rocky* films alongside Sylvester Stallone.

Dan Duva had already spoken to the Morrison camp about a possible fight somewhere down the line, and in the early part of June I had the chance to combine some business with pleasure when I flew out to Vegas for Morrison's WBO world title fight with the veteran George Foreman. At that time the heavyweight title was fragmented. Bowe held the WBA and IBF versions, Lennox had the WBC belt and either Morrison or the 43-year-old Foreman would take the WBO championship after their bout on 7 June, so it was important that I was there.

I travelled to the States with Eugene, David Byrne and another footballer, Mark Bright. I'd been friends with Mark for a few years by this time because he was one of the players Levitt wanted as part of the sports arm of his organisation. At the time of his association with Levitt he was playing for Crystal Palace, but had since moved on to Sheffield Wednesday and when we flew off to Vegas he'd just suffered the disappointment of an FA Cup final defeat by Arsenal, the team who had already beaten them in the Coca-Cola Cup final a few months earlier. We left for the trip on Brighty's birthday and had a great time at the front of the plane, drinking champagne and playing cards with a lot of money changing hands. Eugene tried to persuade singer Roger Daltrey to join us, but had to be content with taking money off of everyone else in our party. We had a great time in Vegas, including a wild night out on the town with movie star, Mickey Rourke, who loved boxing and actually had a couple of fights himself.

We had some fun with Rourke in a table top dancing place called the Olympic Garden, which had some beautiful girls in it, all of whom seemed to be eager to introduce themselves to Mickey. One of them actually asked him if he'd mind going home with her and re-enacting a certain steamy scene from one of his movies. Rourke politely declined but seemed to enjoy our company and his bodyguard, 'Billy Two Guns', was certainly impressed with Eugene. The two of them got into a challenge to see who could 'draw' the fastest and my brother came out on top. Mickey even jokingly offered him a job as a security guard if he ever got fed up working for Lennox, and gave Eugene his hat, which was apparently worth a lot of money.

Later that same night when I was asleep in my room Lennox, who had flown in to watch the Morrison fight, knocked on the door and when I opened it he was standing there beaming from ear to ear, accompanied by two very attractive girls. I think he just wanted to make a point of letting me know he was back safe and sound, while at the same time having a laugh by waking me up after I'd had quite a heavy night on the town.

Morrison made sure of the WBO crown with a points win in what was an unexciting fight, but as soon as it was over I made sure I got Lewis in the ring for pictures with Tommy. Lennox knew there might be the possibility of meeting him in the not too distant future. Dan had already talked to Bob Arum who was Morrison's promoter and on the morning of the fight I had breakfast with Bill Cayton, who was Tommy's adviser. He was also the man who, along with his partner Jim Jacobs, had helped guide the early part of Mike Tyson's career. When Jacobs died, Cayton took charge on his own before a very public falling-out, which saw the emergence of a certain Mr Don King as the new power behind Mike.

But it wasn't all about world heavyweight title fights for me, and the bread-and-butter business of promoting smaller shows back in England was also very important. A couple of weeks after that trip to Vegas my thoughts were very firmly focused on a promotion we were putting on at Pickett's Lock in Edmonton, north London.

I hadn't exactly been on friendly terms with Ambrose Mendy, especially after being thumped in the mouth by him at Crofton Park. In the build-up to the Pickett's Lock promotion I'd received several fairly nasty faxes from him, as well as phone calls, and because of them I'd decided to beef up my security. Although he was banned from the show, Ambrose had said he was going to turn up. It certainly wasn't a pleasant atmosphere. In the end there was no sign of Mendy, but this was also the night where I received one of my out-of-the ring clumps, when Kirkland's partner whacked me while I was at ringside. I remember driving home feeling really down and very stressed out after all that had happened.

It was good to know the show was behind me and the next day I once again began to concentrate on other things when I flew to Atlantic City. I was going to have more talks with Duff about getting the Bruno contest sorted out. Mickey was there with his fighter Lloyd Honeyghan, the former world welterweight champion. Lloyd was a tremendous fighter in his prime and seven years earlier he'd shocked the boxing world by going to Atlantic City to win the title by beating the great Don Curry. Honeyghan was due to fight Vinnie Pazienza, a former lightweight and light-middleweight world title holder, who was as strong as a bull in the ring and a real hell-raiser out of it, as I was to discover some years later.

I slept most of the way on the plane over to the States and felt quite fresh when I got to my hotel, so after a shower and a change of clothes I wandered down to the lobby because I knew the place was buzzing with boxing people. It wasn't long before I met quite a few people I knew and pretty soon got an invite to a private party some very well known boxing people were holding in one of the hotel rooms.

With nothing better to do I wandered up to see what was happening and was quite shocked by what I saw. It wasn't so much what was happening because, let's face it, I'm no choirboy. But it was the identity of the people involved that rocked me back a bit. The booze was flowing freely, which was no surprise, and there were also a few girls in there, who were quite obviously hookers. What did surprise me was that these very well known boxing guys weren't just into drink and women, they were also very keen on snorting cocaine. I was offered some as if it was a cup of tea, and when I declined there were some puzzled looks from a few people.

'You keep going the way you do and you don't even like this stuff?' one of them said, sounding really surprised.

I explained that I'd never been into drugs and instead stuck to drinking some wine as the girls got to work on some of their clients. Believe me, it wasn't a pretty sight, and it certainly couldn't have been the nicest way for the girls to earn their money. Some of the guys in that room were not exactly in the best physical shape of their lives and were quite ugly specimens. But they'd paid their money, or someone had, and they took their choice. It wasn't my sort of scene and I actually began to feel uncomfortable about the whole thing and decided it was probably best if I left.

The negotiations continued with Mickey over the weekend and there was also time for me to win some money off him when I took $5,000 from him in a bet on the outcome of Honeyghan's fight with Pazienza, which he lost in the tenth round. On the same bill Evander Holyfield had a points win against Alex Stewart, which meant the former champion was also very much in the picture when it came to contesting world titles. Panos flew in a day after me and the talks with Duff were just as we thought they might be – difficult.

Bruno might have been uppermost in the minds of the British media at the time as the next opponent for Lennox, but as ever Dan Duva was trying to make sure we had other irons in the fire. He'd arranged a meeting in New York with Bill Cayton to discuss the possibility of Morrison meeting Lennox in a unification fight. Dan believed that having the option of a fight with Morrison might help in the negotiations with Duff.

The talks went well and after working flat-out for 24 hours to get an agreement and provisional contracts drawn up, I left New York knowing that we had put together the sort of deal that not only made great sense financially, but also took Lennox one step nearer to his aim of becoming the undisputed heavyweight champion of the world. Cayton was obviously keen on getting Morrison in the ring with Lennox, and in the end we agreed in principle a deal that would see Lennox earn $7 million.

When news of what had gone on broke a few days later it really stirred things up. The weekend after my meeting with Cayton I attended an HBO party in London which had been thrown on 4 July, American Independence Day. I got a pretty frosty reception from Seth Abraham who said I'd lied and cheated by not telling him what had been going on, while Panos got it in the ear from Duff and Jarvis Astaire. With Bowe also under contract to HBO it seemed pretty clear they would have preferred us to go ahead with a Bruno fight which would leave Riddick clear for a possible contest with Morrison.

I couldn't help chuckling to myself at the havoc we'd caused, but as far as I was concerned the main reason for looking at Morrison was because the fight would be good for the career of Lennox Lewis. He would not only be well rewarded financially, but he'd also get the chance to pick up another title. Naturally there was a bit of stick flying our way in the press, with stories claiming we were trying to avoid fighting Bruno. But that simply wasn't true. During all the time I was with Lewis, he fought whoever was put in front of him and never ducked anyone.

The only fight that was scheduled but never actually happened came about in 1990, when Lennox had been due to take on James 'Bonecrusher' Smith, a fighter who inflicted Bruno's first professional defeat back in 1984. Smith had real punching power and caused an upset in 1986 by stopping Tim Witherspoon in the first round to take the WBA world title. He lost it seven months later against Tyson, but would have been the perfect kind of 'name' opponent to test Lennox. But with posters already ordered for the 22 May contest and Lennox training for the fight, there was a change of heart and it was called off. I think at the time maybe John Davenport thought Smith might not be the right kind of opponent for Lewis.

To explain things a little more and put our side of the story when it came to the Bruno negotiations, we called a press conference at the Café Royal in London, with Panos spelling out exactly what had gone on in our negotiations with Duff in Atlantic City. Dan Duva was also on a phone link from the States to back things up as we went through why a fight with Bruno had broken down. It couldn't have made nice reading for Mickey the next day, but it was the truth.

Although the deal with Morrison was in place and scheduled for either October or November, Cayton then decided it would be a good idea for Tommy to earn some extra cash by slipping in an easy defence at the end of August. As soon as we knew this, things once again started to swing towards taking on Bruno first instead of Morrison. The problem was we still had no definite agreement with

Duff and we needed a big enough venue for such a massive fight. Lennox didn't fancy Wembley Stadium, and we felt that by taking him out of London the fan base would be more evenly split.

Dan got back to Duff to try and sort something out, but Mickey was still intent on making the sort of demands we didn't want to go along with. Over a period of a few days in the middle of July, the phone lines were pretty hot as Panos, Dan and I worked on putting plans in place. We finally seemed to be getting everything sorted out and I even went as far as visiting Cardiff to take a look at the Arms Park, which seemed an ideal venue to us.

Rock Newman almost threw a spanner in the works by talking with Panos and making an offer of $11 million for Lewis to fight Bowe. But it was really all too late. Dan had done some more hard bargaining with Duff to get the thing rolling again, and we'd already had a press conference letting everyone know the Bruno fight was now back on. Lennox was going to get £3 million with big Frank picking up £1 million as the challenger.

Duff was still not happy with things although by this time it wasn't financial matters that were bothering him, it was the venue. Mickey tried to persuade Panos that Wembley would be a much better place to stage the fight, but we were adamant that wasn't going to happen and more to the point, so was Lennox. There was one meeting between Panos and Mickey when Duff was trying to get us to agree to Wembley and Lennox came on the phone and started singing 'We shall not be moved' down the line.

We stuck with Cardiff and the fight was scheduled for Friday, 2 October. As soon as the date was settled the publicity machine swung into action with press conferences on both sides of the Atlantic. Lennox headed off for his training camp in Washington, the same place we'd used in preparation for the Mike Dixon fight a year earlier.

One of my other heavyweights, Julius Francis, flew over as one of Lennox's sparring partners, and there was another young white Polish heavyweight who was working with us named Andrew Golota. He'd won all of his 12 fights at the time and was to go on to build a reputation as one of the division's top contenders a few years later, when his path crossed once more with Lewis in very different circumstances.

Life in camp can be quite boring after a while, so it's nice to get the opportunity of breaking the routine. That's why everyone enjoyed a break when we got the chance, even if it was only to the local prison. To be more precise, it was the Lorten State Penitentiary in Virginia.

We all bundled into cars and a minivan for the drive along the freeway, with Pepe showing off his new pride and joy, a 1966 powder-blue Chevy which actually did tricks by leaning from side to side and rearing up on its back wheels. There isn't a prison in the world that could be called nice, but this place was particularly depressing as we were shown through the entrance with the gates clanking and sliding shut behind us.

The reason we went was to watch some bouts involving the prisoners and Lennox got a rousing reception from the inmates gathered in the sports hall. There were guys there who had sentences ranging from three years to life. Some of them looked real hard cases and the atmosphere they created was amazing. There were also quite a few of the prison 'bitches' sitting at ringside. These were men who actually had breasts and long hair, although some of them still had arms and legs like tree trunks. It was strange to see one of them brushing his hair and putting lipstick on as we waited for the first fight. But these 'Shemales' just seemed to add to the weird atmosphere that included seeing some of the boxers arrive for their bouts chained hand and foot, before having their shackles removed by the guards.

Even the referee was a scary looking guy whose face had obviously been badly burnt at some stage in his life. We were there for more than two hours and everyone genuinely enjoyed themselves. I think it all made us realise how lucky we were to have our freedom, and it's strange to think that all these years later so many of those guys might still be in there.

Towards the end of the camp Eugene went shopping in Washington and wandered into a little toy store. While he was in there having a look around he could hear a sales rep talking to a guy who worked in the shop. The rep was asking to have a chat with the manager, but the guy behind the counter basically told him to get lost and was being pretty aggressive in the way he went about it. The rep eventually left and when Eugene started to ask about some of the goods, the shop assistant again got aggressive and eventually told my brother to get his Limey arse out of the shop. Not surprisingly

Eugene didn't take too kindly to this, but soon did exactly as he was told when the guy bent down below the counter and produced a gun which he pointed at my brother's head! Eugene backed off very slowly and eventually returned to the training camp, but by the time he got back he was seething. I tried to do my best to calm him down and told him to forget it and not get involved. The next morning at breakfast Eugene's mood had changed completely, and he sat at the table with a big grin on his face. I later found out that my brother had not been prepared to let matters rest between him and the shop assistant. After I'd talked to him the night before, Eugene had gone back to the store and found out the guy wasn't so tough when he didn't have a loaded gun in his hand.

I'd worked long and hard on the show to try and make sure everything went smoothly and it would be a success. It was a really hectic time for me both in my professional life and in my relationship with Caroline. She was often unhappy with my work schedule and the way I seemed to put it before everything else. I even had to cancel a planned summer holiday with her because I was so busy. We did manage a short break in New York, although even that was tied up with work because we went out there to attend the wedding of Lou DiBella, who was Seth Abraham's right hand man at HBO. I also wanted to drop in on Lennox at his training camp and then see Tommy Morrison defend his newly won WBO title in Kansas on 30 August.

In fact, it turned out to be the title defence that never was after a farcical night which saw Morrison's original opponent withdraw, and promoter Bob Arum get a boxer called Tim Tomashek to replace him. That might not sound so bad, but the trouble was Tomashek was actually in the audience in Kansas ready to watch the fight. I even heard a rumour that he was in the bar having a drink before he got the SOS call to take on Tommy.

It was a crazy situation with Morrison looking as though he was going easy on his opponent before Tim finally retired in the fourth round. It didn't go down too well with the crowd and there were plenty of boos and jeers, as well as some thrown cups. Amazingly, the WBO sanctioned the fight on the night, but their supervisor was later overruled when they thankfully came to their senses and admitted Tomashek was not championship class.

The good thing from my point of view was that Morrison finished the night without any silly injury, and that meant we were still on course for a unification fight with him once Lennox took care of business against Bruno in Cardiff.

Getting everything together was a 24-hour-a-day business for me as soon as my feet touched the ground back in England. I lived and breathed the contest, from helping to plan the seating arrangements at the Arms Park, to making sure there was a constant stream of publicity to help sell the show. But I also had my other fighters to think about. On 15 September Mickey Cantwell took on Mexican Pablo Tiznado at York Hall for the vacant WBC international light-flyweight title and lost on points. The fight came at the end of a day of meetings and general hassle that included a long and sometimes lively phone call with Bruno's wife Laura.

I have to say that although I really enjoyed the Cardiff fight and the build-up that went with it, the one thing I came to dread was having any kind of conversation with Laura Bruno.

She seemed incapable of talking to me without getting into some kind of shouting match. Whether Frank knew what she was up to, I don't know, and I'm sure she was only trying to look after Bruno's interests. But she had a great ability to rub me up the wrong way no matter how much I tried to make sure everything went smoothly, and we just never hit it off. I found her a difficult person to deal with, and she always seemed to have this desperate need to be in control. To put it simply, I couldn't wait to see the back of her.

But she managed to literally leave her mark on the night of the fight when I walked past her after the contest had ended. Just as I went to speak to her Laura spat in my face. I don't know why she did it but it came as a shock, and I think Lennox's mum was a bit taken aback because she was standing just behind me at the time.

A couple of days after the Cantwell fight Lennox and the rest of the team arrived in from the States to set up camp in Cardiff. We travelled to Wales in a coach and just as we reached the tollbooth on the Severn Bridge, one of the American sparring partners asked me where we were. I told him we were just about to enter Wales and go through immigration. They all got their passports out and held them up, waiting for someone to inspect them. It was hilarious but they couldn't understand what Lennox and I were laughing at.

This was to be the start of the final countdown to the fight and we pretty much moved our entire operation to Wales for the next two weeks. I had a couple of work experience kids from university called Ed Robinson and Robert Norton working for me and they did a great job. Ed later became my full-time press officer and was brilliant, but he also had to put up with some terrible stick from me on occasions.

He was a boxing nut and decided he wanted to have a professional fight some years later, which I promoted. Ed never actually told his mother, because he knew she would be dead against the idea, and I wasn't that keen on it either. The only advice I gave him was to stay down until the count reached eight if he got caught, which didn't exactly inspire confidence in him. He won the fight and after losing another, managed to finish on a winning note before wisely packing it in, but even to this day I'm not sure his mother actually knows he boxed.

I've always been terrible with names and often use the wrong words in conversation, particularly if I'm angry. On another occasion I'd heard that the people in the office weren't too happy with me and had been complaining about the way I'd treated them. So when I found out I had a go at Ed.

'Ed, someone's been making allegations about me,' I told him. 'And I want to know who the alligators are!'

To be honest I must have been terrible to live with at times, and even locked my driver, Eric Guy, in the toilet overnight once because he refused to hurry up when I wanted to get home. But Ed somehow managed to put up with me for more than four years before switching to Frank Warren's office and is now a very successful boxing reporter with Sky TV.

During the Bruno build-up we virtually took over the International Hotel in the city, and I don't think the staff there had seen anything like it before. There might as well have been a conveyor belt in the corridors with the way the local girls were going in and out of some of the rooms. Some of the sparring partners couldn't get enough of the Welsh hospitality on offer. One morning I wondered if a particular sparring partner was in any condition to face Lennox in the gym, after hearing he'd shared his bed with a very accommodating mother and daughter partnership! As you can imagine, a lot of the girls were desperate to get to Lennox, but with my brother on security duty outside his room there was no chance of that happening. Eugene made sure they never got anywhere near the champion.

We were working really hard during the day but some of us managed to let our hair down in a big way at night. Cardiff became a real party place on several occasions and I soon began enjoying visiting places like Jackson's night club, where we later held the after-fight party.

My relationship with Caroline was very rocky at this time and while I was in Cardiff she'd flown to Spain to stay at a villa owned by a friend of mine called Wilf Shereman. It gave her a break and helped me out because I knew she was fed up with the fact that I was away such a lot. I thought it would be better for the both of us if she had a break in the sun and then flew home for the fight.

Although the place was buzzing and I was up to my eyes in the excitement of the fight, there were some nights in Cardiff where I ended up in my room too exhausted to go out on the town. I had a lot of time to think about my personal life and it didn't make me feel all that happy. Although I wanted my relationship with Caroline to go well, I knew in my heart of hearts that it was probably on its last legs.

It seems strange to think now that within the space of a day or so of feeling depressed about the way things were heading with Caroline, I met someone who would change my life in a big way. Her name was Tracey Lewis – no relation to Lennox – and had it not been for a waitress in my hotel all those years ago, we might never have got together.

The waitress happened to ask me what was wrong one morning as I sat in the reception area with a miserable face, looking as though I had all the worries of the world on my shoulders. I told her that despite all that was going on, what I wanted most was to meet a nice girl who I could just have dinner with and talk to. She must have seen I wasn't mucking about and said she had an air hostess friend whom I might like to meet, but she was a bit wary of introducing us because she knew what had been going on in the hotel since we'd all arrived a few days earlier. It must have seemed as though a rock band had hit town and the stories about the girls and some of the sparring partners had obviously done the rounds. But I managed to convince her I wasn't going to jump on her friend and try to take her to bed in double-quick time, I just wanted a quiet evening out with a nice girl.

The lobby of the hotel in Cardiff was always busy during the time we were there, with lots of the press sending news reporters down to Wales in the hope of getting some stories, and young local girls wandering around trying to get to know members of the Lewis team.

A couple of days later I noticed two good-looking young girls as they walked into the reception area of the hotel. One had dark hair and the other was blonde. My waitress friend strolled over with the two of them soon after and introduced us. The brunette was called Kerry and her friend Tracey was the girl I'd been told about. A few days later we went for a meal and then went back to my hotel where we chatted for a while, but it soon became clear that there was no way Tracey was going to stay.

We went for a drink the following evening where there were some journalists who'd arrived to start covering the build-up to the fight. It was a nice atmosphere and it hadn't taken me long to realise I was really attracted to Tracey. It wasn't just the way she looked, although being small, blonde and very pretty certainly helped on that front. But it was also the fact that I found her really easy to talk to and she seemed like such a nice girl.

So you can imagine how surprised I was to learn from one of the reporters that this sweet young girl I had taken a real shine to also happened to be a regular football groupie! To be more precise, what I was actually told was that there was a long standing arrangement between her and a very famous Welsh international footballer.

'A lot of the players are at it, Frank,' I was told. 'It happens when there's an international in Cardiff and the players see these girls whenever they're in town. You should be all right with her tonight!'

I was surprised and a bit disappointed, but then my more basic instincts started to take over. After a few more drinks I popped the question, asking Tracey whether she fancied going back to my hotel room, but she told me in no uncertain terms that she wasn't going to jump into bed with me. She claimed she wasn't that sort of girl, which I thought was a bit rich after being told what she'd been up to in the past.

'I suppose if I was a footballer it would be a different story,' I said.

She looked at me as if I was crazy and asked what the hell I was talking about. When I accused her of being the regular bit on the side for this particular Welsh international, Tracey let her hands do the talking and promptly slapped my face before walking out of the bar.

It wasn't the reaction I'd expected and to make matters worse, next day the journalist from the bar phoned to say he was wrong. Apparently he'd made a big mistake and she wasn't one of the girls who hung out with the Welsh players. I immediately did the only thing I could, and started to leave grovelling messages on her answerphone. Our relationship could have been over before it began, but thankfully she forgave me and agreed to see me again.

Even that date turned out to be a little tricky because while we were out one of the young girls who worked at the hotel spotted me standing at the bar while Tracey was in the toilet. She marched straight over to me and suggested I go home with her and her mum for a bit of fun. It was flattering in a strange sort of way, but I politely declined the offer. But I couldn't keep my mouth shut and as soon as Tracey came back I told her all about it. I got the sort of look that told me she didn't find the story too funny, and then she spelled out in no uncertain terms that if that was what I wanted, I should leave right there and then.

I could tell she wasn't the sort of girl who liked being messed around and by this time I'd told her all about Caroline, but had also said the relationship had run its course and was coming to an end. In my own mind I knew that was true, the only trouble was, I hadn't quite got around to telling Caroline the same thing.

All of this was happening at the same time as I was trying to organise the final few days of preparation for Lennox. He became a very popular figure in the city and did several public appearances where he was mobbed. It was like Beatlemania on occasions and when we visited a youth club it actually got a bit scary because the crowd was so big and out of control. Some little bastard even bit my backside and punched and kicked me as we tried to get Lennox in and out of the place.

It was in the final week of the build-up that we had a really big press conference where Panos decided to take centre stage and made an absolute fool of himself. He got names wrong and tried to make jokes and comments that just didn't come off. After being the quiet man who seemed content to just back the whole Lewis operation and stay out of the limelight, he was suddenly bitten by the celebrity bug.

When I was first introduced to Panos he came over as a confident, out-going sort of person. But the one thing I thought was very different between him and Levitt was the fact that he wasn't really interested in putting himself in the public eye. He seemed content to be running things and stay in the background. His first real public mention had come after the Ruddock fight when Dan Duva had thanked him, and although he'd been more up front since then, he still seemed content to keep a relatively low profile. But that started to change as we negotiated the Bruno deal with Duff and by the time we hit Cardiff, Panos was revelling in the whole world title fight atmosphere. It was fair enough in one respect because he was the money man, but at the same time, he knew next to nothing about boxing or the way the press worked.

It was very different to the way someone like Dan Duva operated. He had so much experience when it came to the sport and the media, but he never went out of his way to seek publicity. If he talked to the press it was because he had to, and things like press conferences were just another part of the business. But it soon became clear to me that Panos was being seduced by the whole experience of being so closely associated with the world heavyweight champion. It was a new world to him and he loved it.

The final few days before a big fight are always tense, with each camp trying to make sure their man gets whatever edge might be going when it comes to the war of words and the mind games that are played. The day before Lewis and Bruno were due to meet we got word that Lennox was going to be served with a writ by Frank's lawyer Henri Brandman for an alleged libel where he was supposed to have called Bruno an Uncle Tom. As far as we were concerned, having the writ served at the press conference was nothing more than a cheap stunt, and after Lennox had posed for the cameras holding the envelope with the legal document in it, he passed it to me and I promptly tore it up and threw it over my shoulder.

NO BALONEY

The big day was fast approaching and as usual I was beginning to feel the strain of it all. Although I was confident Lennox would beat Bruno, no heavyweight fight is an absolute certainty. I knew Frank would really be up for the contest and would fight out of his skin in an effort to cause an upset. I also knew that once again there would be an awful lot of people who would have been happy to see me fail and fall flat on my face. I'd already had a bet with Duff and I'd also promised to walk naked from Land's End to John O'Groat's if Bruno won, so it was more than just my neck on the line.

Caroline had flown back from Spain the weekend before the fight and was due in Cardiff for the contest. It was actually going to go on in the early hours of Saturday morning because of American TV. I let off steam the night before the fight by going for a drink and ended up at Tracey's house much the worse for wear.

But I was up early the next morning because I'd arranged to do an interview for Sky at six. So on the morning of the biggest heavyweight title fight Britain had ever seen, there I was, the manager of the world champion, climbing over a fence at the Arms Park because I couldn't find the right entrance. I'd only had a few hours' sleep and felt like shit, but I was pleased the big day had finally arrived.

Because the contest was going to be staged in the open air, there was always a big concern over the weather. We had plans to deal with rain, but knew that if it got really bad the fight might have to be postponed or even cancelled. Throughout the night it rained and several bouts on the undercard had to be cancelled. One of the fights which did go on was the professional debut of Joe Calzaghe, who was managed by Duff at the time, and the contest was part of the overall deal we'd struck with Mickey. With 45 minutes to go before Lewis and Bruno were due to enter the ring, the canvas had to be swept and covered, to make sure it was in the right condition for the two fighters.

Frank surprised a lot of people by the way he came out and took the fight to Lennox, but it didn't surprise me. The one thing I didn't expect was that Lewis would be so subdued during the opening few rounds. It was as if he couldn't really get into his stride, but I later found out from Eugene that Lennox had been hit by a bad cold before the fight and a doctor was actually called to check him over.

By the end of round six one of the judges actually had Bruno ahead and the other two had it even. That was before class suddenly began to tell in a big way with Lennox springing into action and delivering a left hand shot that shook Bruno down to his boots. As had happened before in Frank's career, it looked as though someone had suddenly turned the lights out and shut the power down in his body. He was still standing but his arms began to dangle by his side and Lennox was able to tee-off punches at his head. It was a great finish by Lewis and one that showed just how ruthless he can be in the ring when he has a man hurt.

It may have been the early hours of the morning and I'd only had a few hours sleep during the previous two days, but I was ready to party. The only complication for me was that both Caroline and Tracey were now in town, and there was also another blonde young lady I was determined to meet.

11. HEAVYWEIGHTS ARE DIFFERENT

THE LADY IN QUESTION WAS PAGE THREE MODEL SAMANTHA FOX AND although I'd never actually met her I really thought she looked terrific. Apart from two obvious physical charms, she also happened to be small and blonde. Too much for me to resist!

It may sound very childish but when I found out she was coming to the fight I got really excited about the prospect of seeing her in the flesh, so to speak. I made sure she was given tickets to the after-fight party and was determined to get to talk to her.

Tracey didn't actually get to see the fight because she was working on the day and got delayed, but I knew she would be around for the celebrations afterwards. In fact, Caroline and Tracey almost came face to face when I got back to the hotel. I walked into the bar with Caroline only to see Tracey standing just a few feet away with her friend. It could have been an awkward moment, but Caroline was in no mood to go on to Jackson's nightclub, and said she felt tired. It was a relief for me because it meant I could go there with Tracey and I also wanted to try and meet Sam Fox.

When we arrived the place was buzzing and everyone was in party mood. We were introduced to Catherine Zeta-Jones and as we walked away Tracey remarked on how attractive she was. 'She's not bad, but she's not blonde,' I said, as I looked around the club for Miss Fox. I couldn't see her anywhere and ended up asking one of the barmen if she'd been in.

'You're too late, Frank, someone's beaten you to it,' I was told. He then went on to say she'd left some time earlier with a former British world title holder who had a real reputation when it came to the ladies. I knew when I was beaten, and to be honest I'm not sure what I'd have done anyway considering I was with Tracey. If I'd gone off and tried to chat up Samantha Fox, I can't imagine she would have been too happy. So my Fox fantasy never got off the ground and instead I concentrated on celebrating Lennox's win over Bruno, knowing we already had another $7 million fight lined up for him.

In the nightclub there was a VIP section which was packed with Cardiff's in-crowd. One of them was an attractive girl called Dawn who stayed for a while before leaving the celebrations with a member of the Lewis entourage. Some time later Dawn actually told Tracey she'd been approached by a reporter asking whether she'd like to sell her story to the newspapers about who it was she was seeing in the champion's team. The same reporter also approached Tracey, but needless to say, she gave him a very short answer that left no doubt about the way she felt.

We announced the fight the next morning at a press conference, telling the media that Lennox would be going into a unification contest with WBO holder Tommy Morrison in the spring of 1994. It was another excellent pay day for Lewis and it also meant that he would get the chance to mop up another title in his quest to become the undisputed heavyweight champion of the world.

I came out of the press conference feeling terrific even though it had been a long night of drinking and celebrating. But as soon as I got back to my hotel the mood changed. I had a blazing row with Caroline in which she claimed I'd been really off with her since the day she'd arrived in Cardiff. She also said she'd heard rumours of what I'd been up to while I'd been in Wales, and it soon became clear she was pretty pissed off with me and with the way our relationship was going. To be honest, I really couldn't be bothered with all the arguing. It seemed as though I'd been down the same road before when I was with Jackie. Maybe a lot of it was to do with me and the way I acted towards both her and Jackie, but at that point I really couldn't be bothered to analyse things too much, and when Caroline said she was going to get the train back to London, I felt a sense of relief.

After she left the hotel I began to cool down a bit and because I knew she'd gone to get the last train out of Cardiff that night, I suddenly felt a bit guilty and decided to check with the taxi firm to make sure she had made it in time. When I phoned they told me she hadn't actually gone to the station, but instead went to a private address. I asked the driver who took her to come over and ended up paying him £75 to take me to the house she'd been dropped off at. It didn't take me long to find out from some neighbours that the property belonged to a wealthy young guy called Scott Thomas. His father had made a fortune out of a pie business, and was actually known in Cardiff as Stan 'The Pieman' Thomas. I later found out from Wilf Shereman that young Scott had been on very friendly terms with Caroline while she'd been in Spain.

I know it's a case of double standards but I was absolutely livid with Caroline and what she'd got up to behind my back, which is a bit rich considering some of my previous behaviour. Although I was really happy in my professional life and things looked as though they could only get better, I also knew I was mixed up in my personal life once again.

Looking back now I believe I got married far too early in my life and it didn't do Jackie or me any favours. I wanted the best of both worlds. On the one hand I felt happy with having a wife and on the other I just wanted to be a single man having fun. Unfortunately, the sort of businesses I was involved in and the lifestyle that I had meant it was very easy for me to stray. It's strange really because I always desperately wanted to have a steady relationship, and then as soon as that happened I seemed to do the best I could to make sure I screwed it up.

By this stage I felt I was at a real crossroads in my life, because although I was really attracted to Tracey, I also knew in my own mind that I seemed to have a problem with relationships. If it was going to work with her I had to be 100 per cent sure this time. I felt like I needed a bit of time and space before I made any real commitment. My solution was to move out of the flat I shared with Caroline in Surbiton and book into the White House hotel in London. For quite a few weeks I lived out of a suitcase.

Apart from having the Morrison fight in the pipeline we were also being kept busy with a book tour to launch Lennox's biography. We went all over the place with him doing different signings. It was all good fun, particularly a trip to Dublin where we all ended up in a nightclub drinking Black Velvet, a lethal mixture of Guinness and champagne. Lennox seemed to delight in getting us all going with the drinks, and then he left before everyone else knowing the rest of us would wake up with terrible hangovers. We also bumped into Paula Yates, the late TV presenter and wife of Bob Geldof. She seemed to take quite a shine to Lennox and after eyeing him up and down told me, 'I'd love to get that man into my bed.' In fact, she did manage it, but only as part of a stunted up interview for a *Big Breakfast* TV programme.

Lennox and I also had an interesting time when we were asked to address the Oxford Union. It was nerve-racking but we both enjoyed the experience and felt glad we'd gone. Lewis got a tremendous reception from the students and was very sharp when it came to taking questions from the audience. All of this was a really pleasant diversion from the business of boxing and from my personal relationship with Caroline.

I knew the situation with Caroline couldn't go on for much longer and it soon became clear things had gone too far. I'd told Tracey when I first met her that the relationship with Caroline was on its last legs, and it was silly trying to pretend anything had changed to make matters better.

Tracey really did mean something to me and she was special. She was prepared to see that what I did for a living was very important to me. There was no shouting or nasty looks when I said I had to go away on business or worked late into the night. It was all very different to what had happened when I was with Jackie and Caroline.

My personal life certainly seemed complicated, but at least I had the consolation of knowing that when it came to the boxing business everything was much more settled. That was until a little-known

HEAVYWEIGHTS ARE DIFFERENT

British-born heavyweight named Michael Bentt upset the best-laid plans we had for the $7 million showdown with Morrison, by sticking Tommy on his arse in Tulsa on 29 October to take the WBO crown with a first-round stoppage. I was thousands of miles away at the time in a Sky TV studio watching in disbelief as the sight of millions of dollars seemed to disappear in front of my eyes.

Bentt's victory wasn't the only surprise in the heavyweight division at the time, because just eight days later in Las Vegas, Evander Holyfield showed just what a great fighter he was by beating Riddick Bowe on points to reclaim the WBA and IBF belts.

So one door might have closed but with Holyfield's victory I knew that another had just opened. Evander was promoted by Main Events and Dan had a good relationship with the new champion. I was in Vegas for the fight, which also became famous because a paraglider landed in the ring during the contest, which was staged in an outdoor arena.

Having felt so disappointed after the Bentt fight I was on top of the world once more, and it was particularly nice to see how humble Rock Newman and Bowe were in the press conference after the fight. In my experience Newman had a habit of treating people like shit, and one of the nicest things about the fact that his fighter had been beaten by Holyfield was that I no longer had to have a breakfast meeting with him the next day.

It was important to plan a new strategy for Lennox and with this in mind we travelled back to Vegas a couple of weeks before Christmas for the WBC convention. There is always so much going on at conventions with some of the biggest players in boxing having meetings and striking deals. The main reason for us going to Vegas was to clear a way ahead for Lewis. We had a private meeting with Jose Sulaiman in which he agreed that we could fight Holyfield, have a voluntary defence and then a mandatory defence. Dan was busy talking to Evander and came back with the good news that he wanted to fight Lennox, so the next stage was to try and work out the mechanics of any possible deal.

When I got back from the States I went to see Caroline who was still living in the Surbiton flat. It was one of those occasions where you find yourself getting a lot off your chest, and we both owned up to seeing other people with her telling me all about Scott. I stayed the night at the flat and the next morning she went off to her mother's place.

As I sat there wondering whether there might still be a chance we could get back together again, the telephone rang. It was an estate agent who asked to speak to Caroline. I found out from him that she'd been to look at a couple of flats with Scott and as soon as I heard that, I knew it was the end for us. I was furious and phoned to tell her she had two hours to collect her stuff, or I was throwing it out. There was no going back as far as I was concerned and I made my mind up that after all the emotional ups and downs I was finally finished with her.

That Christmas was probably the quietest I'd ever had in my life. I took Emma out for a Chinese meal and realised that although she wasn't even 18, she had a mature head on her shoulders and was a really good listener. It was funny pouring my heart out to my own daughter, but I think we both enjoyed the fact that we were spending some time together. I actually wasn't missing Caroline and just felt relieved it was finally over.

The New Year brought another twist to the fight plans we had been hatching when Holyfield decided he was going to take on Michael Moorer before thinking about stepping into the ring with Lennox. We talked about a three-fight deal with HBO and after hearing about Holyfield's plans we began working on setting up a voluntary defence against Phil Jackson, followed by a fight against the mandatory challenger, Oliver McCall. Once those were out of the way we could go into a November contest with Holyfield which would be a unification fight.

As well as boxing, my sporting interests took a new direction just before Christmas when I was contacted by a guy named Oliver Skeete, who was a black showjumper. He asked whether I wanted to get involved in looking after his publicity, and it later proved to be quite a successful partnership. Oliver got some good media coverage and I had a lot of fun helping him. I even had him riding a white horse in the middle of Brixton on one occasion, which stopped the traffic and made a lot of the national press. Oliver became a minor celebrity and was a good rider, but he was never quite in the Harvey Smith league.

All the usual tricks started as soon as we announced the plans for a fight with Jackson. Don King tried to make sure we went straight into a contest with McCall instead of meeting Jackson first. King promoted McCall and he was obviously keen to get his man a title shot as soon as possible. He asked Main Events to pay him $3 million to step aside and also got the WBC to insist that the McCall fight had to go ahead. Main Events refused and took their case to the American Arbitration Society in Miami. All parties were represented at the hearing and they found in our favour, allowing us to fight Jackson. The Jackson contest was set for 6 May, and Lennox would then take on McCall some time in September.

Sorting out Lewis's career always took up most of my time, but it didn't mean I wasn't involved in managing and promoting other fighters. One of the promotions we staged was in Cardiff in January 1994, when Welshman Floyd Havard lost in a super-featherweight world title fight against Juan John John Molina, from Puerto Rico. I had to spend quite a bit of time in Cardiff once again, and that meant seeing more of Tracey. It was a bonus for me because I'd become very fond of her, and although I didn't want to rush straight into another relationship after what had happened with Caroline, there was no denying the fact that I thought Tracey was a bit special.

We had an after-fight party in Jackson's nightclub with Oliver Skeete enjoying himself and clearly taking to the world of celebrity, even if it was only early days for him. As usual there were quite a few girls there who wanted to try and get off with me. Now that may sound conceited, but it was true. It was also true that the only reason they fancied taking me to bed was because I was the manager of the heavyweight champion of the world and they liked the idea of the champagne lifestyle they presumed went with it. I'm not stupid and I don't kid myself. Sure, I was never really short of female company before anyone knew who I was, but once a little bit of fame came along so did a whole load of girls. I have to admit that I was a bit like a kid in a sweet shop a lot of the time, because the temptation was just too great. I'm not proud of the fact that I cheated on my wife and then on Caroline, but it happened and there's nothing I can do about it now.

NO BALONEY

Although I knew I was attracted to Tracey and I'd seen quite a bit of her, I still couldn't resist a pretty girl, or to be more precise, a dozen of them. That's how many I had surrounding me when I had a photograph taken at the party, and when the picture later appeared in a newspaper my mum had a real go at me. She knew I thought a lot of Tracey and could see I was in danger of screwing things up with her if I pulled stunts like having my picture taken with a bunch of women. Not for the first time in my life she made me stop and think. I had to get my act together and decide what I wanted from my personal life, and it soon became clear I wanted Tracey.

We set up camp for Lennox in March in the Pocono Mountains not far from New York. The place chosen was called Caesars Brookdale and it became home to the Lewis team on several occasions in later years. We had a meeting at the start of camp in Lennox's room where I talked about the importance of everyone working as a team, and explained that Lennox was the captain of the ship and we were all there to help him. If the ship capsized, everyone sank with it. It was just my way of saying how crucial it was to make sure the preparation was spot on, because if it wasn't we all suffered.

I had some business to take care of in England and also another promotion in Cardiff which featured the professional debut of Paul Ingle, so I had to leave camp for a while. When I got back to the Poconos it soon became clear all was not well, and the ship I'd talked about in that team meeting was going through some rough water.

Lennox came to see me and said he wasn't happy with the way he was being trained. Harold Knight also seemed unhappy and I got the impression that Correa may have been trying to keep him on the sidelines. Pepe was great when it came to playing to the crowd, but Lennox obviously thought he wasn't getting the sort of coaching he expected. I decided to have a word on my own with Correa and went through a whole range of things with him. I discussed the gym work, sparring and tactics. I told Pepe that Lennox was an intelligent fighter, but I was concerned he wasn't looking the way he should have at that stage in his career. I'd seen Lennox in the gym and thought he wasn't throwing the straight right hand punch that was such a great weapon in his arsenal. I told Pepe every time I'd seen Lennox on the pads and bags, he threw great combinations, but when he sparred all he seemed to be looking for was the big punch. 'We mustn't look for the one big punch,' I said. 'We've got to look for combinations.'

I felt better after talking to Correa but I'm not sure he did. I got the distinct impression he was fed up and he actually began sulking, saying he'd stand down before the next fight and let Harold take over. I don't know if it was his way of trying to get some sympathy from me, or whether he hoped I'd beg him not to go. Whatever Pepe said, I knew there was no way he was going to walk out on the job because it was probably the best one he'd had in boxing, but my gut feeling was that he was the wrong man for Lennox and a change needed to be made.

It takes a very special person to stay in camp and be disciplined for six or eight weeks. You may stay in nice rooms with great facilities, but the place can soon start to feel like a prison. In my opinion, to get to the top in boxing takes a very different kind of dedication to any other sport. The fighters are like gladiators and hours are spent planning, training and talking. Everything is geared towards fighting, and that's why it's so important to have the right people in place.

Halfway through the camp I had the distinct impression Lennox was really training himself. He was basically doing what he wanted, when he wanted. He'd got to the stage where he'd given up on Pepe and looked as though he was paying no attention at all to him. When I spoke to Lennox about the situation, it was clear he wasn't happy with what was going on, but at the same time he didn't really know who else he could get in. It only made me feel more certain that changes had to be made after the Jackson fight. It wasn't the first or last time I heard Lennox say, 'If it's not broke, there's no need to fix it.'

It seemed to me that Pepe was not really a team player and I remember how Harold Knight had asked him once what the game plan was. 'I know what the game plan is,' said Pepe, touching his head with his finger, but there was no way he was going to let on to the rest of the team exactly what it was.

There was some distraction for me with a trip to Vegas, along with Lennox's mum, Violet, to see Evander Holyfield defend his two titles against Michael Moorer on 22 April. With Lennox likely to face Holyfield at some stage, it was important to see the fight and it was also a nice diversion from life in camp. But far from being a happy couple of days in Vegas, it turned into a nightmare as another potential big contest was blown to pieces by a result few expected. Instead of the relatively easy first defence Holyfield wanted, he got involved in a distance fight with Moorer and ended up losing his belts on points. So within the space of a few months I'd seen both the Morrison and Holyfield fights go out the window. It didn't help my mood too much five days later when I flew back to England to witness another disappointment, as Mickey Cantwell lost on points in a European flyweight title fight against Italy's Luigi Camputaro.

When I got to Atlantic City for the final build-up to the Jackson fight I was in need of something to lift my spirits, but the atmosphere in the team was just as bad. I was also hit by a rumour that was circulating claiming that Panos and I would be out of the picture after the fight. On top of all that, Atlantic City must be one of the most depressing places I've ever been to in America. The Casino hotels might be plush and Panos had a suite that you could have done the 100-yard dash in, but having a boardwalk outside that stinks of piss tends to take the shine off the place. The one good thing that did happen that week was the way in which Lennox took Jackson apart in eight rounds to retain his title. The contest also illustrated once again what a vicious bastard he was when he gets a chance in the ring. It's something all great champions have to have.

That fight was also memorable for me because I had breakfast the next morning with a guy I knew as Adrian Ogun from a company called Media Machine who were interested in doing some sponsorship work for Lewis. Adrian had been introduced to me at York Hall by Brian Alexander, who was the Sports Editor of the London *Evening Standard* newspaper at the time. Ogun was a tall, black guy who was very friendly and smooth. He obviously wanted to get involved in the Lewis set-up in some way, and despite his friendliness I couldn't help feeling a little bit uneasy about him. My instincts were proved right over the years that followed, and Adrian's ambition eventually got him to just where he wanted to be.

With Jackson out of the way we could start to move forward with the McCall fight. One of the biggest factors in putting together any major world title fight is the money you get from TV. With Lennox at that time his fights were seen by Sky in the UK and HBO in the USA. But soon after the defeat of Jackson I started to hear rumours that Sky could be ready to drop Lennox and instead plough a huge amount of money into screening eight Chris Eubank fights for a rumoured £10 million. The former editor of *The Sun* newspaper, Kelvin MacKenzie, had moved to Sky and I phoned him and set up a meeting to try and find out what the situation was.

We certainly couldn't afford to sit around and wait for Sky to drop us if that was what was going to happen and so we had to try and pursue other avenues, one of which was Wire TV, a new satellite company who were very keen to get into boxing and show Lennox's fights. After a meeting with MacKenzie I got the impression he wanted everything his way. Some of the discussions got a bit heated and at one point he claimed Lennox wasn't British, he was Canadian. It soon became clear we might be better off elsewhere, so by the end of May a deal with Wire was almost in place.

MacKenzie may not have seen eye to eye with me on that occasion, but some years later when he'd moved from Sky and was in charge of the radio station Talk Sport, we did business again and they covered several domestic shows promoted by us, as well as Lennox's fight with Evander Holyfield. Although we had our differences I liked Kelvin, and it wasn't just because he was a Millwall fan like me.

I'd worked some long hours to make sure everything would be all right with the TV deal and once it was sorted out I was looking forward to leaving the office and getting an early night for once. I'd moved out of the Surbiton flat and was living in the spare room at my mum's council flat in the East End, but on this particular night she was out so I decided to stop off and get some fish and chips to eat while I put my feet up and watched a movie.

When I got back I checked the answerphone and found I had a message to contact Donald Trump in New York. I had to smile, there I was eating fish and chips in my mum's council flat, getting a message from one of the richest and most well known men in the world. When I returned the call I found out he'd heard a story that

I was looking for someone to buy Lennox's contract. I told him the story wasn't true and explained that it must have been a rumour doing the circuit. It showed once again how easily and quickly a story can spread in the world of boxing, even if there's no truth in it at all.

Because so much talking goes on it's very hard to keep things under wraps if you're trying to tie up a deal in secret, but that's exactly what we managed to do in the middle of June, when we called a hastily arranged press conference one Friday evening to announce that Lennox would be fighting Riddick Bowe.

The deal had been hatched by Panos who'd been negotiating with Rock Newman and Bowe's lawyer Milt Chwasky, but Main Events had been kept out of the loop. Panos maintained publicly this was because they also promoted Michael Moorer and he didn't know whose interests came first with them. Privately the move was an absolute disaster for our relationship with Main Events and with Dan Duva, who I felt had been such a help to Lennox's career and to me on a personal basis. There was no doubt it was fantastic money for Lennox, who was due to get £12 million. But what did seem ridiculous was the fact that Panos was ready to let Bowe take £8 million, and he didn't even have a title or anywhere to go. We had the world champion and could negotiate from a position of strength. If the roles had been reversed I know that's what Newman would have done, and it's also what Dan would have done. As it was, we had his father Lou claiming we'd stabbed them in the back, and although Dan never blamed me for what had happened I think he was probably more guarded from then on.

That night I travelled to Cardiff to see Tracey and after a few glasses of champagne at the opening of a nightclub, I managed to get stopped by the local police as I was driving her home. They made some crack about flash cockneys and like an idiot I rose to the bait and came back with a comment about Welshmen and their sexual tastes when it came to sheep. I think the humour was lost on them, but they had the last laugh when I was later banned from driving for a year.

After what had happened in the training camp for the Jackson fight I had a bit of an uneasy feeling as Lennox and the rest of the training team prepared to go off to the Catskill Mountains in the States. The McCall contest was going to take place at Wembley Arena on 25 September, and the American had already been in training for some time when Pepe and the rest of the team got together. McCall was clearly taking the fight seriously and King was going to make sure he went into the Wembley ring in the best possible shape, with Emanuel Steward employed as his chief trainer.

When I got to the Catskills I could see nothing had improved, and if anything it felt even worse. Lennox clearly had no real time for Correa and often seemed as though he would prefer to be somewhere else. I even had a meeting with Lennox where I suggested Harold, Courtney and I could train him and we'd get rid of Pepe, but he was reluctant to do it. I think he knew Pepe would have to be out after the McCall fight, but at that point he just didn't want to make changes.

I wasn't in camp all the time but got regular reports from Eugene on what was going on. My brother and Lennox got on well together, with Eugene able to laugh and joke with the champion in a way a lot of other people couldn't. He wasn't just his minder in camp either, because Eugene would often spend time with Lennox when he was back in England and was on call 24 hours a day.

My brother once told me a great story about the time he was playing pool at Lennox's house and was getting beaten game after game. It got to the point where Eugene was about £300 down to Lewis when Lennox decided it would be a good idea to have some fish and chips, so he asked my brother to go out and get some. While he was waiting for the food, Eugene decided to pop into the bookmakers next door and came face to face with Alex Higgins.

He said hello and asked Higgins what he was up to. By that time in his career Alex was not at the height of his powers in the game of snooker and when Eugene asked whether he fancied a game of pool back at Lennox's place, Higgins accepted. So my brother turned up at the house with Alex in tow, introduced him to Lennox as a mate of his and asked if it would be all right if he joined in. Eugene saw it as the perfect way of clawing back some of the cash he'd lost and suggested Higgins take on Lewis. Alex then went on to produce some brilliant shots and win the game, leaving Lennox looking on in amazement. Eugene knew Lewis hated losing at anything, and told Lennox his friend had been lucky and maybe he should have another game, but just as Alex started to produce a repeat performance, Dennis Lewis came into the room.

'Hello, Alex,' said Dennis.

'You know Eugene's mate as well?' asked a surprised Lennox.

'This is Alex Higgins, Lennox,' Dennis explained. 'The former world snooker champion.'

I think Lennox tried to chase my brother around the table when he realised the stroke Eugene had pulled, but it was typical of the sort of relationship they had, and it was just the same in camp. They spent a lot of time together because it was my brother's job as minder to make sure Lennox got whatever he wanted. They also played chess together and ran in the mornings, so when Eugene telephoned to say Lennox wasn't doing some of the normal runs and was cutting things short some mornings, I couldn't help feeling uneasy about the preparations.

There was also a bit of a problem with one of the sparring partners Pepe had lined up to work in camp. His name was Mike 'The Bounty' Hunter, an American fighter we'd used in a previous camp but someone who seemed to carry a lot of personal baggage with him. The last time he'd been in camp Lennox ended up paying off some of his debts after The Bounty Hunter had been hunted down himself by some heavy-looking characters who were threatening to do some rather nasty things to him.

It all added to the general uneasy feeling I had about things when I travelled back to the Catskills.

The one bright spot for me while I was in camp came in a telephone call from Tracey during early August when she told me she was pregnant. So at the age of 41 and with an 18-year-old daughter, I was about to become a daddy for the second time. It took a bit of getting used to but I was pleased, and quickly let Eugene and Lennox know. At least it was good news and helped to lighten the atmosphere a bit, but by the time I headed back to London to help set things up for Lennox's arrival, I couldn't help feeling concerned. There were lots of things about the preparation that worried me. But Pepe kept telling everyone that McCall was nothing more than a sparring partner, and that Lennox would have no trouble with him. Even I started to believe it, but it was just typical of the way Correa operated. If Lennox threw a decent right hand in sparring Pepe would say how great it was and almost cheer the effort. It's easy to talk a good fight. The hard bit is actually making sure your boxer wins.

Although the contest was set for 25 September, the plan was for Lennox and the rest of the team to fly in three weeks before and set up their base at the Brittania Hotel in Docklands. But a couple of days before all of this was due to happen I received a call from Eugene telling me Lennox wanted to fly home on a separate flight from New York. In the end the training team flew back from Newark, and Lennox went missing for a weekend in the Big Apple. He arrived in London and then went straight to his house for a couple of days. I think it only added to the worries a few people had in the camp about the state of Lennox's mind going into such an important fight.

When I spoke to Lennox he reassured me that everything was fine, although he did have a slight back injury. I told him that if there was even the slightest doubt in his mind that there was a problem with it we could postpone the contest, because we had provision in the contract to put it back for up to 60 days. He said he was fine and Lennox began his daily regime which saw him train at night in the Peacock Gym instead of the afternoons, because the actual fight with McCall was going to be late due to American TV needs.

As I've said, Lennox and my brother had a very good relationship, so when Eugene got a late night call from the police to say an intruder had been spotted in the garden of his house, he was naturally concerned about his girlfriend who had been shaken by the incident. My brother went to see Lennox and told him what had happened suggesting that once Lewis was in bed for the night, he would pop home to the house in Stanmore for an hour or two. But instead of being told it was all right, Lennox told Eugene to get one of his mates to go around to the house, because he wanted my brother to stay in the hotel.

Eugene later told me he couldn't believe Lewis's attitude at the time, but rather than argue the point, he waited until Lennox was asleep in his room and then went to Stanmore, before returning to Docklands early in the morning. Apparently Lennox found out what had happened and began to make remarks about it to my brother when they were on their daily training runs. I think Eugene found it irritating, but he wasn't going to get into a row over it and just wanted the final days to go as smoothly as possible.

In the last couple of days before the fight we did the final head-to-head press conference and once again I got a strange feeling about the contest, because Lennox seemed too relaxed. Although he's always pretty laid-back before a fight, he still has a certain look in his eyes that says he means business. In that press conference with McCall he didn't seem to have the same look, and by this time even Tracey had remarked on the fact that I seemed concerned and anxious about it all.

On the day of the contest I was my normal bundle of nerves. Although I always get jittery it was much more than that on this occasion. I just couldn't help feeling worried. Deep down I felt Lennox had not prepared properly for the fight. There wasn't the harmony in the camp that there should be, and it was clear Lewis had no respect for Pepe as his trainer. The other thing that bothered me was that I knew I was partly to blame for things. I should have been firmer and insisted that Correa go early on in the camp. If that had happened I think Lennox would have accepted it and been happier knowing we were all there trying to help him.

There was an awful lot going on in my mind as I made my way to Wembley, but I thought that once I got there I could at least get into the usual pre-fight routine and it would help calm me down. There was a good atmosphere in the Arena and you could tell there was a lot of expectation. Lennox and his team arrived but the one person I couldn't see was my brother. I asked Courtney where he was and eventually found out that Eugene had walked out of the hotel after going to see Lennox in his room. When I phoned my brother he was at his house and refused to go into any detail about what exactly had gone on between him and Lennox. In the days and weeks that followed the McCall fight I know for a fact that Eugene was offered thousands of pounds by the tabloid press to say what had happened between him and Lennox, but Eugene is not the sort of person to go shouting about things like that, and whatever went on between him and Lewis remains their business even to this day.

HEAVYWEIGHTS ARE DIFFERENT

The fact that Eugene was missing made me feel even more on edge, and the dressing-room didn't have the same sense of unity about it that we'd had in the team before. The crowd gave Lennox a great reception as he walked to the ring, but even that didn't go to plan because somehow they played the wrong music.

McCall was already in the ring, pacing up and down with tears running from his eyes. He'd wound himself up into a real state and was obviously very focused as he attempted to upset the odds. After the first round it started to look as though I had nothing to worry about. McCall might have been strong and determined, but Lennox looked as though he would be able to handle him comfortably using his jab, and then let his classier punches take their toll. But when he came back to the corner there were no great words of wisdom from Pepe. Instead, as the bell sounded for the second round, Correa sent him out with just one instruction.

'Forget the game plan, just go and knock the bum out.'

12. REVENGE IS SWEET

IN THE DAYS AND WEEKS THAT FOLLOWED THE FIGHT I REPLAYED WHAT happened in that second round over and over again in my mind, but it still never made any sense and it certainly never made me feel any better.

Lennox looked relaxed and in control of the fight as he came out and although he had his hands low at times, it looked as though he had the measure of McCall. I suspect that deep down Lewis really didn't believe the American could trouble him and on any other night that probably would have been the case. McCall might not have been in the same class as Lennox, but he had been drilled like a robot by Steward when it came to throwing right hand punches. So when Lennox shaped up to throw a right of his own, McCall shut his eyes in anticipation of what was to come, but at the same time hit Lennox smack on the chin and mouth with a shot of his own.

Any right hook thrown correctly by a heavyweight can have a devastating effect on his opponent, no matter who he is. The fact that Lennox was coming on to the punch at the same time only increased the power and sent him down to the canvas looking shocked and bewildered. The amazing thing was that he somehow managed to get to his feet at around the count of six. He looked dazed and a bit unsteady but managed to nod when the Mexican referee Lupe Garcia asked if he was ready to carry on. For a split second I thought he was going to be able to survive the round, but instead Garcia waved his arms in front of Lennox's face. Lewis had become an ex-world champion after 31 seconds of the round.

He'd also become one of the few world heavyweight champions to be stopped while he was still on his feet. As usual there was pandemonium in the ring, but as well as the shock I suddenly felt a huge wave of anger. Garcia had never been in charge of a world heavyweight title fight and I couldn't believe he'd stopped the contest so quickly without giving Lennox a chance to carry on. I'd seen boxers come back and win fights after nearly being out on their feet in non-title fights. Lewis was the world heavyweight champion, but Garcia seemed determined to stop the fight as soon as he could once Lennox had got to his feet.

As I scrambled onto the ring apron I saw Jose Sulaiman out of the corner of my eye and suddenly started screaming at him claiming he'd cheated us out of our title by giving us a Mexican referee. I was in a blind rage and poor old Sulaiman seemed totally shocked as I pointed my finger at him with a look of pure hatred on my face. One of the photographers managed to capture the moment and the picture made it into several papers with me having a go while Lennox looked on stunned in the background.

I later apologised for what I'd said in the heat of the moment, but a couple of months after the fight I attended the WBC convention in Seville and sitting with his family on Don King's table was Mr Lupe Garcia, which I'm sure was just pure coincidence.

My gut reaction at the time was that the referee had stopped the fight too soon, and I've always publicly maintained that stance. But I have to admit now for the first time that he probably did the right thing. If he'd allowed it to go on McCall might have knocked Lennox spark out with the next punch because he was still groggy. If that had happened it could have spelled the end of Lewis's career at the top, but as things turned out the quick stoppage and all the fuss we made actually helped our case when it came to putting Lennox back in the hunt for his title.

REVENGE IS SWEET

King was in his element that night at Wembley as he taunted us. He finally had a world heavyweight champion again and the fact that the victory had come against Lennox made it even sweeter for him. After 25 unbeaten fights in which he'd never looked remotely like losing, Lewis had finally come unstuck against a boxer who was not even in the same class. It was a stunning loss. With his eyes closed and with one punch, McCall had become a world champion. He'd upset the odds big time. And he'd also put paid to Lennox's hopes of getting £12 million for fighting Bowe.

At the end I felt completely numb and I think everyone was in shock in the dressing-room. I remember mumbling something about having to pull ourselves together, and that the defeat was only a temporary set-back. But in my heart of hearts I just couldn't believe what had gone on. After the post-fight press conference I left the Arena with Tracey. We just kept walking without really thinking where we were going. I was in a daze and didn't really say anything as I tried to piece together what had gone wrong. The tears streamed down my face as I started thinking about the night.

Lennox may have entered the ring as the world heavyweight champion, but he seemed more like a startled kid when he realised his title was gone. I also started feeling sorry for myself. I'd worked so hard to realise my dream of being the manager of the world heavyweight champion, and I knew the knives would be out for me. I'd already seen a few gloating faces at ringside after the fight had been stopped.

We must have walked for a couple of miles before two guys in a car stopped and told us to jump in. They took us back to the hotel in Docklands where there was a party going on but it seemed more like a wake to me. Dan Duva could see how devastated I was and put his arm around me.

'Frank,' he told me. 'Right now you probably feel as low as you've ever done in your life. But let me tell you something. The only thing better in boxing than winning the world heavyweight title is regaining it. Trust me, I've been there. If Lennox wants to carry on, he can become champion again.'

It was good to hear the words from someone like Dan because I had so much respect for him as a man and for what he'd done in

189

boxing, but at the same time I knew that if Lennox was going to get his title again, it would be a long, hard road back to the top.

I eventually went up to my room but couldn't sleep even though I was physically and mentally exhausted. I wanted to see Lennox and went to his room to see how he was. He'd gone off after the fight to have the cut on his lip looked at and I hadn't really had the chance to speak to him properly. When I went in the room he looked like a confused kid as he sat on his bed in near darkness, which was in stark contrast to the way things were after a victory. I told him that I thought I hadn't been strong enough in not insisting Pepe went, but it seemed as though Lennox was already thinking ahead and then he did what he's often done in interviews. He talked about himself in the third person, saying there was no way Lennox Lewis was going to allow himself to be remembered by a performance like the one he'd given against McCall. He clearly wasn't going to call it a day and he wanted his title back.

The defeat had been a sickening set-back for everyone in the camp, but we all seemed to be coming to terms with it in our own way. We were upbeat and positive at our press conference on the Sunday, even when we had to evacuate the hotel after the fire alarm went off. But what really did upset everyone was learning that a planned *This Is Your Life* TV programme featuring Lennox had been pulled because of the defeat. It just showed the way people regarded you when you had the championship belt and how they looked on you without it. The nice thing was that the next day the *Big Breakfast* morning show staged their own form of 'This Is Your Life' for Lennox near his home and the whole mood was very light-hearted and enjoyable.

What wasn't so enjoyable that same Monday was hearing about the treatment my brother had received when he went to see Panos for his money. Eugene may have had a disagreement with Lennox and walked out, but he'd still been in camp with him for the build-up to the McCall fight and was on call 24 hours a day. He'd not only acted as Lennox's minder, but also sorted out an incident involving one of the security guards at the complex and Lewis's mum, Violet Blake. The guard had made an insulting comment to Violet who was always a big part of life in camp. She was great to have around and as well as cooking for Lennox, she was also like a mum to the lot of us in many ways. I've always had a lot of respect and affection for Violet and that applied to Eugene as well. So when he heard that this particular security guard had made a really nasty comment to her, my brother took things into his own hands and physically sorted the guy out before later getting him to personally apologise to Violet.

Eugene might have been upset and had an argument with Lewis on the night of the fight, but that didn't alter the fact that he'd worked long and hard for weeks and deserved to be paid what was rightfully his.

But when he turned up at Panos's office on that Monday morning he was told by Eliades that he was not to be paid because he'd jumped ship. Eugene was probably owed a considerable amount, and could have earned at least that by going to the press and selling his story. But instead he bit his lip and just walked out even though he was fuming. Despite not working with the Lewis team again, he did work for Panos on a casual basis sometimes, but to this day he has never received his money for that McCall fight.

Eugene wasn't the only member of the team to leave, although the next departure was slightly different. My brother walked away; Pepe Correa had to be told to go, and it was Dennis Lewis and I who had to break the news to him.

Pepe later tried to sue Champion Enterprises, the company he had his contract with, but it was soon closed down by Panos who formed a new company headed by him called Panix Promotions. Another writ also turned up at some stage from Conrad Morris and Roger Levitt trying to recoup money from Panos, but also naming Lennox and I because of our involvement in Champion Enterprises. But the action eventually came to nothing, mainly due to the fact that Levitt decided to skip the country and live in the USA.

With Pepe gone we had to get a new man in place. A shortlist was drawn up and we set about the task of trying to get the right man. The trainers on the list were: George Benton, Tommy Brooks, Thell Torrance, Richie Giachetti and Emanuel Steward.

Benton flew in to meet with us and Lewis. He went to Lennox's house and played some pool and then went to a Thai restaurant. I think Lennox liked Benton but didn't seem to 'click' with him and seeing the American down two bottles of red wine while we had our meal amazed me, especially when you think that he was basically there being interviewed for a job.

The idea was for all the trainers to meet with us and with Lennox and to see how things went in the gym as well. We went through all the possibilities, even talking about Benton working with Brooks, the man who I thought might be right for the job, but in the end it came down to a choice between Giachetti, Steward and Torrance.

Steward had been the man who'd plotted Lennox's downfall against McCall, and he had great credentials and experience as a top level trainer. He'd become world famous for his work with Tommy Hearns, but had also trained many top fighters and his Kronk Gym in Detroit was a legend in the fight game. He had also tried to sign Lennox when he'd first decided to turn professional after the Olympics, and Panos and I had a two hour meeting with Manny during which Steward managed to drink two and a half bottles of white wine, each glass being followed by a glass of water. I was beginning to wonder what the deal was with American trainers and wine!

There was no doubt Lennox liked Manny from the start and had respect for him as a trainer. Manny talked a good fight, but his record was there to back up what he said. And seeing him with Lewis it was clear he had the ability to massage Lennox's ego without looking as though he was totally sucking up to him. But we knew that having Manny on board could bring its own problems to the camp. He was used to having his own way, he liked to be more than just a trainer to his fighters and he wasn't going to be cheap.

The good thing was that by the time all of this was going on Panos and I seemed to get what we wanted, a guarantee from the WBC at their convention in Seville. After a fiery debate it was decided Lennox would fight the highest available contender and the winner would then fight the champion. But Sulaiman left the door ajar with the idea that Tyson would become the mandatory challenger if he got a win once he came out of jail following his rape conviction.

I had to eat humble pie over the incident where I'd shouted at Sulaiman following the McCall fight. It wasn't nice, and I'd have dearly loved to have told him exactly what I thought of his organisation, but we were there to help get Lennox's career back on track. I also had to put up with King handing out leaflets with the infamous picture of me screaming at Sulaiman, and accompanied by some fairly unflattering comments, including the fact that I was no friend of the WBC.

The idea was for Giachetti, Steward and Torrance to work with Lennox in the gym to see how things went, but although Torrance politely declined, saying he didn't want to be 'auditioned' alongside other trainers, it was Thell whom Lennox originally plumped for. To be fair to Lewis, Steward was always his first choice but we thought there might be some problems when it came to using him, so Lennox gave his approval to go for Torrance. We even got as far as sending him an offer in writing and air tickets for him to fly into London. But at the eleventh hour Lennox changed his mind and said he wanted Emanuel Steward. Manny was also the choice of John Hornewer, and even though John wasn't part of the selection process, I knew he wasn't backward in coming forward with his opinions when it came to Lennox's career.

I had the job of tracking Thell down and breaking the news to him. We were very lucky that he was a perfect gentleman about the whole thing and just accepted it. Anyone else would have tried to sue the arse off us, and I think they would have had good grounds to have won the case.

We called a press conference to announce the appointment and flew Manny in to meet the media. He loved the whole thing, but the alarm bells started ringing in my head when I heard him say he wasn't just coming in as a trainer, but as part of the management team. I couldn't question Manny's credentials as a trainer and Lennox clearly wanted to work with him, but I knew from day one that Manny's ego wouldn't allow him to be just a trainer, and I couldn't help thinking about the fact that he was pretty close with Don King.

It was Main Events who won the purse bid to stage Lennox's first contest after losing to McCall and once again it was against one of King's men. The fight was going to be against Lionel Butler, a bull of a man who was known as a big puncher, but a bad trainer. We'd come across him about five years earlier when he'd come over to England as a sparring partner for Lennox as he prepared for the

Chanet fight. Butler left his mark on that trip, but it wasn't in the ring. He started to get beaten up in sparring by Lewis and one day just walked out, having clocked up a bill for thousands of pounds for telephone calls and other things.

With my family background, 17 March has always been a little bit special because it's St Patrick's Day. But 17 March 1995 was special for a very different reason and turned into one of the most memorable moments in my life. That was the day Tracey gave birth to our little daughter, Sophie, and to be there at the birth was very emotional for me. Just to make sure the whole thing was a real family affair, I even had her 19-year-old sister there and Emma was as pleased as I was.

Lennox got back into training with some very good sessions in the Kronk Gym, where he showed just what a tough and determined bastard he is, earning the respect of other fighters straightaway. Later in March he set up camp at Big Bear, which is over 7,000 feet above sea level in California. The fight with Butler was scheduled to take place in Sacramento on 13 May, and my big concern was that because the American had a reputation for bad living and unreliability, he might not actually turn up on the night. We actually had a contingency plan in case there was a problem, with another heavyweight named Ray Anis on stand-by, although Manny and I didn't tell Lennox.

Lewis looked sensational on occasions during the preparation for the fight and it was a much happier and better organised place to be with Manny in charge of training. Lennox could still be miserable and sulky when he wanted to be, but that happens with every boxer during training. It was clear to see he was enjoying working with Steward and he had the kind of respect for Manny he didn't have with Pepe.

Although I felt much better and more content than before the McCall fight, I got a letter one morning that shook me down to my boots. It came from Emma and in it she gave me the sort of news I didn't want. 'Dad,' she wrote, 'I'm pregnant.' My little girl was pregnant and I felt a mixture of anger and concern sweep over me. When I told Violet I think she could see I was confused, but said I had to be strong and support Emma, which was always going to be the case. Lennox could see I'd been knocked sideways by the news, but he managed to bring a smile to my face when he patted me on the shoulder and said, 'Never mind, grandad!'

I knew he was trying to cheer me up and he showed how considerate he can be later on in the camp when he suggested that I fly Tracey and little Sophie out to stay with me. He seemed fascinated by the baby when she arrived and spent quite a bit of time with her. It was funny to see this huge man who is capable of inflicting so much pain and punishment on his opponents, sitting there cuddling my baby daughter.

During the course of the camp we'd also managed to negotiate a new deal with Sky TV. It was really started by Sam Chisholm, a tough little New Zealander, who had taken over from MacKenzie. He contacted me one day and asked if we'd like to go back to Sky. 'It's not just because you've got Lennox Lewis,' he said. 'I want to do a deal with you because you're smaller than me, Maloney!'

I got on well with Sam and I think Sky had a lot to thank him for at that time because he had the vision to realise that sport could play such a big part in making them successful. The station really became Britain's boxing channel, and Frank Warren decided to sign with Sky as well. Sam wanted to make sure they went out and got all the top sports people and events. His philosophy has been proved right and after talking things through with Panos we decided to go ahead and sign with them again, after leaving Wire, who were about to close down their operation.

Lennox was certainly in a very different mood when he met Butler to the way he was against McCall. It was a huge fight for Lewis after what had gone on in his last contest and King had done all he could to get under his skin, even to the point of hiring Correa to be in Butler's corner. But after naturally looking a bit cautious early on, Lewis got into his stride and stopped the American in the fifth round. It was the first step in making sure Lennox got his belt back, but as well as the fight it was Dan Duva's quick thinking out of the ring which helped Lewis's cause.

Although we'd got agreement at the WBC convention that if Lennox beat Butler he'd be fighting for the world title, it was clear by this time that Sulaiman was not going to make the sort of public commitment we wanted. With Tyson looming on the horizon after being released from jail, it seemed pretty clear that if Lennox could be kept out of the picture it would make things better all round for Don King.

We might not have been able to get Mr Sulaiman to utter the words we wanted to hear, but Dan managed to get the South African WBC supervisor for the Butler fight up on the top table for the press conference after Lennox had won. He also made sure the whole thing was taped and videoed as the supervisor promised that Lewis's next fight would be for the world title. Game, set and match to us, particularly as those comments came in very handy in a later court battle. As far as I know, that particular supervisor has never been given a job as an official since. I wonder why?

Just as we thought we had McCall in our sights again, our plans were mucked up by none other than the great heavyweight survivor – Frank Bruno. Big Frank might have been bashed about in three previous attempts to win the world title, but by September 1995 he was ready to have a fourth crack, this time against McCall, having had his career resurrected by Frank Warren.

Lennox had kept busy in the summer with a fight in Dublin against Australian Justin Fortune. The contest was arranged to help Manny do some more work with Lewis and the trip went well. The Irish public really took to Lennox and he liked them as well. Fortune wasn't exactly world class and we got some criticism for putting a relative novice in with a former world champion. The outcome was very conclusive as Lennox produced some great uppercuts to stop the brave Aussie in the fourth round.

Probably like lots of other high profile sports, boxing attracts some dedicated followers, and there was a certain young lady named Wendy who seemed to take a particular shine to a lot of the guys involved in the Lennox Lewis team. The morning after the fight in Dublin I saw her wandering along one of the corridors in the hotel, having stepped out of a room belonging to someone in the team. Some time later in New York she revealed to Tracey and my secretary, Sophie, the names of the team she'd slept with and also marked their performances out of ten. I think the girls were quite surprised by her revelations and also by the fact that at another time in her life she claimed to have taken part in a three-in-the-bed romp with a squeaky-clean TV personality.

Not too long after the Fortune fight Seth Abraham at HBO was keen for Lennox to get involved in a series of fights against some of the top heavyweights who were not under the control of Don King. He wanted people like Riddick Bowe, Ray Mercer, Evander Holyfield and Tommy Morrison in the mix along with Lewis. So while Bruno took on and beat McCall at Wembley Stadium on 2 September with a points win to become the new WBC world heavyweight champion, Lennox was preparing in the Poconos for a fight against Morrison a month later in Atlantic City.

It didn't surprise any of us when Bruno won, but once he'd become world champion we knew the problem was going to be getting him in the ring again with Lewis. By this time Tyson was back in action and with Frank Warren as Bruno's promoter it was clear he was likely to favour a fight with Iron Mike. Warren had formed a partnership with King, so the obvious move for Bruno was for him to side-step Lennox and then cash in on a first defence against Tyson, leaving us out of the picture once again. Panos made a $7 million bid to stage a Bruno–Lewis fight, but the offer was rejected.

So we found ourselves with two fights on our hands. The first was in the ring against Morrison, the second was outside the ropes and in the courts, because that was the only way we were going to get what we'd been promised – a crack at the world title.

Tracey came out for the fight in Atlantic City and because I was often busy, she used to spend quite a bit of time with my secretary Sophie. One day the two of them were having a meal together in the hotel we were using, when Emanuel came along and asked if he could join them. Manny then proceeded to blow his own trumpet in a big way, telling the girls about the money he'd earned, the cars he had and the houses he'd lived in. He was in full flow and when he ordered a really expensive bottle of wine, Tracey and Sophie got a bit concerned because they knew they were supposed to stick to a budget. Manny told them not to worry and said he'd pay, but when he'd finished his meal Steward just got up and walked away, leaving the two girls with the bill. I couldn't help laughing when I heard, because Manny had pulled a similar stroke with me in Dublin before the Fortune fight. He'd ordered champagne and food in a club we went to and left me to pick up the tab.

I surprised a few people in a press conference before the fight when I claimed that the loser might just as well cross the boardwalk and jump in the sea, because they'd have nowhere else to go. Tommy quickly said he didn't think it was the case and Violet got a bit upset with me because I believe she thought I wasn't showing enough confidence in Lennox. But I wanted the remark to upset Morrison and add more pressure.

Lennox was always supremely confident of winning and took care of Tommy in six rounds, with the American looking outgunned and outclassed. Morrison did manage to worry Lewis, but that was some time after the fight when we found out that poor Tommy had been diagnosed as HIV positive. Lennox got himself tested just in case, but was given the all-clear.

Just over three weeks after the fight we served writs on both the WBC and Bruno demanding that Lennox should fight for the title before Tyson. It was the first move in what was to prove to be a long drawn out affair, but it didn't go well for us and the High Court threw the action out because they said it was outside their jurisdiction and instead should be heard in the States.

Our cause wasn't exactly helped the next month by the fact that at the WBC convention in Thailand a Bruno–Tyson fight was sanctioned in a vote 28–0. The British Boxing Board of Control abstained because it involved action between two of their own fighters, but Lennox had earned the right and in my opinion they took the coward's way out. A year earlier the BBBC were the leading voice in getting Lennox re-instated as the official challenger, but they seemed to lose their bottle and effectively sat on the fence.

That convention just proved to me what a joke the WBC was in so many ways. It seemed like virtually every convention I'd attended since signing Lennox had been nothing but trouble. Sulaiman seemed to idolise Tyson, and I think he also loved the money the WBC had got over the years in sanctioning fees from his fights. A boxer will pay a percentage of his purse to the organisation if he is involved in one of their fights, and there was no bigger name in boxing than Tyson, so his purses for title fights ran into the millions.

I went to Thailand with Don Majeski, an American who had great contacts throughout the boxing world. In political terms you could call him a lobbyist, and he'd done a good job in helping us with Lennox's career. Don has the ability to get on and deal with lots of different people in the game, and had worked with some big names including Don King. Majeski had played a big part in helping us to establish Lennox in the early part of Lewis's career, and also in establishing his strong position at the previous year's convention in Seville.

He had a great eye for detail and always seemed to act as a calming influence on me. He's the sort of character only boxing seems to attract. He looks quite intense, and has a very pale complexion. The funny thing is that he often sleeps during the day, but is wide awake and working at night – but I'm sure it's just coincidence! He's been a good friend over the years and has taught me a lot about the politics of the sport. Don is also a purist when it comes to boxing. He likes to see the best fighters get their chance to rise to the top, but realises the business side of things often gets in the way.

Frank Warren had made a smart move by going to Thailand with Bruno and it was obvious that Sulaiman was delighted to see his newly crowned heavyweight champion walking around and mingling with people. It made me angry that Lennox had decided he didn't want to go, but there was nothing I could do about it, and despite trying to make our case I knew things were going against us and a Bruno-Tyson fight was very much on the cards.

To try and resolve matters before any voting had taken place the British Boxing Board suggested that Frank Warren and I had a meeting to thrash out our differences and see if some sort of compromise could be sorted out. We had the meeting in Majeski's room and the atmosphere was bad from the first moment. Apart from the verbal battering we gave each other, I honestly think we would have come to blows had it not been for Majeski.

As if to add insult to injury, when I went to my room and got ready to leave the convention I found that a small white box had been put on my bed. When I opened it there was a little memento of the visit, and staring out at me was the face of Sulaiman. I stood there thinking, 'I've just been fucked by him and his organisation, and now he expects me to take this picture home with me!'

Richie Giachetti came up with a great quote after going to a WBC convention when he said, 'The world is full of people who will shove an umbrella up your ass, but some people here will shove it up, then open it just for fun.' As I packed my bags, it seemed to sum up my feelings perfectly.

It was time for us to battle in the courts for what was right, so Main Events, Panos and the rest of the Lewis team began an action which eventually ended in Lennox gaining the right to fight for the title, but incredibly it was to take more than a year before he actually got his chance in the ring. In the meantime there was plenty of fun and games outside the ropes and not all of it was pleasant.

HBO were keen on discussing a new deal with us and Panos flew to New York without me for a meeting with Seth Abraham and Main Events. But it was a short trip. For whatever reason, Panos had sworn an affidavit in an action that Rock Newman was bringing against the cable TV company and naturally enough Abraham didn't take too kindly to it.

Panos walked into the meeting and was told by Abraham, 'You've got two choices. You can either leave through the door or I'll call security.'

'What have I done?' asked Panos. 'I've just flown in on Concorde for this meeting.'

'Well, you can go fly out again on Concorde,' said Seth.

Abraham saw himself as the king of boxing, the man who made it all happen. If you upset him he was like a spoilt kid, and the incident clearly didn't go down too well with him. But he knew he had to go on dealing with Panos, even if he preferred not to have to do it directly, and the man who later became something of a buffer for the relationship was American lawyer Milt Chwasky. Milt had represented Bowe and Newman and it always seemed strange to me that Chwasky should start to play a part in our promotional company, Panix, and later become Lennox's lawyer as well.

The legal battles continued right through into the spring of 1996. But by then the whole Lewis operation had suffered a huge loss with the death in January of Dan Duva. He became ill in October and within three short months had died. It was a real tragedy and a shock to everyone who knew him. Dan had done a tremendous job with Main Events and I knew they would never really be able to replace him. Dan's brother Dino was the man who took charge, and like any other business I'm sure there was a change. Main Events had reflected Dan's way of going about things, and when Dino took over it must have been hard for him.

Just a few days before Bruno's fight with Tyson in Las Vegas on 16 March, Lennox had one of the best knockouts of his career. But it didn't come from a punch. Instead it was delivered on his behalf in a New Jersey courtroom by Judge Amos Saunders. He said that the WBC had treated Lennox unfairly and then accused the organisation of making up their own rules; a thought that had often occurred to me. There was a possibility that the Bruno–Tyson fight might not take place, but instead the Judge issued an order which effectively stopped the winner and the WBC from taking part in a heavyweight title fight against anyone other than Lennox. Saunders stood no nonsense in his courtroom and at one point during all of this he actually threatened to have King and Sulaiman put in jail because of the way they were behaving.

Bruno got beaten in three rounds by Tyson and having taken one title, it was clear King was eager for the new WBC champion to start mopping up the other belts as soon as possible. But as far as we were concerned, if he wanted to do that he'd have to fight Lewis first.

The next fight on the horizon for Lennox was a tough ten-rounder against Ray Mercer, scheduled for Madison Square Garden on 10 May. Mercer was a genuinely tough guy and once again it seemed to me that the TV people were happy to have Lennox fighting the strongest opponents. Maybe it was because out of all the top contenders, Lewis was the one who was not American. It was pretty clear that once you're not the world champion, you lose some bargaining power. The American TV people, who really call the shots anyway, have even more power when you're trying to make sure you get a crack at a world title.

I had a pleasant break from training camp for the Mercer fight when Lennox asked me to go with him to Toronto, where he had an interest in a health club and gym he was opening there. It was a nice trip for me and Lennox was relaxed and happy. We had a meal one evening and he turned up with a really stunning girl, but at the end of the evening he said goodnight to her and we went back to his house. It obviously showed how serious he was about his training for the Mercer fight, but I'm not so sure I would have been so disciplined in the circumstances.

Lennox put in a lot of hard work for the fight and he certainly needed it on the night. It was one of the hardest contests of his career, as Mercer slugged it out and Lewis really had to dig deep to make sure he eventually came out a winner on points by a majority decision, but it looked distinctly dodgy for him in the sixth round.

Around the same time as the fight, things also began to look dodgy for Hornewer. The Mercer fight was to be the last he was around for, with Lennox deciding he'd had enough of the lawyer, whose cause wasn't exactly helped by some of the people in the Panix organisation at the time.

About nine days before the fight, things started to get hot outside the ring, when King went to court again in an appeal against the original decision made by Judge Saunders. When it was turned down, Don was on the phone to Panos trying to see whether he would be interested in a Tyson–Lewis contest. At one point King started with an offer of $6 million and went up to $10 million, but Panos told him he wanted $15 million. It was the start of some long negotiations that went on through the summer, and three days after Lennox beat Mercer, there was another offer from King, this time for $12 million. His thinking was probably influenced by the fact that he'd lost another appeal, this time to the New Jersey Supreme Court, leaving us very much in the driving seat.

Meetings took place on both sides of the Atlantic during the early part of the summer. King and Main Events met in New York, while Panos was talking to Seth Abraham in London. Just to add a bit of spice to the whole situation, we found out from our London-based Panix Promotions lawyer, Peter Crystal, that he'd been approached by a third party who wanted to know whether there was a possibility of Lennox leaving us and joining forces with Frank Warren and Don King. Panos and I actually had a meeting at Crystal's offices with Frank but nothing came of it. We knew there was no way Lennox was going anywhere, but once King found out that was the case it seemed to take the wind out of his sails.

When Panos met Abraham, it was clear Seth was pushing for Lennox to fight Bowe. HBO had made things up with Newman and at the beginning of June Rock flew in to have a meeting. Newman suggested Lennox should get $8 million for the contest, with Riddick getting more than $11 million, but nothing concrete came out of the meeting, and later that month Abraham even came over to speak with Lennox at his house in the hope of getting him to agree to a Bowe fight.

With Tyson chasing the WBA crown against Bruce Seldon in a fight on 7 September it meant we could pursue another route to regaining the world title. If we couldn't agree a fight with Tyson, he would have to vacate the WBC belt and Lennox had the right to be matched with the next highest ranked WBC contender, Oliver McCall, for the vacant title. We decided to inform the WBC and King that we wanted to go straight into a fight for the title and we also asked them to put the fight out to purse bids. It was fun and games all round and when King heard we were going the title route he made another attempt to try and head us off with a new offer.

Just before I was due to fly off and watch Riddick Bowe take on Andrew Golota at Madison Square Garden, King came up with a new plan. The offer to Panos was $4 million straight away; let Tyson take on Holyfield after Seldon, and then Lennox would fight Tyson after that for a purse of $11 million. Taken in total it would have meant $15 million for Lennox, but I told Panos agreeing to such a deal would mean relinquishing the strong position we'd battled for in the courts. Main Events agreed with me and the issue led to some lively correspondence between their office and ours.

The fight between Bowe and Golota will always be remembered for the riot that occurred at the Garden after the Pole suffered a seventh round disqualification for hitting low after looking as though he was beating Bowe easily. All hell broke loose when the bout was stopped, and Lou Duva who was in Golota's corner for the fight, fell to the ground as the fighting continued in and out of the ring. I'd never seen anything like it, and the whole thing was really frightening. I honestly thought Lou might have been killed when he went down, but thankfully he later managed to recover in hospital.

Golota ended up with blood streaming from the back of his head after he was struck by a mobile phone.

We finally left the arena with security provided by Mayor Giuliani, who came into the dressing-room afterwards and made sure we had protection at our hotel all night, just in case there was more trouble from any of Bowe's supporters. The fight made a star of Golota, firstly because he'd beaten up Bowe, but also because he'd used low blows and become the new bad boy of the heavyweight scene.

Meanwhile, King was back on with another plan for us in what was now becoming a real saga. He was willing to pay $1 million non-returnable right away, $4 million when Tyson fought Seldon and another $4 million when Tyson fought Holyfield. Tyson would then have until 31 March 1997 to fight Lennox, who would get $7 million for the contest. The whole package added up to $16 million.

The deal was $1 million more than Panos had asked King for, but I made the point to him that we had to protect Lennox's position and I also asked whether he'd discussed it all with Main Events. Panos told me he was making the decisions as Lewis's promoter and I think the way he carried on only helped widen the rift which seemed to be developing between Panix and Main Events.

I think Panos enjoyed the whole episode and despite what he might have said, I also think he got a bit of a kick out of dealing with someone like King. As far as he was concerned it was another indication that he had 'arrived' in the boxing world. No matter how much he might have played it down, Panos has an ego just like the rest of us, and at this stage I was really watching it grow.

Although there was lots of talk about a fight with Tyson, one very big obstacle could not be avoided. Like all major fighters, the two boxers had American TV backing. The TV people are the ones who actually stop some of the big fights from happening because they have certain fighters contracted to them and they're not going to let them box on other networks, and why should they? Let's face it, managers, promoters and fighters are the ones who make the decision to sign with a network and the reason you sign an exclusive deal is to bankroll your operation. The trouble was that Lennox was contracted to HBO and Tyson's fights were shown on their cable rivals Showtime.

Pretty much as soon as we had that King offer things changed once again and it went quiet until the build-up for Tyson's fight with Seldon, when King started talking to the press with all sorts of figures coming out. The fact was that nothing had been signed, and nothing had been agreed, and our main aim was to get the WBC title back.

Tyson had an easy first-round win over Seldon to take the WBA title, but the WBC belt was not at stake and we later received $4 million in lieu of damages which a lot of the media claimed was step-aside money for allowing the Tyson–Seldon bout to go ahead.

With King unable to agree a deal for Tyson to meet Lewis, we received a letter informing us that Mike had given up the title and purse bids were then set for a Lewis fight against McCall for the vacant championship.

When the bids were opened by Sulaiman at his office in Mexico, King managed to surprise everyone once again by offering over $9 million to stage the fight, beating a Main Events bid by about $6 million. We really couldn't work out how he could afford to bid so much, but as far as we were concerned it meant another big pay day for Lennox.

While Lewis went off to camp I attended the WBC convention in Argentina with Majeski. As usual they didn't exactly go out of their way to help our cause, and there was a crazy situation at one point where they allowed King to have a 30-day extension on staging the McCall fight, which meant it was going to be put back until 11 January. King had actually sent us two contracts since winning the bid. One was for a contest in Nashville in November and the other was for London a couple of months later.

There was no point in Lennox staying in camp once the original November date went out of the window. It meant a return visit to the courts for us, and the familiar figure of Judge Saunders who came up trumps again and ruled that King's bid had become invalid, and the fight promotion would be transferred to Main Events.

We eventually settled on a date of 7 February in Las Vegas and because of the timing it meant everyone would be in camp over Christmas. It was another blow for King who'd seen Evander Holyfield take the WBA title from Tyson on 9 November in sensational fashion with an 11th round stoppage.

Lennox trained on the West Coast in Arizona at the Camelback

Resort in Scotsdale. It was very up-market with great facilities and I was lucky enough to have Tracey and Sophie with me for the holidays. There was a good feeling about the camp, although it wasn't all smooth sailing with Manny. In the early part of our stay there were rumours that he might become Tyson's trainer, even though Steward always denied the story. It didn't help matters one day when Manny cut Lennox's hand with some scissors while he was taking his bandages off. Steward was mortified and couldn't understand it. He said it had only ever happened to him once before and that was with Tommy Hearns before he beat Duran.

At the beginning of January Manny called me in my room and asked if he could come over. We watched a boxing tape and then he started to get some things off his chest. After a couple of drinks in the bar and a few more in the town with me and Mark Roe, the trainer of Julius Francis who was in camp to spar with Lennox and also to prepare for his own European title shot against Zeljko Mavrovic, Manny told me the problems he was having.

He was worried about his relationship with Lennox and thought he wanted too much control in camp. He said he'd always been more than just a trainer to his fighters and he really wanted Lennox to be his masterpiece in boxing terms. It was clear he was concerned and after talking for a while he actually went to see Lennox. He later told me he'd had a heart to heart which he hoped would clear the air, but it was strange to see Manny so concerned.

Lennox worked well in camp but the food at the Resort was superb and I found out that he had been taking full advantage of it with some room service. Lewis was well prepared by the time we travelled to Vegas for the fight with McCall for the vacant WBC title, but he came in at a career heaviest of 17 st. 13 lb, and a few of the press guys from England remarked on the big white shorts he wore on the night of the fight. Manny insisted in public that the weight gain was planned as part of the fight strategy.

I did my usual thing and took the British press out a couple of days before the fight. I almost came to blows with one of them. Things got out of hand between Colin Hart and me as we got into a heated conversation, and TV commentator Reg Gutteridge had to step in to break the whole thing up.

REVENGE IS SWEET

I was on edge as usual. All the Lewis team worked long and hard to make sure Lennox had the chance to regain the belt and everyone knew it was within touching distance. For the first contest McCall had been locked away in a training camp for weeks as he got his mind and body right for the challenge. This time things were very different for the Chicago fighter. A few months earlier we'd heard that he was in a rehabilitation centre after slipping back into some of his bad old ways. He'd had problems with drink, drugs and violence. Nobody was really sure what condition he was in as the fight approached and we heard all sorts of stories about him not being mentally right. But we were given assurances that he would be able to fight, although the alarm bells started ringing when he turned up with three counsellors in tow.

All we could do was approach the job as professionally as possible and that's what we did. The fight was the first time I wore my Union Jack suit, which had been made for me by a tailor in London's East End. I didn't really tell anyone about it except for Lennox and Courtney, but it later became a regular feature of Lewis's fights and the fans seemed to love me wearing it.

The fight itself turned out to be one of the most bizarre experiences I've ever had in the business, and at the end of it you couldn't help feeling sorry for McCall who appeared to have some kind of nervous breakdown in the ring.

At the end of the third round he went on a walkabout and by the fourth it was clear he didn't really want to fight. At the end of the round he had tears streaming down his face and didn't seem to want to carry on. George Benton, who was in his corner, clearly didn't know what the hell was going on as his fighter refused to acknowledge he was even there. But when referee Mills Lane asked if he wanted to fight he said yes and came out for the fifth. After Lennox threw some shots at him, McCall turned away again, and Lane called the fight off, declaring it a technical knockout 'because Oliver McCall refuses to defend himself'.

It was a terrible ending to a world heavyweight title fight, but as horrible as it may sound, my main feeling was overwhelming relief that Lennox had won and had the title back again. The fight did boxing no good at all and it was clear McCall would have been better off in a hospital bed that night instead of a boxing ring. It was the sort of thing that gives the sport a terrible name, and at the press conference later Dino summed up a lot of people's thoughts. 'We have a lot of sympathy for Oliver McCall,' he said. 'Oliver McCall has some problems. The people we're mad at are the people that allowed him to fight and told everyone that he was ready to fight – namely, Don King.'

13. ONCE BITTEN

LENNOX HAD WON THE TITLE BACK AND I COULDN'T HELP THINKING OF THE NIGHT he'd lost it and what Dan Duva had said to me.

It was a special moment and I wish poor Dan had still been alive to see it. We'd gone to so much trouble to make sure Lennox got his shot and he'd done his job, but I also felt a bit sorry for him because the fight was overshadowed by the way McCall had carried on in the ring.

Having breathed a sigh of relief at winning, none of us could afford to relax for too long as we started to plan a way forward, and it didn't take long to realise that King was still casting a shadow over everything. He may have seen Tyson beaten by Holyfield, and then witnessed McCall's defeat by Lennox, but you can never write Don off. He had managed to manoeuvre Henry Akinwande into being the official challenger for the WBC title and we were faced with the prospect of having to meet him that summer in a fight that nobody really wanted.

I remembered Henry from his days as an amateur with the Lynn club in south London. He was a 6 ft 7 in. beanpole of a fighter weighing about 13 st. back then. In fact, the Levitt Group had helped sponsor part of his amateur career and when he wanted to turn professional I had a meeting with him at my pub in Crayford. But I didn't really like his build for a heavyweight because he reminded me of a stick insect and when I heard what he wanted I didn't really take it any further. He eventually turned professional with Mickey Duff, grew into a full-blown heavyweight and then left to sign with King as his promoter. In order to fight Lewis he'd actually given up his WBO version of the world title, having won it against Jeremy Williams 13 months earlier.

Akinwande was an awkward, unexciting fighter and as far as I was concerned the only good thing was that it was another world heavyweight title fight between two British boxers. It certainly didn't capture the imagination of the boxing world, and I knew it was going to be hard to sell it as a spectacle. But because they were both from Britain the obvious place to stage it in my mind was England. We might have been able to pull a decent crowd of around 6,000, but Panos and Dino Duva had other ideas so the contest ended up being staged at Caesar's Palace in Lake Tahoe on 12 July 1997.

It seemed a strange place to have a contest between two British boxers, and they actually fought in one of the Casino's lounges in front of a very small audience which was set up for no more than about 900 people. Less than York Hall could hold.

It had not been a good year for heavyweight boxing. After McCall's problems against Lennox in February, Tyson had added to his notoriety by getting disqualified in the third round of his re-match with Holyfield for biting a lump off Evander's ear. It had happened two weeks before the Lewis–Akinwande fight, and people were saying that boxing needed a contest that would help the sport regain some credibility. Mills Lane, who'd been in charge for Lennox's second fight against McCall, was also the man in the middle for Holyfield–Tyson. Lane then got the job of refereeing the Akinwande bout and must have thought he'd used up all his bad luck when it came to controversial endings. But he made it clear at one of the press conferences that if he had to disqualify a fighter he would.

I'd watched the biting incident on TV during a short trip home to see Julius Francis take the vacant Commonwealth title with a points win over Joseph Chingangu. I couldn't believe what I saw at first, but it just confirmed that you never really knew what was going to happen when Tyson stepped into the ring. I got a bit of stick in some of the papers for saying that I thought the whole thing would probably make him an even bigger attraction and earn him a fortune when he fought again. It may not have been nice to hear, but it was the truth. Boxing is theatre with blood, and when he bit Holyfield's ear Tyson went beyond being a boxing attraction – he became a freak show as well. Like it or not, the public are willing to pay good money to see him perform. Sure they like to see him knock people out, but they also know he's likely to go crazy inside and outside the ring. That's the real attraction to many people.

I also had a bad experience in England in the middle of June, when a fighter I managed named Dominic Negas won the Southern Area cruiserweight title with a tenth-round victory. Normally I would have been delighted, but tragically his opponent, Chris Henry, had to be rushed to hospital for an emergency operation on a blood clot. Thankfully he survived, but things like that make you question the sport and your own role in it. It was the first time I'd been that closely associated with a show that produced such a tragic incident, and unfortunately it wasn't to be the last.

As well as helping to make sure things went smoothly in the final week before the Akinwande fight, I also had another piece of important business to attend to when I asked Tracey to marry me. She'd come out for the fight with the baby and I told her we could get married in the wedding chapel at Caesar's the day after the contest. So as well as the usual round of press conferences and rules meetings in the days before the contest, I had to find time to go and get a wedding licence.

I had no doubt Lennox would beat Akinwande. The only thing I hadn't bargained for was the way he'd win. Akinwande made no attempt to fight and instead tried to hold and wrestle with Lennox until Lane had seen enough and disqualified the challenger in the fifth round. So much for restoring credibility to the heavyweight scene. For the second time in five months I had to feel sorry for Lennox because he'd done nothing wrong and yet had been involved in another stinker of a fight. Lewis actually did get caught by Akinwande during the contest and many of the watching press thought he'd touched down on the canvas.

I also lost out financially because I'd had a bet with Duff, and thought I was about to collect my winnings after the verdict. But Mickey claimed he'd cancelled it and said he'd informed me that was the case, although the news never got through. He'd actually got me to sign an agreement and also insisted on my side of the bet being guaranteed by Dino Duva at Main Events.

Because the contest was in the afternoon there was still plenty of time left to prepare for my stag night. It had been organised by Vince Heckman and two reporters who were good mates of mine, Steve Bunce who worked for the *Daily Telegraph* and Steve Lillis from the *Sport* newspaper. All three were due to act as my Best Men at the wedding the next day. The fight was such a non-event that Lillis later claimed he'd spent more time that week sorting out my stag night than he had covering the contest.

The boys obviously wanted to make it a night to remember for me and after getting a suite in the hotel with a nice big jacuzzi, they suggested I made the most of it and had a dip. So after a few more drinks I hopped in. As well as Vince, Buncy and Lillis, Panos's son Christian was in the room along with Sky commentators Ian Darke and Glenn McCrory. We were all enjoying a drink when there was a knock at the door and two ladies who had been invited by Vince turned up. One sat down and watched TV while she smoked a cigarette, but the other made her way to the jacuzzi where I was sitting with Panos's son and asked which one of us was the bridegroom. I could see where it was all leading and decided it might be a good idea to get dressed and leave the room in a hurry. But just to make sure I would remember my last night as a single man, Vince had somehow managed to hide all my clothes. So there I was stark bollock naked in a hot tub with this girl bearing down on me.

I can think of lots of times in the past when I would probably have closed my eyes and thought of England, but on this occasion I panicked. I grabbed the nearest towel I could find before running out of the room and down the corridor still dripping wet. Apparently Glenn and Darkie left soon after because they had something on that night, but by this time Eliades junior could hardly believe his luck and clearly thought he was in with a real chance as the girl stripped off and jumped in the jacuzzi with him. As far as he was concerned she really fancied him, so you can imagine how surprised he was when she asked for some money if he wanted to take matters further. He obviously hadn't realised the two young ladies were 'professional' girls hired by Vince for a bit of a laugh. The whole thing turned into a farce. It's funny to think it was set up as a typical boys' stag night stunt to get me into trouble. The fact that it all went wrong and nothing actually happened was probably a very good thing from my point of view, because the wedding might have been over before it began.

The one sad moment that day came when I placed a call to my daughter Emma, telling her that I was about to get married. She and Tracey got on really well and I realised she would feel left out when she heard the news. Emma was clearly upset that she wasn't going to be there, but I told her we would see her as soon as we got back to England.

Panos managed to put his foot in things both before and after the fight in my eyes because of a couple of incidents. During one of Lennox's final sparring sessions he showed a real lack of respect for a fighter who was getting the shit beaten out of him by Lewis. Being a sparring partner is hard enough, but Panos didn't seem to realise that.

'Lay him down here in front of me, Lennox, and I'll give the kid an extra $20,' he told Lewis.

In his own mind Panos probably thought it was a bit of fun, but that's because he had no idea how tough it is just to step into a boxing ring, let alone spar round after round with the heavyweight champion of the world. There were a couple of seasoned press guys from England who heard the comment and you could see they were upset by it as well. Colin Hart actually had a word with him about it.

His other gaff came at my wedding reception. Although he was one of the Best Men, Lillis didn't really want to make a speech and instead Panos stood up to say a few words. Once again he managed to misjudge the mood of the room as I've heard him do so many times over the years, and instead of sticking to the usual kind of patter he decided to be a bit different.

'I hope this marriage lasts longer than your last,' he told me in front of all the wedding guests. 'You seem like a nice girl Tracey, so I can't comment on you, but Frank hasn't got a very good reputation. All he wants to do is drink and chase girls.'

I think it was at that point Tracey got up and politely told Panos that he wasn't very good and suggested he stick to making boxing speeches. When he made his cracks about me I had to laugh, because when Lennox had beaten Tucker in Las Vegas more than four years earlier, it was Panos who took both his wife Angela and his girlfriend Rita on the trip and installed them in different hotels. He used to make a joke about it to some of the Lewis team, saying how he had to dash between the hotels in the morning and have two breakfasts!

He also took another young girl with him on another trip and got quite upset when the famous American boxing MC, Michael Buffer, started paying her a bit of attention. Panos actually asked Eugene to go over and have a quiet word in Buffer's ear so that the situation didn't develop any further.

The wedding itself was good fun, and a very happy affair, with my Best Men and me all dressed in very colourful Hawaiian shirts. Just for good measure we also had Caesar and Cleopatra look-alikes present, courtesy of the hotel. Although the reception was a social occasion there was still time for some boxing business to be done, and at one point Panos, Dino, Lou DiBella and I huddled in a corner to discuss the various possibilities for Lennox's next fight.

I was pleased to finally be married to Tracey. We'd planned on getting hitched for some time, but didn't really want a big affair in England, so Tahoe seemed the perfect place and I promised her a short honeymoon as soon as we got home. I have to admit we didn't exactly travel home in style the next day, because although I got an upgrade, there weren't any for Tracey or little Sophie, so we decided to sit at the back of the plane.

At least Tracey and I were together but after the last fight against McCall, I'd been bumped up the front and left her at the back with the baby and my mother. She said she didn't mind and told me to go ahead and take the seat. As I settled down one of the cabin crew said that the singer Lulu was sitting a few seats away from me. I'd always liked her and actually had a bit of a crush on her when I was younger. We got introduced and chatted for quite a while. It was all very friendly stuff and I promised to invite her to a boxing show. When I got off the plane and waited for Tracey I was like a kid who'd just met one of his heroes.

'Tracey,' I said. 'You'll never guess who I met.'

Just at that moment Lulu walked past looking absolutely immaculate after the long flight, and I offered to introduce Tracey to her. As you can probably imagine, the suggestion didn't go down too well, especially as she felt terrible, having spent a restless journey trying to entertain Sophie.

We had to start work on getting an opponent for Lewis's next defence and made an offer of $8 million to the veteran George Foreman, but he insisted he wanted more to fight Lennox and effectively put himself out of the frame. The two other fighters we started to look at were European champion Zeljko Mavrovic and Andrew Golota.

Mavrovic had proved himself to be a good technician at European level and had won all of his fights, including an eighth round victory against Julius Francis in defence of his belt. Golota had managed to add to his bad boy image with another disqualification against Bowe in their re-match in December 1996. The Pole was considered dangerous and unpredictable, and because he was based in Chicago, he had a good following in the States. It all made him perfect box office in the view of the TV executives, and there was a strong push for Lennox to meet him.

I did manage to squeeze in a honeymoon with Tracey, although she had to put up with just a few days in Venice rather than the ten days we had planned. On the third day I got a call on my mobile while we were having a romantic water-taxi ride telling me that I had to go to New York because the fight with Golota had been confirmed. Tracey was really understanding about the whole thing, but I knew that wouldn't have been the case had I married some of the other women I'd known in the past.

We started promoting the fight against Golota with a press tour by train and private jet across America. It was real jet-set stuff and we were pampered and looked after at every stop. I even flew to the States on Concorde with Lennox and it was clear he really fancied the fight against Golota and was supremely confident. He surprised me on the flight when he said he could never see himself losing to a white fighter. It was something I advised him to keep to himself, but more recently Lennox seemed to touch on the subject again in an interview when he was asked if it would be worse getting beaten by a white boxer than a black boxer. 'Yeah, because black boxers have it so hard in the first place, just to get by. It's always easier for the white boxer.'

Lennox proved he had every right to be confident when the fight took place in Atlantic City on 4 October. He produced a devastating display knocking the Pole down and blasting his way to a first-round stoppage. It was a tremendous performance and it really made a lot of his American critics have to eat their words. They had built Golota up as the new monster in heavyweight boxing, but Lennox just went out and destroyed him. At that stage a fight with Evander Holyfield was very much in our sights, but as is so often the case in boxing, what you want is not necessarily what you get. We may have been thinking of a fight with Holyfield in October 1997, but it would be 17 months before we actually got it, and in the meantime Lennox defended his title a couple of times. The first was against American Shannon Briggs and the other saw him take on Mavrovic.

The end of 1997 was a hectic time for me as we promoted a show that caused quite a stir and got me in hot water with the British Boxing Board of Control. It was a promotion that saw Britain's Herol Graham take on Vinnie Pazienza in a super-middleweight fight for the WBC international title. The promotion at Wembley Arena got loads of publicity because of the controversy I caused with our poster for the fight. It had a good against evil theme, with Vinnie happy to play along with anything I suggested. In the end I had him holding what looked like the severed heads of two women. Some people saw it for what it was, a way of promoting the fight, but others were up in arms and the newspapers were full of it. I couldn't have bought the publicity they gave me for nothing!

It wasn't the only time I got into trouble with the Board over one of my promotions. They also got upset once because I started having some of the ring card girls at our shows dressed in skimpy outfits. The punters seemed to love it and I got a lot of publicity because of it as well.

Pazienza was a real character and a promoter's dream for that fight with Graham. He was known as the Pazmanian Devil and he'd do or say anything you wanted to help the show, but he really was one of the wildest fighters I've ever met. Before the actual contest he came over to Britain to start promoting the fight and was out every night drinking and looking for women. He had some outrageous stories including one about a six-in-a-bed marathon sex session. I had to try and keep him entertained, but got so legless one night that when I finally crawled home to Tracey, she refused to let me in and I had to sleep in my daughter Sophie's wendy house – good job I'm small.

On another occasion in Stringfellows nightclub I couldn't take any more booze and gave a friend, who was with us, £200 to look after him for the rest of the evening. The next day I was told the money lasted about ten minutes as Vinnie got some of the club's girls to dance in front of them and peeled off notes like there was no tomorrow.

By the end of the week I was exhausted and asked one of my fighters, Patrick Mullings, if he would mind looking after Pazienza. Pat was delighted because he had a lot of respect for Vinnie and what he'd done in the ring, so I arranged for them to go to Café de Paris in London and they were shown up to the private bar there. They had some drinks and were soon joined by a couple of attractive girls that Vinnie took quite a shine to. But Patrick realised the two were transvestites and quickly told Vinnie. 'So what?' he said. 'We can still have some fun!' Poor Pat didn't quite see it that way and managed to drag Vinnie out of the bar.

The contest with Graham went well for Herol who won on points and went on to fight for the IBF title against Charles Brewer in March 1998, on the same Atlantic City bill which saw Lennox take care of Briggs with a fifth-round stoppage and a great display of punching power. Herol never quite realised his dream of becoming a world champion, and at the age of 38 he just wasn't able to come up with the goods against Brewer, losing in the tenth round. But Herol was one of the best boxers this country has ever produced and a real nice guy. It was a pleasure to work with him.

Lennox trained in Miami for the Briggs fight and it wasn't the usual camp set-up. The work got done but there was certainly a more relaxed atmosphere about things. He did his training but I remember one occasion where temptation seemed to get the better of Lennox. It wasn't girls or booze and he didn't skip camp, but he did order ice cream and apple pie. I think he started to feel a bit guilty because we suddenly all got the call to join him, and he dished out pie and ice cream to everyone.

While we were out there Sky sent a crew over to do some filming with us and their reporter Adam Smith went on a training run with Lennox one day and was really surprised by the conversation he had with him. Lennox had homes in London, Jamaica and Canada. He also had a home in Miami and spent some time there when he wasn't in training. Adam came back and told me how Lewis had chatted to him about the nightlife and girls in the city. He seemed amazed that Lennox had opened up but I think it was just another indication of how relaxed he was about the whole training camp. It didn't surprise me too much, because I knew that Lennox had partied with Glenn McCrory in Miami on occasions.

It was while the Sky people were with us that we nearly had a nasty accident. They wanted to film us on a boat and one of the crew was given the job of setting the whole thing up. I think he must have gone out and got the cheapest thing he could find. It didn't take too long before we started shipping water and the boat began to sink. Everyone fell about laughing but I accused Adam and the rest of his mates of trying to kill the heavyweight champion of the world!

It was after the Briggs fight that I got my first look at a drug everyone was talking about – Viagra. A well known American fight character called Johnny Bos had some on him one day but I resisted the temptation to experiment before curiosity got the better of me a month later in London when I was given two of them by someone.

I kept them wrapped in foil for a while and then after taking Tracey out for a meal and having a couple of glasses of champagne I went off to the toilet and swallowed a tablet. By the time we got home the front of my trousers was like a tent and I couldn't wait to get my hands on Tracey. It was incredible and in the end she sent me into the spare room because I kept pestering her. I was still affected by the tablet in the morning and at one point Tracey actually started whacking a certain excited part of my anatomy with her hairbrush. When the effects of the drug had subsided, so to speak, I was left with a terrible headache and a painful left eye.

Most people would probably have kept quiet about the whole incident, or at least only told their closest friends what had gone on, but I was slightly different. For some years now I've written a weekly column for the *Sport* newspaper, and I decided to tell all to them. My Viagra story was splashed over one of the pages in the paper and to cap it all they even printed a picture of Tracey and me taken on our wedding day. Not surprisingly she hit the roof when she found out and it took days before she calmed down enough to even speak to me.

The ironic thing was I would probably have got away without her ever realising I'd said anything to the newspaper, because Tracey never read the *Sport*. But her gay hairdresser was obviously a keen reader and just happened to ask her if I could help him get hold of some Viagra for him and his boyfriend!

There are three things I remember most from the Mavrovic fight. The first was a change in training camp personnel, the second was how exhausted Lennox was at the end of the contest, and the third was actually being banned from the gym by him during the build-up.

As usual I went out to take a look at how things were going in camp up at Big Bear in the California mountains and it seemed pretty clear there was a bit of a problem between Lennox and Manny. To put it plainly, they just didn't seem to be on the same wavelength, and Lewis wasn't exactly in the best of spirits as he went about his work. But it was still a shock one day when Courtney came to see me and said the 'Champ' wanted me barred from all training sessions.

'Well, you can tell the Champ he can go fuck himself,' I told Courtney. 'He can tell me himself if that's the way he feels.'

Courtney said that Lennox felt I'd interfered and said things about the way he was training. He said I wasn't his trainer, I was the manager and I should stick to doing that job.

'Let him come and tell me,' I said, still shocked by what I'd heard. 'But if that's the case I'll be on the next plane home.'

I couldn't believe it and when I telephoned Panos to tell him he suggested I stayed calm and insisted I shouldn't do anything rash that I might end up regretting. For the next couple of days I couldn't stop thinking about what had gone on and I felt really hurt about the whole episode. But I calmed down enough to keep out of Lennox's way and respect his wishes. If he didn't want me there, I would stay away.

About four days later I decided enough was enough and went to see Lennox to sort the whole thing out and clear the air. We had a good chat and it was obvious he wasn't feeling good about the way training was going. I suggested that I should just go to the gym, stay quiet and make notes. Then after the Mavrovic fight was over I'd go through everything with him and review the way the training and the camp had gone. Lennox agreed and I think he felt better that we'd had a chat. In fact, my relationship with him after our talk was very good and I think he realised that all I ever tried to do was make sure things went well for him.

The change in personnel came in the form of Lennox's old amateur trainer Adrian Teodorescu. The move clearly didn't please Manny too much, but Lennox brought Adrian in and there wasn't too much he could do about it. It made me wonder about Manny's relationship with Lennox if he thought he needed someone like Adrian in the camp. Adrian was a nice guy but very much into being a strict disciplinarian. I also thought he made Lennox work too hard on occasions. Lewis would often train with Adrian in the morning and then with Manny in the afternoons. Adrian paid a lot of attention to fitness and physical preparation and on that front there was another newcomer to the camp named Joe Dunbar.

Joe is a sports physiologist and had worked with several of my other fighters. Courtney Shand knew about him and to his credit suggested it might be a good idea if Joe did some work with Lennox. Unlike Manny, I think the prospect of somebody coming in who did a similar job didn't seem to worry Courtney. He has always been tremendously loyal to Lennox and in his mind he was doing the best for the guy we were all there working for – Lennox Lewis.

The Mavrovic fight went the distance as Lennox retained his title in Connecticut on 26 September in a tented arena. But after the fight as we went to walk out of the ring he told me to stay by his side, and he suddenly began to hold on to me. It was soon clear that his legs had almost given out on him and he looked really tired when we finally got him back into the dressing-room. Lennox had to do a lot of work in the fight and when I spoke to Joe he wondered whether Lewis had come down from Big Bear too late to benefit from the training he'd done at altitude.

14. COURTED BY THE DON

WHEN LENNOX STEPPED INTO THE RING AGAINST EVANDER HOLYFIELD AT Madison Square Garden on 13 March 1999 for the undisputed heavyweight championship of the world, it was the end result of a process that had been started more than a year earlier.

Even before the fights with Briggs and Mavrovic, negotiations for a contest with Holyfield had taken place. As Evander's promoter, Don King was in the thick of it along with our promotional company, Panix, Main Events and Jim Thomas, who was Holyfield's attorney and adviser.

In December 1997 we met at King's offices in Florida to try and finalise our side of the contract that would see Lennox and Holyfield meet for the undisputed world heavyweight title. A little over a month earlier Evander had added yet another chapter to his amazing story when he beat Michael Moorer and claimed the IBF title to add to the WBA version he already held.

I went to Florida knowing that if any deal was going to be done I had to get agreement for a $10 million guarantee for Lennox because that was the figure we had talked about. The idea was that if that could be done we could give our agreement to the fight, and King would then try to sort things out with Holyfield before taking the whole package to HBO.

There was already a bit of friction between Panos and Dino Duva because having started to talk to King about the possibility of a fight with Holyfield, Panos hadn't exactly fully included Main Events, and I'd noticed that their name was actually missing from one of the early contract drafts that were faxed between King's office in Florida and our own in London.

The negotiations were heated at times, but mainly between Panos and Main Events. At one stage King suggested we sort things out between us while he and his lawyers left the room. It was such a crazy situation and because none of us really trusted King, we decided not to use the office in case we were overheard and Patrick English suggested we all went outside to carry on the discussions. I think Don was amused by the whole thing and all the petty arguing that was going on. He didn't really care so long as he got a deal, but I can remember making eye contact with him during all of this while the others were talking and arguing among themselves. King leaned back in his chair smiling and with his right hand made a gesture to let me know how he felt about it all. He clearly thought they were all acting like a bunch of wankers and I could understand why he did.

The other thing I remember most from that day was seeing Thomas with his feet up at one point and noticing he had a hole in his shoe the size of a 50p piece. Here was the adviser and lawyer to one of the richest sportsmen on earth, and he wore a shoe with a gaping hole in it.

Eventually Main Events called it a day and left the meeting, but Panos and I stayed on and somehow managed to get an agreement. Don was obviously pleased to have at last made some progress on the deal and the next day he invited us to his house for a barbecue. When we got there King told us we'd be surprised at who the chef was going to be, but despite the fact that he was Lennox's trainer it was no real surprise to see Manny Steward turn up and cook food for everyone, as he often sang Don's praises to us. King's house was amazing and he also had a guest cottage in the grounds that was bigger than most people's homes. Manny told us how Don let him stay in the guest accommodation whenever he was in town, and then

King showed us around the main house. I have to say it was magnificent and tastefully decorated. The rooms were huge and he had a bath that was bigger than my lounge at home. Don told us the furniture and all the decorating ideas were down to his wife who wasn't around that afternoon.

'That's her,' said King, pointing to a picture on the wall of a woman shaking hands with President Clinton. One of the people who worked for King then told us that the President had wanted Don to have dinner with him that weekend.

'That's right,' boomed Don. 'I said I can't have dinner with you, Mr President. I'm having dinner with my friends from England. Panos and Frank are flying in! I must get my priorities right. Doing a deal with my new partners is more important than having dinner with the President of the United States.'

It was all good stuff and only King could have come out with a crack like that. He even managed to have a word with Tracey that afternoon when I phoned to let her know what flight we were catching. Once again Don was at the top of his game, laying it on thick as he grabbed the phone off of me. 'You beautiful, beautiful woman,' he said as his voice got louder and louder. 'You're going to have riches beyond your dreams now that little Frankie and I are partners.'

Tracey took it all with a pinch of salt but it was just another example of the way King operates and the fact that once he's in his stride, there is nothing on earth that can stop him. If there was an Olympic event for talking, he would have won gold many times over.

After a dash to Miami airport in one of King's Bentleys, Panos spotted Mike Tyson at a check-in desk and decided to march over and introduce himself. He told him he represented Lennox Lewis and he'd just sorted out his part of the contract for a fight with Holyfield. 'Beat him up for me,' said Tyson, who didn't know who the hell Panos was, and probably thought he was dealing with some crazy English guy who'd had too much Florida sun.

You can never be sure of anything in boxing and on Christmas Eve I had a call from King saying the fight couldn't be made because HBO didn't want to pay the numbers. Of course one of those numbers could have been the money King wanted out of the deal. But it didn't stop him phoning again the next day to wish me and my family a Happy Christmas. He was on the speaker phone for ages and little Sophie seemed fascinated by this continuous noise that was coming out as he carried on talking and laughing all the way from the States.

The deal may not have been done at that stage but the new found friendship between us began to bear fruit in other ways. Panos obviously liked the idea of dealing with King and I think he got a kick out of it. He used to like telling the press how he dealt with King and made it sound as if he always had the upper hand in negotiations with Don.

'I meet the Don Kings of this world every day in liquidations,' he claimed in one interview. 'They're very clever people. But you don't give in. In our negotiations Don can be very strong for five hours but once he realises he can't get past you he gets tired very quickly, and you can get your way. He doesn't know my weaknesses, he can't manipulate me, that's why we do a deal.'

One deal that started to excite Panos in February 1998 was the possibility of forming a company with Don called Kingpan. There were quite a few draft agreements and proposals which went backwards and forwards across the Atlantic, but although King was keen on getting another partner in Britain after splitting up with Frank Warren, a company was never actually formed. But we started to have a lot more to do with King and it seemed like I was talking to him virtually every day, and through him we were able to put some decent fights together.

As well as the Briggs and Brewer world title fights in Atlantic City, we also staged a big show in Hull on the same night as part of a pay-per-view event for Sky, which featured two world title contests involving British boxers. Unfortunately, both of them lost the IBF fights, with Paul Lloyd being beaten in two rounds by Tim Austin at bantamweight and Terry Dunstan losing out in the 11th round against Imamu Mayfield at cruiserweight.

As part of the build-up to the shows Sky wanted to do an interview with King and I arranged it for them. But by this time there were stories all over the sports pages about King having a bust-up with Tyson in a hotel car park and it looked as though their relationship was rocky to say the least.

'I'll do the interview for you, Frankie, but I'm not talking about Tyson,' Don told me. Of course, as soon as he got the opportunity Sky's Paul Dempsey started asking about Tyson, and King had to fend him off as he tried to stick to other matters.

'They tricked us, Frankie,' said Don when I spoke to him later that day. 'They kept asking about Tyson, but I did all right. Tyson's a silly young man who spends money like water, but there's no money coming in at the moment. All my enemies are out to get me and they're saying bad things about me in the press, but at least I have my friends in England like you and Panos.'

Panos and I were on pretty friendly terms with King at the time. At the 1997 WBC convention in Torremolinos we'd had some fun with him after Don hit town with his party. We went out one evening with King in great form as he joined in the flamenco dancing on stage, twirling around with his hands holding dollars instead of the fans the girls used. At one point he actually fell over and seemed to bounce straight up again, still holding the dollars in his hands before dishing them out to the dancers and thanking them for letting him join in.

At the end of the evening we went back with King to his room and both Panos and I thought he looked exhausted as he went into his bedroom. But before too long he'd emerged dragging a huge case. When he opened it we saw that it was full of books. It seemed to be packed with biographies and works by philosophers. For more than four hours we sat there while Don talked and quoted us sections from the books. By the end of it all he was wide awake and we were the ones who were exhausted.

If there's one thing I've learned over the years about King it's that he's relentless when he wants something. It doesn't matter to Don if he gets knocked back a few times, he just keeps going in the belief that he will eventually get what he wants. It may take days, weeks, months or years, but he doesn't give up, even though anyone else would consider it a lost cause. Whatever you think of King, nobody can deny he's a very intelligent man who is prepared to work 24 hours a day. Making deals is like food and drink to Don, and that was why I always thought a fight with Holyfield was a possibility somewhere down the line.

What I hadn't bargained for was the fact that as well as getting Lennox's signature on the dotted line for a contest with Evander, it was also King's intention to get me to sign a deal with him.

Although the possibility of a fight with Holyfield had been hanging in the air for a while, nothing had been agreed or signed and we were looking at either Lou Savarese or Moorer as possible opponents for Lennox's next defence if nothing could be done with Evander. In the first week of October I got a call from Don Majeski telling me that Don King wanted to see me in New York. By this time I knew that King was thinking of making me an offer he hoped I couldn't refuse.

The subject of working for him had started to come about as we spoke to each other regularly over the previous months. As I've said, King had started to talk to us at the back end of the previous year when we'd tried to negotiate a Holyfield fight. We continued to work together on other things and although Don had cooled a bit in his relationship with Panos, he was friendlier than ever with me. I'm not kidding myself, because I know that as usual King was probably looking at the bigger picture. He wanted to stage Holyfield–Lewis, and I knew he had tried for years to win Lennox over, so maybe he saw me as a route to doing just that. Over the years of dealing with King I have seen Don use his flattery on other people in the Lewis camp as well. He was always very nice to Violet Blake, and as well as obviously being on friendly terms with Manny, he also seemed to get on well with Prince, a member of the Lewis team who was involved in merchandising.

At that time, for whatever reason, I was suddenly in the position of being courted by him and I couldn't help being curious about exactly what he was going to offer. Panos knew I was going to see him and the other reason for flying to the States was to try and move a fight with Holyfield further along the road. In fact, I got the impression that Panos wouldn't have minded me joining King because that would probably have put me out of the picture with Lennox.

The trip got off to a bad start because when I got on the plane there seemed to be half of Frank Warren's office staff on the same flight going to America on business and I obviously didn't want to let them know what I was doing, and then Majeski phoned me in New

York to say King wasn't going to be there and instead asked if I could fly down to his office in Florida. When I eventually met him the next day, he was his usual self.

'Hey, it's Frankie, my new associate from England,' said Don as he burst into the room followed by a couple of his lawyers. It didn't take long for him to get down to business and ask me how much I was being paid at Panix Promotions. When I told him what it was he said he'd double it and before I knew where I was it began to sound like I was already a general in King's army. The figure on offer to me that was quoted in the English press was £250,000, but in actual fact it was lower than that. He wanted me to sign some form of agreement there and then, but despite all the flattery and the speed at which everything had happened, I managed to interrupt him long enough to say I wanted my lawyer to see any proposal before I made a decision. King said that if I did work for him I wouldn't just be leaving Panix, it would probably also mean my time with Lennox would be up as well. It was a possibility that had also crossed my mind and I knew I had a lot of hard thinking to do. I had a lot of loyalty towards Lennox and wanted to be there when he fought Holyfield.

When I got back to England I took King's proposal to my lawyer, Bernard Clarke, to look over and left it with him. My head was buzzing with what was going on and that evening I phoned Lennox's mum, Violet, to let her know about my meeting with King because I didn't want her reading all about it in the papers and getting the wrong impression. As far as I was concerned, I wasn't being disloyal to Lennox in any way, all I was doing was listening to an offer that had been made to me, just as anyone else in their right mind would do.

Panos was quite happy for me to keep talking to King because he knew we were edging towards getting a deal done for the Holyfield fight. He also had another reason for not wanting to deal too closely with King. During the week of the Mavrovic fight Panos had called me to one side and said he had something to tell me. He told me that for some time he'd been having talks with some black Muslims, who claimed they were some of Tyson's closest aides, about the possibility of Mike being handled by Panix and because of that he didn't particularly want to have too much to do with King.

The weekend after my trip to the States, King went to France where he had a couple of fighters boxing, and the plan was for him to stop over in London to see if we could thrash out an agreement for Lennox to fight Holyfield. Don phoned to say he'd be coming in on Eurostar and could I meet him at Waterloo Station in London. When he stepped off the train King looked quite subdued and tired, but once he went through the doors and saw some photographers and press waiting for him, he was a changed man. Suddenly he was the Don King everyone knew. The cigar was out, he started making victory 'V' signs with his hand and with that unmistakable voice of his began quoting Churchill. Within seconds he'd attracted the kind of attention only film or pop stars get, and I don't think the famous old station had ever seen anything like it. King is a born showman – give him a crowd and he'll perform.

We went straight into a meeting with Panos to try and negotiate the Holyfield deal, and about six hours later we had something agreed in principle. At one point King screamed at Panos over some points and told him he didn't want options on Lennox's next fights, all he wanted was a re-match clause or the first mandatory defence of the WBA belt which was against Akinwande, and if that didn't happen then Lennox would have to give up the belt.

'All I want, Panos, is him!' said King pointing to me. 'I'm taking him with me. That's part of the deal.' King then went on to accuse Panos of betraying him and doing deals with Dino Duva and HBO. It was the usual sort of verbal blast you expected from Don at some time during any negotiation, but I also knew from my conversations with King that he wasn't exactly an Eliades fan so he focused his attention on me and Dennis Lewis who was also in on the negotiations. I think Don had a lack of respect for Panos because he saw him as someone who didn't really know the boxing business. We celebrated the deal with a massive meal that both Panos and King got stuck into. If there was one thing at which Panos was Don's equal, it was his food intake.

Don flew back to the States ready to get to work on promoting the fight which would unify the heavyweight championship, leaving me with a heavyweight decision of my own to make. Should I stay, or should I go?

15. A BUM DEAL

IT WAS STRANGE TO THINK THAT ONLY FIVE YEARS EARLIER KING HAD CALLED me a mental midget and now he wanted me to work with him.

I knew that the name-calling back then was just part of the hype that goes on in the sport, and it had actually helped to put me on the boxing map in a funny sort of way. It was another example of how things change in boxing. Your enemy one day can be your best friend the next.

To be perfectly honest, having King phoning all the time to try and pressurise me into making a decision was something I could have done without. Of course it was flattering and it also gave me a genuine job option, but the fact was I wanted to concentrate on making sure Lennox actually got a crack at Holyfield. We all have egos and ambition. I wanted to be the manager of the undisputed heavyweight champion of the world.

I managed to avoid Don for a while but then got a call on my mobile while I was in Jersey for an amateur boxing show. He started having a go at Panos and telling me how he could offer me so much if I went to work for him and then he suggested meeting up. 'I hear you're in Jersey,' he said. 'That's perfect, why don't you fly down to me or I'll fly up to you and we can have dinner.' When I explained that I wasn't in New Jersey, but on an island near France, it didn't put him off his stride at all. He just kept pummelling my ear with his usual non-stop talk. 'It sounds like a beautiful island and I want to visit there some day,' he told me, even though he didn't have a clue what it was like.

The Holyfield deal was moving on and both Panos and I knew we had to keep at it in order to make sure nothing went wrong. We flew to New York for another meeting and left thinking everything had been sorted out, but then there was a hitch over the guarantee for Lennox, with King claiming HBO did not want to cover the full $9.5 million, so Don was talking of a cut to $7.5 million. To be fair to Panos, and Main Events, they worked hard to make sure King eventually did guarantee the other $2 million by getting him to agree to a letter of credit to be put in place on 1 March.

With the fight date set for 13 March at Madison Square Garden it was important to get the publicity bandwagon moving as quickly as possible, and King organised press conferences at the Garden and then across America. We travelled in style on a private Boeing 737 jet that the New York Nicks basketball team used. As usual King was in his element and as we were waiting at the Garden for the press conference to start Don looked across at Lennox.

'Hey, the invisible champ,' he said. 'Lennox Lewis, your time has come. You're going to learn to love me. I'm going to grow on you, my brother. You'll learn to want me.' It was all done tongue-in-cheek, but at the same time I couldn't help feeling King was still hanging in there in the hope that sooner or later he would win Lennox over.

He also claimed that he was the only promoter who could have put the show together. 'Who else could sell a black guy with dreadlocks who plays chess?' he asked me, referring to Lennox, and I had to admit that the more I saw of him and the way he worked, the more you had to agree that he was a master promoter. It was all about selling, all about hype and nobody did it better than King.

A new addition to the team for the press tour was Adrian Ogun, who was by this time working closely with Lennox's brother Dennis on commercial matters. I had always got on well with Dennis since he appeared way back in the Levitt days. Roger didn't seem too sure about his involvement then and it was rumoured Levitt used to tape his phone calls without his knowledge, something I only found out about after the collapse of the Group. Although Violet was Dennis's mum, he had a different father to Lennox, a man named Rupert Daries, who had once worked as a masseur to Frank Bruno and who was around when Lennox fought for the world title in Cardiff. When I first met Dennis he shared the same surname as his father, but later decided to legally change it to Lewis.

As we set off on the press tour Dennis was not in the happiest of moods because of a clothing sponsorship deal with French Connection UK, or FCUK as the label said on their products. Dennis hadn't actually done the deal and found out about it very late on. Panos had concluded the deal because he knew the guy who owned the company, but the whole thing had been set up by a marketing guru named Trevor Beattie. The thing had been on-going with a couple of guys Panos had brought in to his office doing the early ground work. But when Dennis found out he went mad, claiming that procedures he'd laid down had not been followed properly. Then he accused Panos of not showing him respect.

It was an amazing outburst by Dennis and whatever the rights and wrongs of it I was just pleased I had nothing to do with any of it. This whole thing had happened before we set out for the States but Dennis's anger was still simmering below the surface. He called me over when we boarded the plane to start the press tour and began going on about the run-in with Panos again. I think he just wanted me to see everything his way, but I obviously didn't give him the answers he wanted because I soon found myself being grabbed by the neck by him and he looked as though he was going to thump me. I couldn't believe what was happening and didn't understand why Dennis was having a go at me. The next day he was as nice as could be and later back in London he apologised to me, but as far as I was concerned it was another indication of the way things were changing in the Lewis team.

It wasn't the same happy, close-knit group we had been a few years earlier and if I was honest with myself, I'd reached the point where I didn't have the same kind of enthusiasm for the job. I still did it to the best of my ability, and despite all the stuff that was going on with

King, there was no way Lennox could have questioned my loyalty. It was just that I had an uneasy feeling about certain things. Like it or not, Dennis had changed in many ways, and then there was Adrian Ogun. Very smooth, very charming, but he had the ability to make me feel uncomfortable. Adrian was ambitious and very driven. He had obviously been desperate to get involved with the Lewis team all those years ago when I'd been introduced to him at York Hall. By the time we started the press tour, people were asking me who he was and what his job was in the organisation.

Having got the press tour out of the way it was important for Lennox to settle down to his training in the Poconos. As usual I planned to flit between the camp and England during the build-up, but before I paid my first visit King travelled to England for a court case he was involved in against Frank Warren. Although they had enjoyed a good partnership, Frank and Don had split by this time and were going through the courts to settle their dispute, but while he was over King also did a deal with my help for Talk Sport radio to cover the Holyfield–Lewis fight, breaking the stronghold that BBC radio had on boxing. He also took the opportunity to put more pressure on me to sign with him.

My lawyer Bernard Clarke and I had a meeting with Don and his two American lawyers, Charles Lomax and John Worth, but nothing was signed and the night ended on a hilarious note with King and his party causing uproar in a Knightsbridge restaurant as they stood around their table and sang the American national anthem at the top of their voices. King also did some TV and press work while he was over, each time mentioning how great it was going to be having me working with him. Considering nothing had actually been signed it was all a bit premature to say the least, and I'd already told him that I wanted to get the Holyfield fight out of the way first before making any decisions.

When I went to camp I was pleased to see that everything seemed to be running smoothly. Lennox was relaxed and Manny seemed a lot more focused. Adrian Teodorescu was still part of the team, but this time he was little more than an onlooker.

The FCUK gear caused a bit of a stir at the resort and I was actually asked to go and see the manager one day because he said there had been complaints from some of the guests about Lennox and his team wearing labels on their gear which said FUCK. When I pointed out that it stood for French Connection UK and was spelt FCUK he burst out laughing and apologised. But he obviously wasn't the only one who thought it looked a bit too much like another four letter word because New York taxis were actually stopped from advertising the company on their cabs.

Later on in the training programme Lennox made it clear he wasn't happy with some of the sparring. Since losing to McCall, Lewis liked to vet the sparring partners he had and it could often make things a bit awkward. It was important everything was right for the build-up to such a big fight and we changed things, including bringing in Jeremy Williams for the last three and a half weeks of camp at a cost of $10,000. Apart from Lennox training in the Poconos, I also flew my featherweight, Paul Ingle, out to the camp for a while as part of his preparation for a world title challenge against Naseem Hamed that had been set for 10 April in Manchester.

While we were in the Poconos Colin Hart came out to do a piece for *The Sun* with Lennox. He spent some time at the camp and then did an interview with him. I've had my ups and downs with Harty over the years, including some heated rows like the one in Las Vegas before the McCall fight. But I've always had respect for him as a boxing man. When I have disagreed with him it has usually been because I've been defending Lennox or one of my other fighters. Colin is never short of a word or two and always seems to have a story to tell, so I quite liked having him around for a few days to help break up some of the boredom that always sets in during training camp.

Colin did his interview with Lennox and told me it had gone very well. He said Lennox had talked openly about his sexuality and denied the gay rumours that had been circulating for some time. Then in typical Harty fashion he said, 'Mind you, Frank, it wouldn't bother me whether he was gay or not, so long as he can fight!'

Colin flew back to England pleased with his story, but a few days later all hell broke loose when I discovered what his paper had done with the piece. As I've said, rumours about Lennox had been around for a while and during the course of his interview Colin Hart had actually made just that point.

'You mean the ones about me being gay?' said Lewis. And then Lennox went on to tell Colin, 'I must say I find it comical. But let us put the silly rumours to rest once and for all. I'm certainly not gay. I love and adore women. I date girls and do not date boys.'

That should have been that and the story itself was fine but the thing that really upset me and the rest of the training camp team was the fact that alongside it was a panel saying if you have been a girlfriend of Lennox or been out with him, let the paper know about it. Something like that gave any nutcase the chance to have a go.

I immediately sent a letter to the *Sun's* Sports Editor, Paul Ridley, letting him know in no uncertain terms how upset I was by what had gone on. I knew that although it was Colin's story he had no control over headlines or the fact that they'd decided to stick the panel alongside the article.

Ridley obviously realised how upset I was and sent me a fax:

> Dear Frank. If we trapped a nerve with you and Lennox then I apologise. Colin assures me Lennox was comfortable with the piece, and was happy to put the rumours to the sword. The invitation to former girlfriends may have been a bit O.T.T. I can assure you we will not pursue it.

To be fair to Lennox he just laughed the whole thing off, but it wasn't the first time I'd had to deal with such a rumour and it wasn't to be the last. In fact, I had once found out about a Sunday newspaper's intention to investigate a story that I was supplying rent boys to Lennox. I knew the whole thing was ridiculous because I had done no such thing. But when I found out about it I could see they were seriously thinking of doing a story. I actually did a bit of undercover work myself, taping the reporter in conversation as he tried to set the whole thing up with my driver, Eric Guy, even offering to pay him for his help. In the end nothing came of it but it just showed the lengths to which some papers would go to get a story, even if there was no story there in the first place, and I let Dennis, Adrian and Panos know about it as well at one of our weekly meetings.

I felt a bit sorry for Colin Hart because he'd just been doing his job and he had the guts to ask Lennox directly about all the rumours and give Lewis the opportunity to deny them. I heard some years later that at the *Sun's* annual Christmas do in 1999 Colin was given a framed copy of the article for his efforts in getting the story with a caption on it saying 'Bottle of the Year!'

There was some needle creeping in towards the end of the camp with Williams, who was a genuinely funny man out of the ring, trying to take a few liberties during sparring with Lennox. On one occasion he seemed to pull Lennox to the floor and when Lewis tried to get his revenge by tripping Jeremy, Williams just flipped him over. Apparently one of Jeremy's other talents was martial arts, and he'd used Lennox's own weight to make sure he tumbled to the ground. Lennox actually did get his own back on Williams with some vicious shots once they continued using more orthodox boxing methods.

Manny, who had once worked with Holyfield, was very upbeat and confident about the prospect of facing Evander, and he told me he thought it was a very easy fight for Lennox if he did things right on the night. 'He's got to go in there and dominate with his jab,' he said. 'He's got to make sure he dominates Evander from the word go.'

Although I'd felt a little bit disillusioned at the start of the build-up for the Holyfield–Lewis fight, it was mainly due to the internal politics of our own Panix organisation. The fight itself was something I'd dreamed of for years, and it was my chance to be the manager of the undisputed heavyweight champion of the world. If Lennox won I knew that what ever else happened, I'd made my own little bit of boxing history. Despite the fact that I'd been involved at world level for ten years, I still felt the need to prove myself. So when I arrived in New York for the final week of the fight build-up, I was as excited as I'd ever been. I've always loved the city and to be right at the centre of such a huge sporting event was a bit special.

I was determined to enjoy every minute of it and with so many British supporters out there the place seemed to have even more of a buzz than usual. Tracey flew out with Sophie and we stayed in the New York Palace along with the rest of the Lewis team, unlike the last time he'd fought in the city against Mercer. Then the camp was split between two hotels; the plush New York Palace where Lennox and some of the other members of the team stayed and the more downmarket Southgate Towers.

NO BALONEY

On the Wednesday before the fight Vince Heckman and his wife flew out and brought my Union Jack suit with them. We'd pulled a bit of a publicity stunt during the time I was in camp by saying that I'd lost the suit. Sky had a designer one made for me which cost around £1,500, and I was happy to wear it for a time, but there was no way I was going to have anything other than the original for the fight, and Vince was under strict instructions to make sure he brought it with him.

The next night I took the press out to a steak restaurant and King came along too. Once again he talked about me going to work for him, and I had to play the whole thing down. After the meal I suggested to Tracey, Vince and his wife Eileen that we went to a club and we ended up in a table top dancing place called Scores. Once again there seemed to be Brits everywhere and they all wanted to talk about the fight. We even got invited into the VIP section of the club where Rod Stewart was sitting with some very pretty blonde girls. Although we didn't know each other, Rod greeted me like a long lost friend and immediately started asking me how I thought the fight would go. He even suggested we could go for a party back at his hotel. We didn't go but it was good of him to ask and the evening was just the sort of thing to help you unwind a bit before such a big event, even though it was spoiled by the fact that I somehow managed to lose my wallet and credit cards during the course of the night, and spent most of the next morning trying to put a stop on them.

If discovering I'd lost the cards was a shock on the Friday, it was nothing compared to what hit me 24 hours later on the morning of the fight. I got an early call from a reporter who was in New York to cover the contest for a Sunday newspaper back in England.

'Frank, I'm phoning about a story the office have got hold of in London,' he said. 'Apparently you've been sacked!'

At first I couldn't quite take in what he'd said. It was clear from the way he said it that he was serious, but the words made no sense to me.

'What are you talking about?' I asked him.

'It's Panos,' he said. 'He went on TV last night and basically said that you're out as of today, and the worst part of it is that the interview was recorded last month.'

A BUM DEAL

When I heard what he said I was in shock and my mind was racing. I asked him to tell me exactly what the story was and he read the Press Association release to me as I listened on the other end of the phone.

> Lennox Lewis will wake up to rumours of a split in his camp today, just hours before he bids to become undisputed world heavyweight champion against Evander Holyfield in New York. Lewis's promoter Panos Eliades launched an astonishing verbal assault on the fighter's manager, Frank Maloney, in an interview which was broadcast last night on LWT's *Nightlife* programme. In the interview, which was recorded last month at Highbury prior to the Arsenal v Sheffield United FA Cup match, Eliades suggests Maloney will be 'out' as soon as Lewis's fight with Holyfield is over. Eliades, clearly aware that he was being filmed and that the feature was due to be shown last night and speaking in the presence of Lewis's brother Dennis, said: 'Don't even start about Frank Maloney. He's out, he's out. If this is showing on 12 March, Frank better not be watching this, because he'll be out on 13 March.'

After hearing what he said I felt numb and then very angry. I tried to call Panos in his room, but he'd put a block on calls getting through to him. I told Tracey what had happened and then stormed out of the room to go and see Eliades. I couldn't believe what was going on and at that point I felt like smashing my fist into his face. Luckily, by the time I'd got to his room I even managed to surprise myself by the way I stayed in control. After my thumping on his door, Panos eventually answered it in his underpants and could clearly see I wasn't happy.

'What's wrong?' he asked.

'Panos, if you want me to go just tell me,' I replied.

When I explained what had happened he denied all knowledge of it. I actually went and got a copy of the story to show him, but he still claimed he didn't know anything about it. The stupid thing was that at that point I actually wanted to believe him because the alternative made me so angry and was too hurtful. I'd sweated and slaved to help get Lennox to this point and now it seemed as though some of the people closest to me in the Lewis team were plotting to get rid of me.

Panos was eventually persuaded by all the English press to give them an interview in the hotel lobby, but not before he'd told Charlie Sale from the *Daily Express* that he wasn't going to speak until he left. Things between Panos and Charlie had become personal because Sale had tracked down Panos's wife Angela, who was staying at the Plaza hotel, while Eliades and his girlfriend Rita were at the New York Palace. Just for good measure Panos had also brought Lydia, the woman who seemed to be his spiritual adviser and office manager, out to New York and she was staying at the Palace as well.

When he eventually did talk to the press Panos claimed that it wasn't true that I was going to get the boot and also seemed mystified by the whole thing. The relationship between him and me had been strained for some time, and we'd had ups and downs over the years, but I could never have expected anything to hit me like that on the morning of the fight. He tried hard to smooth the whole situation over and make fun of it, insisting everything was fine, but as I left for Madison Square Garden to check a few things out my stomach was in knots. I felt emotionally drained and it wasn't even midday.

I tried to act as normally as I could but by this time the rest of the Lewis team had heard what had gone on, and it wasn't a nice feeling. The good thing about going to the Garden was seeing all the Lewis supporters. They were in a great mood and started chanting my name when they spotted me. Whatever had happened I knew I had to put it all behind me and concentrate on what was the biggest day in Lennox's career. We'd both come a long way since we first met ten years earlier at Heathrow, and I wanted this to be a special day that we could both look back on and feel pleased with. Lennox had often used his stock phrase of 'being on a mission' as he tried to become undisputed champion. My job was to make sure he accomplished that mission against Holyfield.

With 21,000 in the Garden that night the atmosphere was electric and as usual Lennox had brought tremendous support from Britain. Fighting for the undisputed heavyweight championship of the world is the ultimate in sport as far as I'm concerned, but if Lennox was nervous he certainly didn't show it before the fight, and settled down for his normal pre-fight snooze when we got into the dressing-room. There was quietness in the room, with a sense of purpose and expectation. You tend to get to the venue at least an hour and a half or two hours before the contest is due to take place. Once you're there it's a case of everyone going about their separate routines. There's always a lot of tension and it was no different in New York. I could see and sense the fear in people's eyes. The only real exception seemed to be Lennox, who was very calm but focused.

A lot of people find it amazing that he can walk into the dressing-room before a big fight and go to sleep, but he's always done it and it must help him to prepare. Although it was such a big fight, the usual preparations had to be made. Manny got on with cutting the strips of tape that are used to bandage Lennox's hands before he puts his gloves on and Courtney checked the water bottles, while our cuts man made sure he had ice in his bucket. I've never been very good at sitting around before a fight and ended up doing my usual thing of popping in and out of the room as I chatted about anything to anyone who happened to be around.

With 15 minutes to go I changed into my Union Jack suit which always seemed to be a signal for everyone to move to the next level of preparation. It was as if we were going to war and the atmosphere changed as we all realised the moment to enter the arena was drawing close. Manny called Lennox, Courtney, Harold and me into the bathroom area away from everyone else. He told Lennox that we were his closest team and that this was going to be his moment of destiny. We all said a little prayer together and I thought it was a moving moment that Manny handled well.

There was a knock at the door calling us into the corridor for the walk to the ring, and at that point the room started to get louder. People started shouting, 'Champ, it's your party. Nobody's going to gate crash it. We've worked eight hard weeks for this. Let's go!'

As soon as we left the room we were herded into a holding area while the security people checked on who exactly was going to be walking to the ring. They seemed to have a problem with us having our usual flag-carrier taking the Union Jack into the ring. There seemed to be so many people in the entourage, half of whom I didn't recognise, and I couldn't help thinking about the time he'd made his professional debut almost ten years earlier, when there was just Lennox and three others walking to the ring at the Albert Hall.

As we stood there you could suddenly hear a tremendous roar from the British fans as they caught a glimpse of us all on the giant TV screens that were positioned in the main arena, and as we started to walk the wall of sound hit us. I've never led a team out for an FA Cup final at Wembley, but I can't believe it can be a more electric feeling than the one I experienced that night. The noise was deafening and getting to the ring was chaotic to say the least, as some of the security people seemed to try and take the flag away from the guy who was carrying it at the front of our party. We eventually managed to step between the ropes and despite Lennox being concerned that the ring was not as big as he'd wanted it, he soon settled down and began to prowl around like a lion eagerly awaiting his prey. Although I tried to look as relaxed as I could, the butterflies were shooting around in my stomach as I leaned against the ropes waiting for the usual pre-fight announcements.

It seemed to take ages before the ring was cleared and then it was just Lennox and Holyfield standing there staring at each other, both desperate to throw a punch and ease some of the tension out of their bodies, as they finally got the chance to set about the task they'd trained so hard for, by becoming the undisputed heavyweight champion of the world.

I took up my usual position in the corner and after the first few rounds I could feel my whole body start to relax as Lennox began to take control of the fight. He boxed beautifully and Holyfield never really had an answer to the jabs Lewis threw. It was a great feeling to know Lennox was boxing so well, but at the same time I couldn't help hoping that nothing would go wrong to spoil it. As the rounds progressed I had Lewis winning it easily, but as the bell sounded for the last round my stomach began to knot again. He was so close to winning, I just wanted him to make sure he did nothing silly in the final three minutes.

When it was over I breathed a sigh of relief and then a feeling of expectation took over, because I knew he'd done it. After all the ups and downs, the court cases, the sweat and the tears, he was about to be crowned king of the heavyweights. He'd got his place in history and as his manager, so had I, or at least that's what I thought. At the end of the fight I had tears in my eyes because I was so sure Lennox had won, and I even shouted across to Violet telling her he'd won. I could see from looking at Holyfield's corner that they felt their man had lost, but seconds later I knew I was wrong as confusion turned to anger.

The South African judge Stanley Christodoulou scored it for Lennox 116–113, but amazingly judge Eugenia Williams thought Holyfield had won it with a score of 115–113. Crazy as that was, the score that really knocked the stuffing out of me came from Britain's Larry O'Connell, 115–115. The contest was a draw and each champion kept his belts. The uproar that broke out after that was unbelievable. I was so angry I could hardly control myself. I grabbed Lennox and said, 'Fuck this, we've just been robbed!' I just kept shouting at anyone who could hear me to get Lennox out of the ring. He'd been robbed and even when we got back to the dressing-room he still didn't seem to be able to understand what had happened, or take in the injustice of it all. He kept asking what had happened and I told him he'd won the fight but they hadn't given it to him. It was as if we'd won the lottery and then lost the ticket. None of us could quite manage to take it all in.

As far as we were all concerned, despite the fight ending in a draw, he was now the undisputed heavyweight champion of the world. But as one American said to me, we'd been given a bum deal.

16. LENNY WON LAST NIGHT

THE IMPACT OF THE RESULT DID NOT FULLY SINK IN ON THE NIGHT OF THE fight but I soon began to realise how people felt about it.

In the press conference following the contest my emotions were running high and I said some crazy things, including the claim that even Stevie Wonder or Ray Charles could have seen that Lewis won the fight. I also said that Prime Minister Tony Blair should break off diplomatic relations with the Americans. In fact, the Americans were just as upset by what had gone on as we were. They seemed to feel ashamed about everything that had happened and New Yorkers in particular were really up in arms. The fact that King was the promoter of the show also added to the mix of it all, but as far as he was concerned the bigger the controversy the bigger the re-match. Even before the dust had settled King was thinking ahead.

Don stood up at the press conference holding court as he always did, but I was still seething and at one point I told everyone that we were leaving because I wasn't going to listen to any of his bullshit. Holyfield stood there looking as though he'd been beaten up in the street by a gang, and was clearly in pain. Lennox hardly had a mark on him, other than a couple of small cuts caused by Holyfield's head.

I think he was still in a bit of a daze after not getting the verdict he deserved, and it was obvious from the mood of the press that they felt Lewis had won as well.

When I eventually left Madison Square Garden I was still trying to come to terms with what had gone on. It was a strange feeling because although Lennox hadn't lost, it was the flattest I'd felt after one of his fights since that terrible night at Wembley against McCall. It was all such an anti-climax. I left the Garden with John Dillon, one of the English reporters who were out for the fight, and as we walked down 5th Avenue an American woman stopped to ask if I was British. There I was, still dressed in my Union Jack suit, and she came out with a question like that! For the first time all night I couldn't help laughing.

I wandered down to one of the parties that were being held after the fight, but it was all very subdued and after a couple of drinks I went back to my hotel. I'd always wanted to be the manager of the undisputed heavyweight champion of the world, and I felt the verdict that night had not only robbed Lennox, it had also robbed me.

If we needed any confirmation of the way people felt about the verdict we didn't have to wait too long. The next day the papers were full of it. It was front and back page news with headlines like, 'It Stinks' and 'Robbery'. It seemed as though everyone who was anyone had been asked what they thought including the Governor George Pataki and Mayor Rudy Giuliani.

There were plenty of people willing to scream that the fight had been a fix, especially as Williams had been appointed by the IBF, the same organisation whose boss, Bob Lee, was already under investigation by the FBI following allegations that he had accepted money from promoters and managers in return for moving fighters up the rankings. I have to say that I thought her scoring was ridiculous but although there was an eventual investigation into what had gone on, it seemed to me that she was simply not up to the job and didn't have enough experience of judging world title fights. Having said that, even a novice could have seen that Lennox hammered Holyfield in the fifth round, but somehow she'd managed to give it to Evander.

LENNY WON LAST NIGHT

The repercussions of what had happened in New York just seemed to rumble on and on. It was a massive story for days after the event. Poor Larry O'Connell really got some stick because so many people in Britain just couldn't believe he'd scored it a draw. I've known Larry for years and he's as straight as they come. He just marked the fight as he saw it at the end of each round and I think even he was surprised his scoring came out as a draw. Although he'd been robbed of the win, Lennox suddenly gained more credibility and popularity among a lot of the boxing people in the States and his general profile in America grew because of the incident. In many ways getting the controversial verdict turned out to be one of the best things that ever happened to him.

After the fight I managed to fly back on Concorde which had been chartered by a bunch of fans. The deal was that I would get a free trip back if I went on it and wore my Union Jack suit and had a chat with some of the passengers. Tracey agreed that I should take up the offer, but I did feel a bit guilty as I was ushered through at the airport and looked across to see my poor wife standing in line at another check-in with little Sophie and my mother.

The publicity rumbled on when we got back and towards the end of the month Lennox and I were invited to watch England's 3–1 European Championship win over Poland from the Royal Box at Wembley. We also got to go on the pitch and I met Sir Geoff Hurst. He's always been a hero of mine after those World Cup final goals against West Germany in 1966 so I asked for his autograph, but he joked that he should be asking for mine after all that had happened. I really enjoyed the whole experience and I think Lennox did as well, although he didn't stay until the end of the match.

There was no doubt he was in demand and he agreed to do another appearance at a music awards event and the BBC Sports Personality of the Year show. The day after the Sports Personality show, Lennox was due to attend a Boxing Writers' Club lunch in his honour, but failed to go along. It didn't go down too well and one of the writers, Ian Darke, commented, 'a sheepish-looking Frank Maloney tried to cover for him saying he had flu, but I am not sure even he believed it.'

As well as trying to get things moving on a re-match with

Holyfield, I had another world title fight to plan for, with Ingle's challenge to Hamed. Because of all the fall-out from the Holyfield contest, I wasn't able to spend as much time in Scarborough with Paul as I'd hoped. Ingle was the local hero there and had a tremendous following. He hated being away from the place and although he tolerated the trip to the Poconos as part of his build-up, you could tell he couldn't wait to get home again.

It probably didn't help matters too much when Paul and his party seemed to go missing for a couple of days and arrived in camp late. It was all down to the fact that their plane had developed trouble over the Atlantic and they had to make an emergency landing in the Azores. I think they thought they'd had it at one stage when the plane dropped several thousand feet in a matter of a few seconds.

Paul travelled to the States with his brother Dean, trainer Steve Pollard and a friend named Rocky Rowe, who is a larger-than-life character. At over 6 ft and as hard as nails, Rocky is a former marine who now owns a hotel in Scarborough and had been a supporter of Paul's since his amateur days. I loved Rocky's hotel from the moment I stepped foot inside the place. It's not swanky but just provides basic accommodation with signs on the doors of rooms warning people not to wet the bed! It was a bit of a shock to some of the boxers I took up there when they found they were staying in a room that had three or four beds in it. Things are never dull when Rocky is around and as soon as I checked in after travelling north for the Hamed build-up, he had me out on a night-long drinking session.

Just over a year earlier Rocky had caused a stir when he hosted the weigh-in for Ingle's Commonwealth featherweight title defence against Trust Ndlovu from Zimbabwe. Patrick Mullings was also on the bill in a fight with Bulgarian Martin Krastev for the IBO super-bantamweight title. Paul and Pat both won, but it was Rocky's style as the Master of Ceremonies which will always stick in my mind.

As well as being a hotel Rocky's place, The New George Inn, also has a large dance area on the ground floor and it was there that we decided to hold the weigh-in. Patrick was being billed as the gladiator and so I got John, a young lad from my office, to travel up to Scarborough with me and dressed him in a Roman gladiator's uniform. Just to add a bit of spice to the occasion, Rocky decided it would be a good idea to have him enter the room on a white horse. Everything was going well until the poor horse saw all the press lined up and the photographer's flash lights started to pop. At that moment the horse bolted, the kid who was riding him got thrown to the floor and there was chaos as everyone tried to get out of the way in case a hoof hit them in the face.

During that same trip Rocky decided it was time for a night out and took me and my press officer, James Russell, to just about every pub and club that was open. In one of the clubs there was a DJ playing music, but I could see there was something a bid odd. It turned out the guy was having a sex change and although he was dressed like a woman, there was no disguising the fact that he was pretty tall and quite muscular.

James and I eventually lost track of Rocky and we wandered off on our own. After visiting a few more bars we were heading back to the New George when we heard someone shouting out to us. We turned round to see the sex-change DJ standing in the road and he asked us if we fancied another drink. We'd both had so much by then that we decided another one wouldn't do any harm, so we followed him back to his flat.

When we got there I think both James and I thought we might have made a mistake. Our host, or hostess, produced two dirty mugs with wine in them for us to drink, and then started showing me a bunch of magazines containing information about changing your sex. After disappearing for a while the DJ came back and without batting an eyelid asked which one of us wanted a blow job.

Now we might have drunk half the alcohol Scarborough had on offer that night, but I can assure you that within a split second both James and I were stone cold sober. James's face was a picture when I told him I was pulling rank and that he'd have to get to know our new friend far better than he could ever have believed when we first saw him in the club.

When we explained that neither of us were too keen, things started to turn nasty and the DJ went into the kitchen before returning with a massive carving knife. It was at that point that he left his feminine side behind as he chased us down the stairs and out on to the street. Luckily we managed to get away without any harm coming to us, but if anyone tries to tell you what a quiet little seaside town Scarborough is, don't believe them. It can be wild.

After a few days of Rocky's hospitality in the build-up to the Hamed fight I was grateful for a break from the nightly boozing when I had to head back to London for Julius Francis's bout with highly rated heavyweight prospect, Danny Williams, who was promoted by Frank Warren. Julius was having a real purple patch in his career and at the age of 34 he had already won against another unbeaten heavyweight three months earlier, when he stopped Pele Reid in three rounds. Reid had been unbeaten in 13 fights and Danny was unbeaten in 15 contests when he stepped into the ring with Francis to challenge for the British and Commonwealth titles at the Albert Hall. Once again Julius did the business, gritting his teeth to win on points just a week before Ingle's fight in Manchester.

It was a great win and I was in a really happy mood as I travelled back to Scarborough that night in Eugene's car, but my mood soon changed when my brother told me that Panos had given my mum the sack from her job working in the Lennox Lewis College. My mother helped out there and enjoyed being involved at the place because she loved boxing and quite often there would be fighters staying, or training at the college. It seemed to be working well, but Eugene told me that she'd been told to go by Panos and my brother felt he'd been heavily influenced by the views of Lydia, the woman whom Eliades often consulted for spiritual guidance.

When Panos arrived at our hotel in Manchester on the morning of the Hamed fight I confronted him. For the second time in a matter of weeks I felt myself raging inside at what he'd done. It wasn't quite the same feeling I'd had in New York when my own sacking had been at the heart of the matter, this time I felt sickened that he could be so petty and not even bother telling me.

When I told him that I'd heard what he'd done to my mother, his excuse for not letting me know was that I'd always said I didn't want to be involved in any business to do with the college, but this was different, this concerned my own mum. He later told a journalist that he'd given my mother time off and not sacked her, but if that was the case it must have been the longest holiday ever known because she never went back. Despite all of his excuses I left him in no doubt about how I felt and how upset I was.

'Professionally I've got to work with you, Panos,' I told him. 'But I don't want anything to do with you socially. You're nothing but a control freak.' It was a phrase Dennis had used to describe Panos to me when we were on the press tour for the Holyfield fight. I suddenly began to agree with him.

I was surprised at the way I'd managed to stay so calm, but I heard that Eugene's reaction wasn't quite the same a few days later when he paid Panos a visit and exchanged a few choice words before threatening to throw Eliades through a window. Things did calm down with Panos eager to try and make it look as though everything was fine when the two emerged from his office, but as far as my brother and I were concerned Eliades had shown his true colours in a very personal way.

To make matters worse Ingle lost the title challenge against Hamed when he was stopped in the 11th round. However the defeat did no harm to his career, with the way he fought helping to establish him at world level, and seven months later Paul became a champion in his own right when he took the IBF featherweight title against Manuel Medina.

A little over a week after the Hamed fight I was in the hunt for glory again, but this time it was on the football field and not in the boxing ring. Millwall had managed to reach the final of the Auto Windscreens Shield at Wembley against Wigan. I know it wasn't exactly the FA Cup final, but it meant a lot to me and to all Millwall fans. Any supporter loves to see his club at Wembley and it gave the fans a chance to have a great day out at the famous old stadium.

I'd arranged to go with a few friends and meet up with David Byrne at the Hilton Hotel near the ground. Former Millwall heroes Neil Ruddock and Terry Hurlock were there and Ian Wright turned up and decided he wanted to come and sit with me in the middle of all the Millwall fans. It was amazing to see the reaction of the supporters as they suddenly realised who he was. Wrighty loved every minute of it and at one point was leading the singing of the famous Millwall anthem, 'No one likes us, we don't care.'

It says a lot for the sort of character he is that he had supporters eating out of his hand and chanting his name. Apart from his days at Arsenal, Ian had played for Crystal Palace and at the time of the Wigan match he was turning out for West Ham – not the most popular of clubs with Millwall fans. But he's a real south Londoner, and they loved his passion. He even ended up giving his baseball cap away to a kid who asked for his autograph, and he lived every kick of the game. Unfortunately the day didn't have a happy ending, because Wigan got a last minute winner, but I think every one of the 55,349 crowd enjoyed their day out.

I've always loved supporting Millwall and six years earlier I was a guest along with the former Labour party leader John Smith at their first match after moving to a new ground. During the course of the season I was asked whether I might be interested in staging some boxing at the ground and I mentioned this to an American TV executive. Unfortunately I picked the wrong game to try and impress him, because when I took him to see a play-off match with Derby at the New Den the locals were a bit restless with the result and there was a near riot!

Going to Wembley certainly helped me to unwind because at the time I was continually being wound-up by Panos and his antics. He might not have been aware of it but our relationship had become strained to say the least.

The business about me being sacked when I was in New York certainly didn't help matters, and even though he'd tried to brush it off as no more than a misunderstanding, the whole thing had sewn seeds of doubt in my mind about what was really going on behind my back. As I've said before, throughout my career as manager of Lennox, I always felt I had to try and prove myself in some way or other. There had been attempts to undermine me as a person and my position with Lewis, but I'd survived and could hold my head up knowing that I'd done a good job.

I'd made compromises along the way just like anyone else has to in life, but I was finding it harder to live with some of the politics that were going on at Panix Promotions in general and with the Lennox Lewis team in particular. It wasn't actually Lennox that I had a problem with, but some of the antics of those around him like Panos and Manny Steward. The fact was that I had to deal with Panos on a daily basis and I saw even more of him because he'd moved the Panix operation to his offices at Bloomsbury Square. Panos was an intelligent man and he'd achieved real success in his own field of accountancy, but I'm not sure he ever really fully understood the boxing business.

I disagreed with a lot of what went on and with the way he went about things. His ego seemed to be getting bigger by the day and the fact that he'd sacked my mother from her job at the college made things more personal. I know it might be easy to say that I should have walked away if I was so unhappy, but it wasn't that easy. What would I have walked away to?

I was the one who had found a way to sign Lennox all those years ago, and I was also the one who had played a major role in helping to make Panix Promotions what it was. Sure it was Panos's money, but even he knew that without my know-how when it came to the boxing business, the company would not have been the success it was. I'd always liked Panos and we'd got on well in the beginning, but although you expect any relationship to have its ups and downs, there seemed to be more downs than ups by this time and it started to feel as though the whole thing had run its course.

Although I hadn't exactly been bosom buddies with Frank Warren since we split and was probably seen as his main boxing rival in Britain, we'd started to have some contact during 1999, mainly due to the fact that Julius Francis had beaten a couple of his previously unbeaten heavyweights with those victories over Pele Reid and Danny Williams. Frank and I had discussed the idea of an informal arrangement that would see our two promotional companies working together on occasions. We called a press conference to announce the move and got plenty of coverage, with the papers talking about how British boxing's bitter rivals were about to start working together and at the same time wondering how long the 'marriage' would last.

On the morning of the conference Panos tried to talk me out of it and when I suggested that he ought to come along as well, he said Lennox wouldn't like the idea. Sure enough the next day Panos had a word with me to say that Lennox had told him he wasn't keen on the whole thing.

NO BALONEY

To Frank and me the move made perfectly good sense because we knew that his Sports Network company and Panix Promotions were the top dogs around. We could put together the sort of fights the public wanted to see, and it was better to work with each other than against each other. We felt it would make business sense because we would both benefit.

This was all going on at the same time we were in negotiations with Don King about a way to try and stage a re-match with Holyfield for later in the year. With all the publicity that came with the controversy over the draw in New York, Lennox was now seen as a victim on both sides of the Atlantic. Virtually everyone thought he'd won the first fight, but the fact was that it had been called a draw and because of it there was a whole heap of money still to be made out of the two boxers fighting again. If there's money and heavyweights involved you can be sure that King will be in there somewhere, and as soon as the verdict had been announced at Madison Square Garden, the little dollar signs must have been rolling in his brain. He'd made money out of the first fight and he wanted the chance to do the same again with the second.

There was the little matter of a possible indictment hanging over King, but he's not the sort of man to let that worry him, despite the fact that HBO didn't want him involved if that were to happen. Panos had also gone on the record in a TV interview with Sky saying there were major doubts about a Lewis–Holyfield re-match happening, but Don still ploughed ahead determined that he was going to be the promoter and confident he wouldn't be indicted.

King wasn't the only person being looked at by the authorities in the States and as part of an on-going FBI investigation into boxing poor old Don Majeski found himself the subject of an early morning visit by the Feds. After interviewing him it soon became clear to Don that they thought he was some kind of 'middle-man' who had possibly been used to sweeten officials with cash. They asked him if he'd ever paid officials and Majeski was completely baffled by the questioning and what they seemed to be accusing him of. He even offered to take a lie detector test to clear his name and hired a lawyer to sort things out for him when he remembered what the FBI might be talking about. At the time Lewis fought Golota, Don had helped

Panos out by paying some of the officials, but it was all innocent stuff on Majeski's part. They'd needed money for expenses which they were entitled to for working at the fight. Don had simply paid them for Panos, and it was all legal. Poor old Majeski had been looked at simply because he'd done his job, but the FBI had their teeth into the sport and, as Don said to me, 'They look at everyone in boxing as guilty until proven even more guilty!'

With nothing finalised regarding a re-match, despite King talking about a date of 13 November, we had to start thinking about possible options and one of those was meeting the unbeaten giant, American Michael Grant. Panos and I, along with Dennis Lewis, had a meeting with Grant's manager in New York just before Michael fought Lou Saverese. At one stage Panos talked about a possible promotional contract with Grant, but after seeing him in action I was pleased nothing came of it. I was also convinced that if Lennox ever met Grant it would be like taking candy from a baby for Lewis.

The American was big and looked the part, but he wasn't exactly quick and everything he did seemed to be in slow motion. Lennox watched the fight with us and walked out after four rounds as Grant went about getting another win with a really mechanical performance.

It was while we were watching one of the earlier heavyweight bouts on the same show that a smartly dressed guy in a suit came over to where we were all sitting and asked, 'Which one of you is Mr Maloney?' He turned out to be an Assistant District Attorney and he said he'd like me to talk to the DA's office about the first Holyfield fight and what went on. I told him I'd be happy to at a later date because I was due to fly home the next day, but nothing actually came of it, because I asked them to pay my fare if they wanted to see me and they quickly lost interest in having our little chat.

Things weren't quite the same for Panos. He wandered down to us at ringside saying he'd been served with a subpoena and they wanted him to come back at the end of the month to give evidence. He actually seemed quite proud of the fact, as if it was one up on what had happened to me.

That wasn't the only surprise for Panos during the trip. We were staying at the New York Palace and decided to go to a nearby restaurant. As we sat at our table a man with thinning hair who looked a little overweight wandered past us. I didn't really recognise him at first, but the large cigar and moustache soon gave him away – it was Roger Levitt.

He'd set up a business in New York with offices not far from our hotel and despite all the problems he'd had in England with the fraud charges and the collapse of his Levitt Group, he'd been trying to get back into big-time boxing with a match between Larry Holmes and George Foreman which never actually came off. We said hello to him and he nodded back without anything being said before wandering inside to the bar. But when Roger's wife Diane came past it was a different story. When Panos tried to speak to her she looked directly at him and simply said, 'I don't talk to scum.' So any thoughts Panos might have had of letting bygones be bygones went straight out the window!

I flew back to England to see Julius Francis get a win against Scott Welch, as he avenged an earlier defeat and also defended his British and Commonwealth titles. While Panos continued negotiations for a possible Holyfield fight, I spent a couple of weeks in the former Soviet State of Georgia helping one of my heavyweight prospects, Georgi Kandelaki, prepare for a contest against Kimmuel Odum. It was an amazing experience for me and I found the whole thing so different to anything else I'd done in boxing.

Kandelaki was only beginning his professional career with me and wasn't well known at all, but he was worshipped in his own country where he'd become a huge hero because of what he'd achieved as an amateur. Georgia is a very poor country, but I was treated like a king and the people were some of the friendliest you could ever wish to meet. Although there seemed a lot of poverty all around me nobody appeared to complain, and they just got on with their lives, most of the time with a smile on their faces. Kandelaki's morning runs were incredible because we regularly used to have about 100 people trailing behind, just so they could be close to their hero.

I stayed in a place called Gori which was where Kandelaki came from and was also the birthplace of Stalin. My boxing agent, Philippe Fondu, and I seemed to be the only people staying in our hotel, but one day I returned to find it surrounded by armed troops and I only managed to get to my room with the help of the manager, otherwise I wouldn't have got past the front door. I found out the reason for all the security was the fact that a high-powered minister had been entertaining some 'friends' overnight in his hotel suite. We weren't even allowed into the dining room for breakfast the next morning until he was gone, although I did have the compensation of being moved to his suite once he'd departed.

I was looked after really well in Gori and the hospitality of the people was tremendous. I used to get invited to meals that would go on for about four hours and throughout the course of them there would be almost constant toasts. I once counted 48 toasts at one particular meal before I started to feel quite ill after drinking the potent local wine.

Although Georgi was from Gori the fight with Odum was being staged in the coastal town of Batumi, and we had a six-hour drive with armed guards when we moved there to prepare for the contest. As soon as we reached the town a new set of guards took over and we were met by a heavily armed man dressed in black who was the head of security for the region.

We stayed in a tennis complex which also had a hotel facility and I noticed a heavy security presence. The reason for it was that the local Governor had a VIP guest visiting him, who turned out to be Hillary Clinton's brother. I was introduced to him and he went to the fight which was watched by about 15,000 screaming fans in the open air. Kandelaki got his win in a ring which had been specially imported from Germany at a cost of $50,000, and the next day Georgi and I were guests of the Governor, when he presented us with some gifts as souvenirs of our stay.

My whole involvement with fighters from what used to be called the Eastern Bloc came about some years earlier through Fondu. He's the sort of character that only a sport like boxing could produce. Philippe is originally from Belgium and although he's a boxing manager and agent these days, he's led a colourful life, including a stint big game hunting in Africa. He's also a qualified dentist but that job came to grief after a couple of unfortunate incidents with patients. The first was when he gave an injection to one of them and then spent so long on the phone arranging a boxing contest that by the time he went to work on the poor guy's mouth the anaesthetic had worn off. The second was when he got so carried away he actually forgot to use an injection. Not surprisingly Fondu went into boxing on a full-time basis after that.

I first met him at a boxing convention in Jamaica and then some years later I noticed him on TV in the corner of Martin Krastev, a Bulgarian who became European super-bantamweight champion. I contacted Philippe and the first time I used some of his boxers was on a show in Hull. On the day of the show I arranged for Fondu and the fighters to be picked up at the airport and driven all the way to Hull in a van. After the contests were over Philippe asked me where their hotel was and I told him there wasn't one – they were going straight back in the van. It's a wonder he ever wanted to be involved with me again, but despite some disagreements we've maintained a working relationship ever since, and I began to pay more attention to the fighters coming out of the East.

One of those who came over in 1996 caused quite a stir. We billed him as 'The Beast From The East', and it didn't take too much imagination to realise why when you saw him. He was a Russian heavyweight named Nikolai Valouev who stood over 7 ft tall and weighed in at more than 22 st. He had a chin that was wider than my shoulders.

I got some great publicity with him when the bed he had in his hotel room was too small for him, and we had the press down taking little and large type pictures of me standing on a chair next to him so that our heads were at the same height.

He fought at Battersea against a boxer from Barnsley named Neil Kirkwood, and the Beast won in the second round after stepping over the top rope when he made his ring entrance. My matchmaker Dean Powell and I had a bit of fun at the weigh-in when we told an American fighter we'd signed, named Cedric Boswell, that Valouev was the man he was going to be facing.

'I ain't fighting that motherfucker!' said Cedric as he eyed the Beast up and down.

Dealing with some of the people from Russia and the East has been a bit different for me. But even to this day I really enjoy it, which is more than could be said for one particular guy I met from Russia who introduced some fighters to me. It seemed that some of his 'associates' back home didn't approve of the business he was doing and he ended up in a hospital bed for three months after being badly beaten up and having his legs and jaw broken. He later died in hospital of a massive heart attack.

As I've said the hospitality I got in Georgia was fantastic and it's been the same in other places like Bulgaria, although in their case it didn't stop with a meal and some wine.

For a time Fondu and I co-managed a Bulgarian fighter named Tontcho Tontchev who had won a silver medal at the Atlanta Olympics in 1996. Philippe and I were invited to Bulgaria after we launched Tontchev's professional career and were entertained by a guy who was quite a big shot out there.

One evening we were taken to a restaurant in a fleet of black limos with armed guards and when we got there the place was empty except for our host and his friends. We sat down and started the meal before Fondu leaned over to me and said the guy wanted to show me something downstairs. We all trooped down to a room below and lined up against the wall were ten beautiful girls.

Philippe told me my host wanted me to pick one of them. It was obviously his way of trying to make me feel at home and there was no point in trying to decline the offer, because I got the distinct impression this man was not someone you wanted to upset. Just as I was about to leave and return to the table with my new dining companion, the guy said something else to Fondu and I waited for the translation.

'Frank,' said Philippe. 'He wants to know if you're a real man. Can't you handle more than one woman? Pick another one.'

So in order to maintain diplomatic relations I chose another girl and then sat down to finish the rest of my meal, but when it was over it wasn't only the bodyguards who got in the car with me. My host insisted that I took the two women back with me to the hotel.

I sat in the car wondering how on earth I was going to get out of the awkward situation I was in. Then I remembered the strict rules my hotel had and the way they wouldn't let anyone in who wasn't actually staying there. But when we arrived that all seemed to change, and when the hotel security approached us the two bodyguards who were with me opened their overcoats to reveal a mini arsenal hanging from the lining inside. Then they escorted us to my room and insisted the girls go inside with me.

When I closed the door I quickly explained as best I could that I was a happily married man and didn't want the kind of sexual desserts my host had obviously had in mind after the lavish meal in the restaurant. I told them they'd better go, but the girls were afraid that if they reappeared too soon they would be in trouble. So for the next hour the three of us sat on a couch watching TV and drinking a bottle of champagne that had also been provided, before I gave them $100 each and said I hoped they hadn't been offended!

The summer of 1999 wasn't all work for me and I managed to get away for a family trip to Portugal with Tracey and Sophie. By coincidence Frank Warren was out there at the same time. When he found out where I was staying Frank suggested we meet for lunch at a beach-side fish restaurant which could only be reached by walking across a bridge. After a couple of drinks we were soon talking about the old days and getting on like long lost friends.

The wine flowed, followed by white port, and by the end of the lunch neither of us could stand up properly. We even ordered a couple of cigars at the end of the meal, and neither of us smoke! We staggered back and were leaning against each other for support, singing the theme tune from the film, *Bridge over the River Kwai*. We talked about a lot of things that day but by then we were already on friendlier terms than we had been for years. We'd even had a football match between Frank's company and Panix that Lennox played in and I actually scored the winning penalty.

Needless to say I felt dreadful the day after my lunch with Frank and had a terrible hangover, but I couldn't afford to lie around in bed because although I was on holiday I was still working at trying to arrange a world title fight for Paul Ingle. I was on the phone constantly during the trip, but Tracey didn't complain, although maybe if she had I wouldn't have clocked up more than £1,000 on my mobile phone bill.

The money was worth it in the end because I got Paul his shot against IBF featherweight champion Manuel Medina, and the best thing was that I managed to secure him home advantage, because the fight was going to be staged in England. It meant paying Medina a lot of money but it gave Paul a distinct edge to fight in front of his home supporters and he also got around £70,000 for the challenge instead of the £30,000 he would have got for a European title fight against Steve Robinson.

The on-off saga of Lennox's re-match with Holyfield also ended during the summer with Panos finally agreeing a deal with King for the fight to be staged in Las Vegas on 13 November, and as part of a double-header for TV we later agreed to stage Ingle's challenge against Medina in Hull on the same night.

After all the fuss over King and the possible trouble he might get into it was ironic that Don eventually rode out the storm as he had done so many times before, and instead it was Panos who got a rude awakening one morning when the police turned up at the house of his girlfriend Rita to ask some questions as he opened the door in his pyjamas.

Panos was charged with dishonestly obtaining money for his insolvency firm and after spending a night in the cells, he was given conditional bail and then had an extra security condition of £100,000 imposed to allow him to take part in the build-up to the second Holyfield fight. Eliades was eventually cleared at Harrow Crown Court more than two years later, but at the time of his arrest King couldn't help having a pop at him.

'Even if I was to get indicted tomorrow, Panos has beaten me to it,' claimed Don. 'He's made getting indicted palatable at HBO, the TV network bankrolling Lewis and Holyfield.'

While Panos might have had his problems, my main concern was making sure everything went smoothly for Ingle and Lennox. Although Paul had done some of his early training for the Hamed fight in the Poconos, it was clear he preferred being in Yorkshire, so all of his preparations for the Medina contest were done on familiar home territory.

When I went to the States to see Lennox I got the distinct impression that all was not well in the camp. I couldn't exactly put my finger on what it was, but there just seemed to be quite a few niggling issues. The good thing was that Lennox was ploughing on with his training, even though he told me one day that he wasn't happy with some things and that there would be changes made after the Holyfield fight.

It seemed that relatively petty issues were getting to people and when Panos told me to stop some of Manny's training camp expenses because he'd gone off to help Naseem Hamed for a few days, it only added to the uneasy undercurrent around the place. I actually believed Panos was in the right to do it, but Courtney and Harold thought it was the wrong thing to do. I have to admit it certainly didn't help matters.

Panos was also in the habit of telling people to do things and claiming that it wasn't just him who wanted it done, but Lennox as well. He was always going on about how he and Lennox were partners, but from some of the things Lewis said to me it didn't always come across that way, and I think Lennox got a bit fed up at times with the way his name was being used. I also got the impression that Adrian Ogun was paying more attention to matters and playing a more prominent role. When I did speak to Lennox in camp, it sounded to me as though he wanted to take more control of everything after the Holyfield fight.

For my own part I have to admit that by this stage I was starting to take the easy way out. If I'd wanted, I could have been constantly bickering with Panos about all sorts of things, but I let them go. I just wanted to get on with my job and make sure I got the money I was entitled to. It was a strange feeling in many ways because I knew in my heart of hearts I wasn't as enthusiastic about the whole operation as I had been.

The thought of Lennox fighting for the undisputed heavyweight championship again should have had me buzzing during the build-up to it, but it wasn't until I actually got to Vegas for the final week leading up to the fight that I felt some excitement. Even then it didn't seem like the old days, and that kind of saddened me. I'd been with Lennox for ten years and had worked my arse off to get him to this point, but just as both of us were so close to realising our different dreams, I started to feel like an outsider.

It didn't help a couple of weeks before the contest to be given an ear bashing down the phone by Lennox because I'd revealed his travel plans to HBO. At one point he asked me whether I'd thought about how it might affect his security, and the fact that someone might jump out at the airport and try to stab him. I shook my head in disbelief as I listened to him, but I put it down to the fact that the fight was getting nearer and he was maybe feeling edgy.

When I got to Vegas I started to feel better about the whole thing and began to enjoy the build-up. I'd gone on record as saying that if Lennox lost I would run around Times Square naked. At one of the press conferences in the week before the fight King pulled out two little pairs of panties for me to use in case Holyfield won. To try and trump him, I suggested that if Lennox won, King should have his famous hair shaved off, but he wouldn't hear of it and instead hit me with a bet that really took the wind out of my sails.

He said he'd donate $100,000 to a charity of my choice if Lennox won and I'd have to do the same if Evander came out on top. Now although I had complete confidence in Lennox's ability to get the job done, I've always said that in heavyweight boxing anything can happen, and the thought of having to pay out that sort of money left me speechless. I had to agree to the bet but several people told me later that I went white and my mouth dropped open when King came up with his little idea. Because of the way things were later to turn out I didn't have to worry about finding the money, but my charities are still to receive the $100,000 from Don – perhaps he's been too busy!

I did have a laugh at King's expense later on in the week, although he didn't really know anything about it. At the weigh-in all the Lewis supporters started singing whenever King was talking. 'Listen to them, Frankie,' he said to me. 'Even your fellow countrymen love me.' And he started to wave back at them without really knowing what they were saying. One of the security guards eventually asked me what the chant was.

'They're actually singing "you fat bastard, you ate all the pies!"' I told him, and he burst out laughing as Don continued to smile and wave at what he thought was his new British fan club.

The day of the fight started early for me because I decided to get up at three and wander over to another hotel where they were going to show England's football match against Scotland on a big screen. The atmosphere in the hotel was amazing, with all the England fans who'd travelled to Vegas for the Lewis fight singing and chanting as if they were back on the terraces. I had a seat in the VIP section with some of the press, but decided to go down and watch the match with the other supporters. England won 2-0 and I got carried out on the shoulders of some of the fans. When I got back to my hotel I hoped it was the first part of a happy treble that day. An England win, followed by Ingle becoming a world champion, and finally Lennox getting crowned as the undisputed heavyweight king.

Because Paul was fighting in England it meant the contest was taking place in the middle of the afternoon Vegas time. I wasn't able to watch it, but I'd arranged to listen to the commentary from one of the Sky TV trucks and I have to say that it turned out to be one of the most exciting moments I've had in boxing. It was weird only being able to listen and not see anything, but it didn't stop me getting totally wound up in the whole thing. From what was being said it was clear that Paul was doing a good job and winning the fight. But just when I thought it was all going to plan, I heard them say in the very last round, 'Ingle's on the floor!' For a split second there was no way of knowing how bad the knockdown was, but he managed to recover and stay on his feet for the rest of the fight.

It was an amazing feeling to hear the judges' scores read out from 6,000 miles away in Hull and suddenly realise that Ingle was a world champion. I started jumping around in the back of the truck like a little kid. Having Paul win a world title meant so much to me. He'd been with me from the very first day he'd become a professional, and I'd guided his career knowing that I had a special fighter who was capable of reaching the top.

I thought about what it must have been like in Hull and wished I could have been there with him. It's a very special feeling for a manager when his fighter becomes a world champion, and I regretted not being there but there was nothing I could do. Just as it had done for the previous ten years, Lennox's career took priority over everything else, and all my other boxers knew that. It was just that my relationship with Ingle was special and being there to see him win would have meant so much. Instead, I had to be content with a few mumbled words down the telephone and a promise that I'd celebrate with him when I got back to England, before turning my attention to Lennox and the biggest fight of his career.

LENNY WON LAST NIGHT

There wasn't much said on the journey from the Mandalay Bay Hotel where we were staying to the Thomas and Mack arena for the fight. Once again you could feel the special atmosphere in the air that occurs whenever there is a world heavyweight title fight taking place. Lennox's dressing-room was quite subdued, but that was more to do with the fact that everyone in it felt we were there to take care of some unfinished business.

'Come on, Lennox,' I said just before he was due to leave the dressing-room. 'Make Holyfield eat your jab.' I was convinced that another performance similar to the one Lewis had produced for the first fight would see him win the contest this time. Holyfield had no real answer to Lennox's jab, and I thought it could really open things up for him. But the fight wasn't really like the first encounter. Instead Lennox chose to mix it up and make it more of a 'rough house' affair. The tactics worked for him and justice was eventually done when he was given the verdict at the end of 12 rounds.

While we waited for the verdict I walked around the ring staring out at all the faces in the crowd to catch their reaction. I remember seeing Frank Bruno sitting at ringside. He winked at me as if to say, 'He's done it, Frank', and there were a lot of other smiles and nods from people who obviously felt the same way.

It's very difficult to describe how I felt when Lennox was crowned undisputed heavyweight champion of the world that night, but probably the biggest emotion was relief. After all that had happened in the first fight, I just wanted to make sure that we weren't robbed again. There were actually a few press guys who thought Holyfield had won, but there was no way I could agree with that. Lennox had won and deserved his victory.

One of the nicest moments for me was when Lennox told me later that he'd heard me throughout the contest screaming instructions and willing him on. It meant a lot to me to know that he appreciated it, and I think he maybe realised how much him winning meant to both of us. When I hugged him after the verdict I couldn't have been happier, but there was still a bit of a hollow feeling, despite it being a special moment for both of us.

However, there was still some controversy to come after the fight when we discovered that there was a dispute over sanctioning fees with the IBF, and because of that their belt was missing. To be honest, it wouldn't have mattered if all the governing bodies had taken their belts away. The whole of the boxing world knew Lennox Lewis was the undisputed heavyweight champion, and that was what mattered. In simple boxing terms, he'd beaten the man who'd beaten the man.

It was a great moment and it was particularly nice for me because I pretty well had all my family out there with me, including my father. I'd managed to persuade him to come even though he hates getting on a plane and seems to think he should have been born with wings if he had been meant to fly.

After the fight and press conference I wandered over to the Hard Rock Café where there was a celebration party going on. It seemed a shame that a lot of the fans couldn't get in to help celebrate as well, but that's the nature of many of the after-fight parties. I only stayed for a while and had a couple of drinks, before accepting an invitation from some English guys to go to a local 'pub' and say hello to some of the supporters who had flown out for the fight. I think they were surprised to see me turn up, but it was nice to go there and mix with the punters.

After about an hour I felt mentally and physically drained. I went back to the hotel with Tracey and suddenly felt overwhelmed by everything. I thanked her for being there with me through it all and putting up with all my moods and problems. It made me realise how lucky I was to have ever found her and as we lay in bed together my mind started racing.

For ten years I'd pursued a dream. I pursued what everyone thought was impossible. A kid from the back streets of Peckham, a kid without any real education, a kid who'd hustled his way through life. Right at that moment I was at the top of the boxing world. I was manager of the ultimate sportsman, the heavyweight champion of the world.

I couldn't comprehend what it meant. I had mixed feelings. I just kept thinking about how I'd finally achieved what I set out to do and yet it began to seem like a bit of an anti-climax. There was a hollow feeling there, because rightly or wrongly, I'd felt since the first Holyfield fight that my relationship with Lennox was changing. I think there was a bit of a battle for his attention between Panos and Adrian. I just began to feel that I wasn't really part of the decision-making team as I once had been. In many ways I was more excited by Ingle's win than Lewis's. I thought about all of the in-fighting that seemed to be going on and my role in the whole set-up. I'd got where I wanted to be, but after such a long journey it didn't feel the way I thought it would. At the same time I knew that whatever else happened I'd been a part of history. I'd managed two boxers who had won world title fights on the same day on different continents.

I walked over to the window and gazed down at the neon-lit Las Vegas strip. My mind wandered back to the day I'd signed Lennox and how excited I'd been. Those early days were so different for both of us. When he'd first come back to England the Levitt Group didn't really know where he should stay until I suggested it would be a good idea to have him living close to me in Crayford. He was given a house just a few minutes away from the pub I had and must have been just about the only black guy around there at the time. It must have all seemed so strange to him, but Lennox immediately settled in and the locals really warmed to him. Kids would congregate outside his house waiting for an autograph, and he'd never disappoint them.

He would often pop over to the pub for a typical Sunday lunch and spent a lot of time reading to Emma and playing with her. He'd sometimes pick her up from school and drive home with the windows of his Mercedes wound down and music blaring out from his stereo. They were good memories but everyone moves on and changes. That night in Vegas, for whatever reason, I just had a gut feeling that having achieved what we'd set out to do, my time with Lennox was coming to an end.

I just lay there in the darkness of the room and eventually drifted off to sleep. The next thing I knew it was daylight and my arm was being tugged by my little daughter Sophie. She was only four years old but had become a regular at all of Lennox's world title fights.

'Guess what?' I said to her. 'Lenny won last night.'

But all she was really interested in was getting me to take her downstairs for something to eat and drink. I might have been the manager of the undisputed heavyweight champion of the world, but on that morning after the night before, Sophie made sure she brought me quickly down to earth and put everything into perspective.

17. FULL CIRCLE

I DIDN'T REALLY HAVE TOO MUCH TIME TO START THINKING ABOUT THE HOLYFIELD victory because I went straight from Vegas to the WBA convention in Panama, and then on to watch Michael Grant beat Andrew Golota in Atlantic City.

While I was at the convention I decided to push the boat out and do some entertaining which included a night in a club with the son of the organisation's president and a whole load of other people who tagged along. They gave us a private room at the back of the club and the champagne soon began to flow. It was a real boys' night out and it all got silly with everyone having a lot to drink. But I soon sobered up when I asked for the bill. I'd stuck my credit card behind the bar at the start of the evening and was struck dumb when they told me I owed $7,500! I quickly asked for a recount and finally it came down to around $5,000 which has still got to rate as the costliest piece of entertaining I've ever done. I think that night is still talked about by some people, but as Lennox was the heavyweight champion of the world it was the sort of thing that was almost expected of you. Entertaining is all part of life at boxing conventions.

I had another funny experience in a club when I got back to

England. Lennox decided to merchandise a range of men's underwear with his own brand name on them and we had the launch at a club in the West End of London. After all the press stuff had been done Lennox and I went up to the bar and started drinking cocktails. Before I knew where I was I woke up in my bed at home with a terrible hangover and couldn't remember anything about what had happened the night before. I was due to go to the 21st birthday party of Panos's son, Christian, that day and knew Lennox would be there as well. I began to worry that I might have disgraced myself and embarrassed him in the process, so when I turned up for the party I was a bit sheepish. I managed to spot Courtney and asked him what had happened.

'I don't know, Frank, but you were well out of it,' he told me. 'I had to stick you in a taxi and send you home.'

'Did Lennox get upset with me?' I asked him.

But Courtney just laughed and said that Lennox hadn't been far behind me, and was well gone too. We came to the conclusion that maybe someone had spiked our cocktails because we'd both got into such a state and we couldn't remember having that much to drink.

Having finally become the undisputed heavyweight champion of the world, the one big fight out there for Lennox was a mega-pay day against Mike Tyson. But we knew that the fight was probably a long way off and the more immediate prospect was a contest against the giant Grant. While I was in Vegas for the Holyfield fight, Tyson's name had come up because it was becoming clear he was looking to have a bout in Europe.

There was talk of him fighting in England or Germany and pretty soon our promotional company, Panix, had become involved in all the various scenarios. After talking to Main Events it was decided we should put a proposal to Tyson's manager, Shelly Finkel, of $1.2 million for us to be the promoter in England and I suggested Julius Francis, who was the British heavyweight champion at the time, could be a possible opponent. At the same time Panos began to insist that if we didn't get the fight Julius wouldn't be allowed to take on Tyson for another promoter.

I agreed it would be good for the company to get the contest, but at the same time I was determined to make sure I did the best for Julius.

After all, I was his manager and there was no way I was going to let him be denied the best purse of his career just because of petty politics.

It was no surprise to me when Frank Warren's name got thrown into the hat as a possible promoter. He had a good relationship with Showtime, the American TV network who bankrolled Tyson and screened his fights. Frank had also had some promotions screened on Showtime and dealt with Jay Larkin, the guy who made the decisions for the company when it came to boxing. So once Frank was in the frame I knew he was the most likely promoter to stage any Tyson contest in Britain. I also knew that Jay was not the biggest fan of Panos.

Before the fight with Ruddock he'd tried to do a deal with us but it hadn't worked out. There was also an incident when we were out of contract with HBO and, having talked about the possibility of signing with Showtime, Panos basically walked across the road and used it to get something better out of Seth Abraham. Jay accepted that as part of a way of negotiating a good deal, but I had no doubt it must have left a bitter taste in his mouth. It was also a fact that Panos was a HBO promoter, and Tyson was not going to be allowed to fight for someone who had such close ties with a rival TV organisation.

Once Frank became the favourite, Panos began telling Shelly that unless Panix got the fight, Julius wouldn't be the opponent. As far as I was concerned it was something he had no right to say. I assured Frank and Shelly that there was no problem with Francis fighting Tyson, but Panos somehow seemed to see this as disloyalty on my part.

The truth was that Panix was never seriously in contention to stage the contest and when Frank Warren was eventually confirmed as the promoter, Julius was offered $500,000 to face Tyson at the MEN Arena in Manchester on 29 January 2000. It was a great pay day for Francis, but ironically he might have been able to get even more. The figure was arrived at after Panos had mentioned it when he thought he might be staging the event. Once the fight went to Warren that was the amount Showtime were working on and even though I tried to get it increased, there was no more money in the kitty.

The decision to allow Julius to take the fight seemed to be the beginning of the end for me with Panos. He clearly thought I should have said no, but that would have been unfair to Julius and I wouldn't have been fulfilling my role as his manager. It was my job to help him earn money as a professional fighter, and stepping in the ring with Tyson would give him more than he'd ever earned for a contest before.

When Panos implied that I'd been lying, I told him if he thought that was the case he should pay me up and sack me. I knew I'd done nothing wrong and the fact was that part of my management percentage from the contest was going to go to the company and not into my own pocket.

I had a row with Panos when he accused me of not acting in the best interests of the company and of being disloyal. What he seemed to forget was that I'd helped to build the organisation. Sure, it was his money behind everything, but it was my boxing know-how which contributed to making us into a real force.

It got to the point where I began to feel as though I was on trial and Panos also said Lennox was not happy about what had gone on. Even Dennis Lewis chipped in by saying his brother thought I was being disloyal. To make matters worse Julius had a girlfriend who had once worked for Lewis as his secretary and had left under acrimonious circumstances, which saw her take her case to a tribunal.

I actually spoke to Lennox and he asked me some questions that I thought were a bit strange. He seemed to think I was doing something wrong by allowing Julius to fight. I pointed out to him that I was acting as a manager should. If someone comes along and offers you loads of money for your fighter, it's your job to take it for him. In many ways it was no different to what had happened in Lennox's own career. After all, Don King had forked out cash for Lewis in the past and we were happy to take it, despite the fact that he was a rival promoter.

I felt hurt by the fact that Lennox questioned my loyalty. I'd had countless opportunities to be disloyal to him in the past if I'd wanted to cash in, but I'd never done it and yet suddenly I seemed to be the person whose honesty was being questioned.

Not long after all of this, rumours started to circulate in the press about me being sacked. It was clear something was about to happen and one day I got a call from Panos asking me to go down and see him in his office. He immediately said he wasn't going to sack me, but that there were going to be some changes made. He claimed he'd had a two-hour meeting with Lennox and they'd discussed the situation, with the general feeling being that I'd let the camp down.

He went on to tell me about certain cuts in my promotional and management money that he claimed were going to take place. Panos said that from then on I wasn't going to be allowed to have anything to do with promoting, and also claimed that I couldn't advertise my website. Then he asked me to sign a confidentiality clause.

I think it was at that point I started laughing even though I was really angry about what he'd said. I just couldn't believe what I was hearing from him. The whole thing seemed so ridiculous. I sank to my knees in front of him, put my hands together and said, 'Panos, please sack me.'

He seemed genuinely surprised by what I'd done and immediately claimed it was Lennox's idea that I should sign a confidentiality form. I told Panos to get Lennox to come over and ask me to do it. The whole thing was a joke. I'd worked for Lewis for ten years and hadn't signed anything like it before, so there was no way that was going to change.

As far as I was concerned it seemed to be more about me and Panos than anything else. By this time I was convinced that Eliades and his ego had no room for me. Whatever he said to my face I was certain he wanted me out of the equation as far as Lennox was concerned.

I'd had my run-ins with Panos in the past, including one occasion in his office where I tried to grab him around the throat when we were having a meeting concerning Scandinavian fighters and TV and had to be restrained by former European heavyweight champion Steffen Tangstad. It was just one of a series of incidents between us, but the latest accusations really made me feel sick.

It was pretty clear I was no longer going to have the same role within the organisation, but I wasn't going to let it get to me and it was a relief to escape from all the office politics by going into training camp with Julius. We decided to set up camp with the Army in Aldershot and things couldn't have gone better as Francis concentrated on preparing for the biggest fight of his career.

The whole idea of Tyson coming to England for his first ever fight in the country created huge interest, but it also created a problem because of his rape conviction. There was talk that he shouldn't be let in to Britain, and for days there was huge interest by the media, as the debate raged on. I got in on the act by getting Julius to write a letter to Prime Minister Tony Blair, asking for Tyson to be granted entry, and pointing out how unfair it would be to Francis if he were denied the chance to earn so much money. It wasn't the first time I'd been involved in writing to Downing Street, because I'd asked John Major to consider Lennox for some sort of honours award in the past, only to receive a polite standard reply.

But things eventually swung our way with Tyson when he got the official nod from the Home Office and the promotion went ahead. The whole event was massive from start to finish, and I have to admit that Frank Warren did a brilliant job with it. Tyson stopped traffic wherever he went in London, where he set up camp before travelling up to Manchester for the actual contest.

We didn't do too badly in the publicity stakes, with Julius getting tremendous coverage as I talked up his chances of causing an upset against the former world champion. If I'm honest I have to say that my head always had the American winning, but in my heart I was hoping Julius might just be able to pull it off. I was criticised in some quarters for one of the stunts I pulled in the run-up to the fight, when I managed to do a deal to let the *Daily Mirror* newspaper have advertising space on the soles of Julius's boots. People seemed to think it was an indication that I believed he would get knocked out, but it was a purely commercial deal which would have been silly to turn down.

The Francis team went up to Manchester a couple of days before the fight in a mini-bus, and we had an interesting encounter at one of the service stations on the motorway, when we came face-to-face with some of Tyson's entourage, including the character known as 'Crocodile'. He was Mike's chief cheerleader who wore battle fatigues and sunglasses and always bad mouthed the opposition. He tried it on with us for a moment but quickly came off second best, with Julius's trainer Mark Roe really getting into the swing of things by having a real go back as he made sure the 'Croc' shut his mouth.

Tyson was already in his hotel when we got to Manchester, but we caused a real stir in the street outside as Julius jumped on top of a police van with hundreds of fans around him. He raised his arms and started waving at them all, while we told the crowd to support their own British heavyweight champion against Mike. We actually needed the police to break the thing up, but it just added to the excitement of the occasion.

On the morning of the fight I woke up early and went to buy all the newspapers, before quickly making the decision not to let Julius see any of them. It was pretty clear not one gave him a chance of defeating Tyson. There was no way I was going to allow negative thoughts to enter his head, so I told the rest of the team that on no account should Julius be allowed to read anything about the fight. I tried to take his mind off matters and give him another mental boost that afternoon by taking him to be introduced to the crowd at Old Trafford as we watched Manchester United. We also received some words of encouragement from Sir Bobby Charlton.

But actions have always spoken louder than words when it comes to boxing, and despite all we'd said leading up to the fight, it was pretty clear on the night that Tyson was in a different league to Francis. We had always known that was the case, but the idea was to try and make things difficult before seeing what happened. Although Julius had been cast as the sacrificial lamb, he went out and took the fight to Tyson, but couldn't stand up to the sort of attacks that came his way and was stopped inside two rounds.

After it was over I said that Francis had gone for a shoot-out, but unfortunately hadn't loaded his guns. The good thing was that Julius hadn't been hurt, he'd earned a lot of money and he had also become a mini-celebrity. I'd enjoyed being in camp with Francis, who is one of boxing's genuine nice guys, and I'd also enjoyed being involved in the whole promotion.

Although Lennox's next fight was due to take place in April against Grant in New York, we had begun planning ahead by lining up a July bout in London against South African Frans Botha, who was promoted by Frank Warren.

We had a meeting in February to try and finalise a deal with Frank for Botha to fight and I couldn't help noticing how Warren handled the whole situation. Panos was his usual over-friendly self during the meeting and immediately asked Frank what he could do for him.

'It's not what you can do for me, Panos,' said Frank. 'It's what I can do for you.'

As he said it Warren set the tone for what followed. It soon became clear that Panos needed to come up with the sort of figures Frank wanted or the deal just wouldn't happen. Warren eventually got the money he wanted and the fight was pencilled in.

As preparations for Lennox's training camp got underway, there was another indication that my time with Panix seemed to be coming to an end. Panos said it had been decided between him and Lewis that I should stay in London to help with some shows rather than go back and forth to camp as I always had done. I was also asked once again to sign a confidentiality form and informed by Panos that my name was to be dropped from the promotions. It was no longer going to be 'Frank Maloney for Panix Promotions'. In future it was simply going to be 'Panix Promotions'.

It wasn't a big deal really, but it just showed the way things were going for me within the organisation. As far as I was concerned it was all about power with Panos. He claimed I just didn't like him taking more control of his company, but it wasn't that. We seemed to have reached the point where we just couldn't work with each other. I was beginning to even dislike the sight of the man.

Although I was the manager of Lennox Lewis, I began to feel I was manager in name only. It should have been the happiest time of my life, with Lennox having achieved what we'd both striven for by becoming the undisputed champion, but instead everything felt flat and going to work was not a pleasant experience.

I might not have been welcome in the Lewis training camp at the time, but I did have to go to the States to testify in a court case. It concerned the WBA taking away their belt from Lennox because he had not gone ahead with a contest against Henry Akinwande who was the mandatory contender. We were contesting the fact that Lennox should relinquish the belt, but the simple fact of the matter was that Panos had agreed to such a defence as part of the deal he struck with King for the return fight with Holyfield, despite the fact that Pat English, the Main Events lawyer, disagreed with the clause. You didn't need to be a legal expert to realise that we were going to lose the case, and that's exactly what happened.

My appearance in the New York courtroom was brief with King's lawyer, Peter Flemming, only asking me a few questions, while some of the others were really put through the wringer. Flemming gave Milt Chwasky a real going over, and Milt was actually warned by the judge to watch his behaviour, or he could find himself in a cell for the night.

During a break in the proceedings I asked Flemming why he'd been so easy on me. 'When someone gets into the witness box and is clearly telling the truth, there's no need to be hard on them,' he told me.

Back in London I had a surprise waiting for me and when it came it seemed like another nail had been knocked into my coffin. By this time we had started to have weekly staff meetings. I'd managed to avoid a lot of them, but on this particular occasion I couldn't get out of it. Once again the subject of signing a confidentiality form was brought up, and Panos asked me if I was going to sign one. I could tell from the way he spoke there was something more to it, and then he hit me with the news. He said Lennox had told him that if I didn't sign the form I couldn't go to training camp, and that anyone who didn't sign wouldn't go to the Grant fight at Madison Square Garden.

I felt my stomach knotting and I think I also began to shake a bit, but I didn't want the rest of the people in the room to see me lose control. I did manage to mutter a reply, saying it would be a bit difficult to keep me away because I also happened to have two of my other fighters, Paul Ingle and Scott Harrison, on the same bill.

Panos suggested I call Lennox and so did another member of the organisation, Prince, who had become part of Lennox's inner circle in the camp. On the way home I felt like crying, but held back the tears because James, my press officer, was driving the car and I didn't want to let him see how badly the meeting had affected me.

I had the distinct impression I was going to be out of the picture after the Grant fight, and once again the rumours circulated in the press that I was likely to be sacked. But in a telephone press conference with Lennox he was asked about my position by one of the journalists and came out with the 'If it ain't broke, don't fix it' line.

Despite all the talk there was never any real doubt that I'd be at the Grant fight and after arriving in New York at the start of the week leading up to the contest I finally got to see Lennox at one of his work-outs, and I also went to his suite the next day for a chat. To be honest I felt a bit awkward, which was crazy considering what we'd both been through over the years, but things got easier and he was very friendly towards me. It seemed as though nothing had ever happened, and it made me wonder exactly what was going on behind the scenes.

One of the more unpleasant things I'd had to do for Panos during the lead-up to the Grant fight was telling Colin Hart that Lennox wanted him barred from the Madison Square Garden show. Lewis had phoned the office in London one day saying he didn't want Colin at the fight, and Panos immediately asked me to take care of the situation by telling Harty. When I passed the message on to Colin he told me to tell Panos that there was no way anyone was going to stop him from being there. He even checked with the Garden to make sure his credential would be waiting for him on the night.

But when it got to the week of the fight Colin was told by Panos that Lennox didn't want him to attend a pre-fight press conference in his suite. Harty had just retired from *The Sun* newspaper, but was there as a freelance and the rest of the British press said they'd boycott the conference if Colin wasn't allowed to go along. Hart insisted that they all had their jobs to do and that they should go to the conference without him. I'm sure he thought the whole thing was down to Panos, but it was Lennox who instigated it all.

I think there had always been some friction between Colin and Lennox. I remembered the time Lewis fought Golota and an American journalist named Tim Smith had asked Colin about Lennox and whether he was as popular as Frank Bruno. Harty said he wasn't, but that he was more successful.

Smith then went up to do an interview with Lennox and happened to say that Colin Hart had told him he wasn't as well liked as Frank Bruno. Lennox wasn't too happy with Harty and he wanted me to phone the BBC and get Colin removed from being part of their team covering the fight. But the next day Harty made a point of going over to Lewis after his workout and telling him exactly what he'd said to Smith. It ended with Lewis and Colin shaking hands but I don't know if it helped their relationship.

At the final press conference for the Grant show Panos seemed to be a bit put out by the fact that Ingle publicly thanked me, but failed to mention him. 'I'm the one who put you on the card,' Panos told Paul. But what Eliades seemed to forget was that Ingle and I went back a long way and he'd been with me since turning professional. There had been a classic moment soon after Paul, who was managed by me and promoted by our own Panix organisation, won the British title against former world champion Colin McMillan in 1997. He went to a Boxing Writers' Dinner and sat on the same table as Panos. 'Hello, son, what's your name and who do you fight for?' asked Eliades.

Panos also managed to put his foot in it when he and I were given a joint Manager of the Year award by the American Boxing Writers' Association a couple of days before the Grant fight. He compared the event to a mafia convention during his speech and you could almost feel a sigh of relief from everyone in the room when he finally stopped talking and sat down.

The show in New York was a tremendous success for British boxing. Lennox took care of Grant inside two rounds, Ingle got off the floor to stop Junior Jones in the 11th and defend his title, while young Scott Harrison had a points win over former world champion, Tracy Patterson. After the show I had a great night celebrating, but it wasn't at the Lennox Lewis party. Instead, I decided to join Paul, Steve Pollard, Rocky Rowe and the rest of Ingle's travelling fans in a crazy night of drinking. I might have missed out on him becoming a world champion, because I'd been in Vegas with Lennox, but I more than made up for it in New York.

If the New York promotion was a success, the Panix promotion back home at Wembley on the same night was a financial disaster and just to make matters worse, the top of the bill saw Robert McCracken lose his WBC middleweight title challenge against Keith Holmes. Panos had kept me away from the promotion until the final two weeks when he even offered me a bonus to try and rescue the show because it was going so badly, but by that time it was too late to save it. Apparently it was a terrible promotion and Jose Sulaiman said as much after witnessing it first hand.

After Lewis beat Grant we went straight into planning the Botha fight, which was going to take place at the London Arena on 15 July. Right from the start I knew the show was going to be a hard sell, because in the build-up we were going to be competing against the Euro 2000 football championships, tennis at Wimbledon and also the return visit to Britain of Mike Tyson for his fight in Glasgow with Lou Savarese. We had tickets priced from £750 to £50 and Panos kept telling me how we had to sell the show, and how important it was to let Lennox see we were doing a good job.

Once again I didn't go to camp with Lennox and instead stayed in London working my arse off in an attempt to make sure the London Arena promotion was a success. I did it for my own professional pride and not out of any sense of loyalty to Panos. We were still working together but the relationship was very brittle.

I had plans for Lennox to help boost ticket sales and interest by coming in to London a couple of weeks before the show and getting plenty of publicity. I wanted him to do some TV work, visit his old school in east London, go for a walkabout and tour around in an open-top bus. But Adrian Ogun, who seemed to have a big say with regard to Lewis and what he was doing, wrote to me saying Lennox wasn't going to be able to do anything other than the bare essentials and he eventually arrived back in England with about a week to go before the fight. His big grumble when he got back was the fact that he didn't see any posters advertising the fight, but I knew we'd spent a fortune having them put up all over the place. After sending someone to check, we found there were over 2,000 posters in the London area.

After the weigh-in in the open air at Covent Garden, Lennox really laid into me verbally for allowing pictures of his house in Hadley Wood to be taken for an article in the London *Evening Standard*. He hated having his privacy invaded, but it was a positive piece giving the show good publicity. The whole thing had been cleared and partially set up by Adrian and his own brother Dennis, who by this time was not really in the picture too much, with Ogun emerging as a major player in the Lennox Lewis team.

It wasn't the only picture idea we didn't see eye to eye on, because I also suggested having a photo session with a girlfriend of Lennox's named Aisha who had caused a bit of a stir with some reporters before the Grant fight. There had even been a story about them in the paper, but nothing was done before the Botha show, although about a week after it there were pictures of the two of them at a pub in Basingstoke in *The Mirror* newspaper.

Lennox had an easy second round win over Botha, but the show was really the beginning of the end for Panos as his promoter. We'd had terrible trouble trying to sell the seats and in the end had to discount a lot of them. From a personal point of view I couldn't really get excited about the night and didn't even bother to change into my Union Jack suit for the contest.

The one light-hearted moment came from a story Frank Warren told me. Apparently Frank had asked Panos if he could have a VIP seat for Minnie Driver. 'Why can't you just give him a cheap ticket?' he asked Warren, thinking he was talking about a cab driver and not the famous actress.

To the outside world it probably seemed like a great show on the night, but internally there were lots of things going on. There was still a lot of bad feeling between Panos and me and at times I felt like I could have happily strangled him. I'd always accepted that it was his money and his business, but it was his attitude that I found so hard to take. Two days after the win over Botha, Lennox sent a letter which both Panos and I got a copy of. It was basically the first step in him taking control of his affairs. He made it clear that he didn't want anyone to start making plans on his behalf and that he was going to take some time to look at the options and possibilities open to him.

When I got my copy I actually thought it was a letter telling me I was sacked, because at the time I really felt out of the picture. I wasn't sure what was going to happen to me but I wanted the chance to clear things up with Lennox and find out exactly where I stood.

In the end I wrote a letter to him in which I said my position as his manager had been undermined and that I hadn't been able to act in my rightful capacity as I'd been cut out of all negotiations. I told him there were a number of points I wanted to discuss with him and I then posted the letter off to Adrian for him to pass on to Lennox.

Panos became very suspicious of the letter he'd been sent by Lennox and sensed his position might be changing. He also thought Adrian now had a very strong role within the Lewis team, and it was clear he was beginning to feel threatened.

I had a face-to-face meeting with Lennox at his house along with

Adrian and told them about the way I felt and the fact that I was constantly battling with Panos. I went over the whole Julius Francis episode, and told him there was no way I'd been disloyal to him or the Panix company. I also told him that I'd had an offer from Frank Warren to go and work with him as a consultant. There was also the King offer still floating about and another from an internet firm who were interested in getting into boxing.

I explained to Lennox that I liked being his manager, but I didn't want to do it if it was going to be in name only. Once I'd got all of that off my chest I felt a lot better, and it was the first time I'd had a serious conversation with him since the first Holyfield fight. Since that contest I'd felt as though I was just making up the numbers. Lennox told me that he wanted me to work closely with Adrian, and soon after the meeting I got a call from Ogun saying how pleased Lennox was with the way things had gone.

I also got a call from Panos who was clearly rattled by developments and wanted to know about my meeting with Lennox, but there was no way I was going to go into what had happened. He seemed much friendlier than he'd been for a long time and claimed that the two of us would have to be strong and stick together, because he was worried about Adrian and the influence he seemed to have.

From being out in the cold I felt as though I was starting to get involved with Lennox and his career again. As negotiations for his next fight against David Tua began, Adrian and Lennox were keen to understand more about the way big fight deals are put together.

I had made plans to have a holiday in Portugal and I was pretty certain in my own mind that when I came back I'd wave goodbye to Panos. The offer from Warren was something we'd talked about a year earlier during our boozy lunch on the beach. Having told Adrian and Lennox about it and got their blessing if I did decide to leave, it was really just a matter of saying yes to Frank.

We'd started off together all those years ago and there had been a few run-ins along the way, but I felt comfortable about the prospect of teaming up with him once again. It was as if things had gone full circle for me, and I felt that a weight was about to be lifted off my shoulders.

18. BLUNDER IN AFRICA

BEFORE I WENT TO PORTUGAL I'D HAD YET ANOTHER CLASH WITH PANOS OVER the way Panix was being run. I believed he was signing a lot of boxers who nobody else really wanted and as far as I was concerned it was no way to build for the future.

I told him I was going away and would think things over while I was on holiday. Either I'd come back and carry on with him, or it would be the parting of the ways. But the truth was I'd really already made my decision.

While I was in Portugal I spoke to Adrian, who in many ways seemed to have taken over the role Panos used to have with Lewis, and was assured by him that my position with Lennox was safe. It was clear by this time he was a very strong player in the Lewis camp and he told me to go ahead and start setting up the training camp for the Tua fight which was scheduled for November. Lennox and his new boxing company, Lion Promotions, were going to be putting the show together at the Mandalay Bay Hotel in Vegas. It had surprised me that when I'd had my chat with Adrian and Lennox about what my involvement might be in the future, they hadn't seemed interested in me going to work at Lion Promotions for them and maybe taking my fighters with me, even though they knew I'd had enough of Panos. But after thinking things through I felt a whole lot better about my situation knowing I was going to make a fresh start with Frank Warren, and at the same time become more involved once again with Lennox.

A few days before I was due to fly back to England I got a call on my mobile phone while I was sitting with a friend in a bar. It was Panos and he didn't waste too much time telling me what was on his mind. 'I don't want you coming to the office. You're barred,' he said. He then went on to accuse me of stabbing him in the back over various things and was verbally laying into me when I stopped him in his tracks.

'Panos, you're not going to stop me from coming in,' I told him. 'I was going to see you anyway because I want to hand in my notice – I'm leaving.'

As soon as I explained I was going to walk away from it all anyway, his attitude changed. It was as if he thought I was saying it just to have a go back at him, but my mind was already made up. I knew I was joining Frank Warren and his Sports Network company.

Despite what Panos had said there was no way he was going to stop me from turning up to collect my personal belongings from the office, and although I was relieved to have finally made the decision to leave, I have to admit I felt very sad at the way it all ended. I'd put an awful lot of my life into the company and helped to build it as a major force in British boxing, but I felt as though I had to go. Staying there would have been bad for my health, and I might have ended up doing something I regretted.

A few days later my driver Eric Guy picked me up at my house and drove me to my office at Panix for the last time. I think Eric could see how subdued I was and he cheered me up by talking about some of the times we'd had in the past when I would constantly sack him over something really silly and he would just ignore me and turn up again the next day. He also reminded me of the times he'd drive Lennox around when he first arrived in this country and he would tell Eric to be careful because there was a million dollars in the car. When Eric asked him where it was, Lennox would simply say, 'It's me!' Even back then Lennox knew how important he was to everyone.

As I travelled into London that morning all I was concerned with was getting my personal belongings out of the door and finally saying goodbye to the man who'd managed to make my life hell. I spoke to Panos as I cleared my things and he said that although I was going we shouldn't fall out. That was fine by me because for the first time in about 18 months I actually felt relaxed. I was about to start a new chapter in my life and leave all the hassle I'd had at Panix behind me.

Frank Warren and I had a press conference in early September to let everyone know I was joining Sports Network, and I had to fend off the expected questions about my relationship with Lennox and whether I'd still be his manager. The fact of the matter was that Lennox and Adrian were quite happy for me to work with Frank and didn't see any conflict in what I was doing.

I explained to the media that my relationship with Panos was like a marriage that had run its course and we were just going our separate ways, but once things had been announced with regard to me teaming up with Frank, Panos started talking to the press claiming I'd been sacked and there was even a suggestion that there had been some financial irregularities surrounding the reason for my departure, which was absolute rubbish. The story was run in the press and one paper had to pay out in a settlement I had with them and also gave me an apology. The simple truth was that I'd had enough and needed to stop working with Panos.

When I first got to know him things were fun and he never really used to interfere or tell me what to do, but that changed as the years went on and towards the end life with him got worse by the day. It was like living with a dictator and the irritating thing was that I believe he never really understood the boxing business. But he certainly seemed to like being involved in it and also being in the spotlight. Panos actually managed to pick up an award as Co-manager of the Year along with me, when he heard I'd been nominated by the American Boxing Writers' Association, even though he'd never managed a fighter in his life. There were countless times where I thought the company could have really benefited and got stronger if the right boxing decisions had been made, but ultimately he was the one who said yes or no to things.

For example, it's funny to think that Lennox might not have been our only world heavyweight champion if Panos had been willing to take more of a gamble on John Ruiz. I came across John when he was used as a sparring partner for Lennox in his build-up to the first McCall fight. Eugene had told me Ruiz had looked quite good and was fast for a heavyweight. I told Panos that it would be a good idea if we started to sign some of the American heavyweights and it would help to build our stable of fighters.

We worked out a deal and he had a few fights before getting badly beaten in the first round by David Tua, but we were able to slowly bring him back from that set-back and there was no doubt in my mind that he had potential and was worth keeping. But when it came to re-negotiating his contract, Ruiz wanted $100,000 to sign. Panos wasn't happy with the amount and so I suggested John should get $50,000 up front and the other $50,000 could be in the form of a loan that Ruiz could repay over a period of fights.

Eliades still wasn't happy with the idea and didn't want to take the gamble, so John went off to Don King and immediately got the $100,000. To be fair to Don he also agreed that Ruiz still had two fights left with us and that the money would only be paid once those were out of the way. This whole thing happened around the time Panos was talking to Don about the idea of forming Kingpan, and I think at the back of his mind he thought any deal would be covered by their possible partnership. But Kingpan never materialised, Ruiz duly went off to be promoted by King and eventually wound up as WBA heavyweight champion. Panos claimed on several occasions that he was going to sue over the affair, although nothing ever actually happened during my time with him.

We also had another American fighter named Montell Griffin on our books. He was a decent kid and we managed to get him into a WBC world light-heavyweight title fight with the great Roy Jones, who was later to take the WBA crown from Ruiz after moving up to heavyweight.

Griffin fought Jones in March 1997 and Panos was telling everyone that his fighter was going to cause an upset. He even told me that he'd had some kind of spiritual message that Griffin would win. Amazingly Griffin did get a win and became a world champion, but only because Jones was disqualified in the ninth round. Panos really thought he'd cracked it and in a sense he had because we got unbelievable money for the re-match, but I knew lightning wouldn't strike twice and Jones got a first round win.

Panos asked me what he should do next with Montell and I told him that in my opinion we should hand Griffin back his contract. There was really nowhere he was going after that, and the TV people didn't seem interested. But Panos ignored what I said and went ahead with getting more fights for Montell. In the end Eliades used to complain to me about the amount of money it was costing with Griffin, but he could have ended up much better off financially had he taken my advice.

The impression I got with Panos was that when God gave out brains, he believed he was the only person in the room. He seemed to have a really patronising attitude to a lot of people in the game, including me. He was the sort of guy who'd made a lot of money and wanted to let you know he had. It got to the stage where I couldn't stand being in the same room as him. I got the feeling that towards the end of our relationship Panos was hoping Lennox was going to sack me, but the irony was it was he who ended up going first.

When I left Panix I felt very bitter about the way things had gone and I have to admit that I hoped they would start to crumble following my departure. In the end that's exactly what happened and it wasn't too long before they ceased to be the major force in the boxing world they had once been.

For the first time since the drawn Holyfield fight I found myself back in camp with Lennox as he prepared for the Tua fight by training in the Poconos, but apart from discussing his defence I soon found out there was another reason for Adrian and him wanting me there.

We had a meeting in Lennox's room and it was all very friendly. He asked me about a number of points to do with boxing and Adrian asked how things were going for me with Frank Warren. Suddenly Lennox wanted to know how much he paid me. I told him it was 3 per cent of the purse, and he then asked whether I thought I was worth that sort of money. I must admit that I was bit surprised by what he was saying, but I told him that I believed I was definitely worth it, and then spelled out exactly what I did for him.

But it was clear Lennox thought my job was going to be easier for me with the new set-up he had in mind and although I honestly thought my percentage was more than deserved I ended up agreeing to take a cut. Adrian actually told me that Panos had been speaking to Lennox and had suggested I ought to get a flat fee for each Lewis fight I was involved with, but I told Ogun that if that had happened I would have walked out.

I knew I'd swallowed my pride by taking the cut, but the truth was that I still wanted to be involved just as I had been from day one. The reality was that Lennox was coming to the end of his career and there weren't too many fights left for him. There was still the possibility of a big pay day against Tyson, and there was no way I wanted to miss out on that. I also had a genuine loyalty towards Lennox, even though I had to wonder why saving 1 per cent on me was so important when you think of the sort of money he has made in his career.

Don't get me wrong. I owed an awful lot to Lennox Lewis and my association with him had given me the kind of money and lifestyle I could have only dreamed of at one stage. But the fact remained that I was probably one of the worst paid managers of a world heavyweight champion there has ever been in terms of the percentages I took. If my money had been cut a few years earlier I probably would have reacted differently, but I was older and wiser. I had also had enough of constantly battling with Panos, and having made a fresh new start, I wanted my life to be as free from hassle as possible.

After the meeting, Adrian said I'd handled the whole thing very well and as the two of us flew off to Mexico for the WBC convention we chatted about the sort of role I would have in the new set-up. It was clear Ogun was going to have a lot of influence, but he didn't really know the boxing business and I got the impression he was eager to pick my brains over certain issues. I knew from day one that he was a calculating sort of guy and it seemed as though he'd finally managed to get into the kind of position within the Lewis camp that he'd craved since I was first introduced to him back in 1994.

Although things were very amicable between Adrian and me it soon became clear I was only really going to have a bit part to play when it came to the career of Lennox Lewis. I was there as his boxing manager, but my main role seemed to be keeping the press sweet. In real terms it was Adrian who had taken over. His job description may have said business manager to Lennox Lewis, but in reality he appeared to be a lot more than that. The two seemed very close and it was obvious Adrian had Lennox's ear on a whole range of things.

When I arrived in Vegas for the fight Adrian had arranged for me to stay in a suite for the week, but I soon began to feel more like an invited guest than anything to do with the Lewis team. It seemed to me as though there were three different camps. Adrian, Panos and Main Events. Everyone was very nice to me and I was told that I was a valued member of the team, but if I'm honest I felt like no more than a whore when it came to my involvement in the fight. I turned up, took my money and went away again. I didn't really feel as though I contributed much, but that wasn't my fault, it was down to the way the whole operation was run.

On one occasion I turned up outside Adrian's suite and told the bodyguard on the door my name. 'Frank who?' he asked me. Talk about feeling like an outsider. To be fair to one of the other guards, he actually did recognise me and told them to let me in, but it didn't help me feel any more comfortable.

Lennox jabbed his way to a points win against Tua, a short powerful fighter who was reckoned to have one of the most explosive punches in the heavyweight division. It was a professional performance, but not a very exciting one. I couldn't blame him for that and had often said that it didn't matter how you won, just so long as you got the victory. As with so many contests in his career, Lennox had worked out what he needed to do and he wasn't going to take any risks.

I have to admit that while I was in Las Vegas I wondered whether I should walk away from the whole thing. Although I was still part of the Lewis team, I felt as though I was on the outside looking in, and it didn't make me feel very comfortable. The excitement I'd had in the beginning wasn't there any more and I knew I was Lennox Lewis's manager in name only. For the first time I didn't have any of my family out there with me for the Tua fight, and I actually ended up feeling quite lonely.

The link-up with Frank Warren had gone well and I was beginning to enjoy the boxing business again. It was easy to see why he'd been so successful once I started to work closely with him again. Frank is extremely smart and astute. He's got a lot of courage when it comes to doing business and is prepared to take the sort of risks needed in the game if you are going to make it to the top. The set-up at Sports Network was very professional and the company promoted the biggest shows in Britain.

Three months after joining Frank we put on a show in Sheffield which featured Paul Ingle defending his world title against South African Mbulelo Botile. It should have been one of the best nights of my life, instead it turned out to be one of the worst with poor Paul fighting for his life in hospital.

I've always made it a policy not to get too involved on a personal level with my boxers because it can affect your judgement and can often end in disappointment. But I have to admit that I had a special relationship with Ingle, or 'Paul Ingles' as I always referred to him.

When he turned professional with me I knew he was a bit special and his amateur record showed what a great pedigree he had. He came from a tough estate in Scarborough where he lived with his mum and brother. In many ways he reminded me of Lennox in the sort of relationship he had with his mother, because both were devoted to their respective mums.

Paul was a real hero in the town even before he became a professional and over the years I think he did a tremendous job for the place and did an awful lot of charity work locally. He had his mates and liked to hang around with them when he wasn't training for fights. He would sell a tremendous amount of tickets and even if he was fighting in London, he'd have hundreds of fans book themselves on coaches and travel down for the contest.

Although I'd moved away from Panix I was still representing Paul and the fight against Botile had gone to purse bids which Sports Network won. My formal agreement with him as his manager had come to an end and he didn't want to sign another one with me, preferring to have me looking after his boxing interests and letting others organise things like his merchandising. In reality not very much changed and I still took my agreed percentage of his purses. The Botile contest was set up to take place at the Sheffield Arena and although he was a world champion, I knew from past experience that there was no way Paul was going to go away to a training camp. I got on well with Ingle, but if there was one thing which we disagreed on it was the way he prepared for a fight.

Don't get me wrong, Paul always trained hard, but he also liked to have a drink and enjoy himself with his mates when he wasn't preparing for a fight. Having been associated with Lennox Lewis and the American fight scene for such a long time and seen the way he shut himself away in camp, I felt that kind of preparation was the right way to go about things for a champion. I knew Paul hadn't liked his time in the Poconos before his fight with Hamed. He seemed to believe that if he was going to feel mentally right before a contest he needed to stay and train locally, whether the fight was for six rounds in the early part of his career, or a world title.

I wasn't happy with the situation but accepted that he preferred to stay near home and do his work with Pollard. He also had a conditioner named Neil Featherby as part of his team and another guy whom he'd brought in as his dietician. I wasn't around for his training on a daily basis, but whenever I checked I was told everything was going to plan.

On the day of the contest Ingle told me Panos had been on the phone and wanted to walk Paul into the ring because he was his promoter. I thought it was a bit of a cheek because he could have contacted the office direct and asked himself, but I left a couple of ringside seats for him. Although the Ingle team didn't want him in there, he eventually managed to get into Paul's dressing-room, but the amazing thing was that by the start of the fight Eliades had gone and didn't even stay to see the contest.

After just a couple of rounds I could see that Paul didn't have his normal spark and he looked a bit sluggish. By the end of the 11th round I knew he was getting beaten, and I told Pollard that the only way I thought Ingle could win was by a knockout.

But in the next round the unthinkable happened when Paul got hit by a great shot from the South African and collapsed. It wasn't just an ordinary knockdown and he actually sat up and then rolled over. If I'm honest, I can't really remember what happened after that, because everything seemed to be a blur. I felt numb because I knew Paul was in real trouble and the medical people quickly rushed him off to the City's Royal Hallamshire Hospital.

A guy called Robert Battersby, who was the consultant neurosurgeon, removed a blood clot from Paul's brain as we all waited at the hospital that night. Like everyone else at that point I didn't know how serious things were or whether Paul would live or die. But he survived the operation and as the days went on the news got better and he got stronger. Mr Battersby tried to reassure me that what had happened could have occurred at any stage in the fight. Logically I knew that it meant had Paul not gone out for that last round and collapsed he might well have gone home and then had trouble later in the night. As terrible as it was, at least he got first class treatment on the spot at the Arena and that could only have helped, because time can play such an important part.

In the early hours of the morning following the fight I called a meeting with Pollard and Neil Featherby to go over what had happened leading up to the contest, but the dietician who had become part of the Ingle team wasn't there as we talked things through and tried to make some kind of sense of the horrible thing that had happened.

I still felt in a state of shock about the whole business for a long time after it. I started to question my own role in the affair and also wondered about boxing itself.

At one point I was actually on the verge of giving up boxing and then I went to my brother Eugene's gym for their Christmas party. After working for Panos on and off and then helping out on security when Ingle fought Hamed and Julius took on Tyson, Eugene had decided he wanted to get more involved in boxing again and started to manage and promote boxers at a gym in east London. I sat there surrounded by some of my young fighters and they helped me put everything into perspective. They all said that boxers knew the risks they took when they went into the ring and that I shouldn't blame myself. I knew what they were saying was true, but at the same time, having witnessed what happened to Paul, it was difficult to come to terms with. I have to say that talking to them made me feel a lot better, but there were still nagging doubts in my mind about what had happened.

The BBBC launched an inquiry into the whole sad episode and both Frank Warren and I had to talk to the board. However, because they were not licensed by the BBBC at the time, neither Featherby nor the dietician were called to give evidence. I also did my own investigation by asking Joe Dunbar to go over Paul's training and the methods that were used to prepare him, and as a result of the Board inquiry the weight of boxers preparing for championship fights is monitored much more closely. I'm confident in my own mind that I know some of the answers to the questions I had following what happened.

Perhaps I should have paid more attention to Ingle's preparation, not so much in the gym under Pollard, but in the general way he went about the business of getting himself in shape for the contest. I think people realise now how important it is to monitor fighters and the way they prepare for contests, but as those fighters had told me in Eugene's gym, you can't live with a boxer 24 hours a day.

Happily Paul has continued to make progress since that night and I know he wants to stay in the sport and perhaps train fighters, but it's a long hard process for him. I helped to organise a charity football match and dinner for Ingle some time ago and there was a lot of goodwill on show from the people of Scarborough for someone who was a real hero.

But one of the things I have noticed when I've been up there since the fight is how quite a few people have changed. Not people like Rocky and Pollard who will always be there for Ingle, but others in the town. When Paul was fighting and winning world title contests everyone wanted to know him. Once you're no longer at the top some people don't seem as interested as they once were; they only like being associated with success.

Paul will always be a special fighter to me and I'm glad he achieved what he did and became a world champion. What happened on that night in Sheffield was tragic, but he's not bitter or twisted about it. Ingle is a born fighter and he has the strength and character to continue to re-build his life.

In February of 2001 I began to get involved in what was to be Lennox's next fight, defending his titles against American Hasim Rahman. Having felt completely out of it at the Tua show I wasn't sure what to expect next, but it became clear that Adrian wanted to involve me more for the Rahman fight. It was originally going to take place in Vegas, but then Ogun put a deal in place in South Africa.

He telephoned and asked me to go out there with him for a couple of days to look over the place and see what I thought. The venue itself seemed fine with decent facilities and accommodation, but my biggest concern was the fact that Lennox would be boxing at altitude. The fight venue at Benoni in Carnival City was 6,000 feet above sea level, and after making inquiries I was told that ideally he should have six weeks acclimatisation, although four weeks would probably be enough. But after talking to Courtney I found out there would be a problem with Lennox coming out early, because he was contracted to appear in a cameo role for a film called *Ocean's Eleven*, starring Julia Roberts and George Clooney.

The other problem was that Manny Steward was going to be in Naseem Hamed's corner for his fight with Marco Antonio Barrera in Vegas just two weeks before the scheduled 21 April contest between Lennox and Rahman.

We returned to London and announced the fight at a press conference. There was a bit of spice added to the occasion when I was asked to read out a statement which effectively said Panos was no longer Lennox's promoter. I have to admit I enjoyed breaking the news to the media, and I couldn't help feeling some satisfaction that after all the bullshit I'd had to put up with towards the end of my time with him, it was Eliades and not me getting the elbow.

Panos wasn't slow to have his say when he heard the news, alleging he was owed money from the Botha and Tua fights. 'Lennox has changed,' he said in the press. 'He is not the man that you think he is. I gave him the crown and he has taken my head.'

He was clearly bitter about the whole thing and it was the start of a legal battle with Lennox for breach of contract which was eventually settled in the American courts a year later, as Lewis counter-sued, alleging fraud and racketeering before being awarded $8 million.

Having had the visit to South Africa and heard all about Lennox's film commitments I sat down and wrote a memo to Lennox and Adrian outlining a compromise. 'We need to be in South Africa for no less than 21 days,' I wrote. 'We should arrive in South Africa on Saturday, 31 March 2001 to start training on the Monday.' I also listed what I believed were the main problems. 'Time difference, flying time, altitude (a big one),' I noted.

Lennox went off to his training camp in Las Vegas to prepare for the fight and although I heard that he'd claimed he would be on the next plane out once Rahman went to South Africa, when the American did fly to Carnival City four weeks before the fight, Lewis decided to stay in Vegas. He didn't seem at all concerned the challenger might be getting some valuable extra time to get used to the altitude.

I arrived in South Africa a little over two weeks before the contest to make sure everything was all right and prepare for Lennox's arrival. In a press conference the day after I got there Lennox sounded very strange on a link from America. He kept on telling Rahman he was going to knock him out, but it was the way he said it that made an impression on me. He was emphasising every word and sounding really arrogant. When he was asked about the altitude he virtually dismissed the idea that it might be a problem.

Lennox stayed on in Vegas and watched Manny work Hamed's corner as he got bashed up and defeated by Barrera. It was a bad defeat for Hamed who was outclassed and out-fought by the Mexican. It was also a bad start for Manny in what was to be an eventful couple of weeks, which later saw him sacked as Naz's trainer.

Lennox and his team arrived on the Tuesday following the fight, which was 11 days before the contest with Rahman. The entourage surrounding Lewis seemed bigger than ever, and just to add to matters he also had a full-time South African security team to make sure everything went smoothly. I doubt if George Bush could have had better protection than Lennox had on his runs, with everything worked out like a military operation.

If the security side of things went smoothly, the same couldn't be said of our relationship with local boxing promoter Rodney Berman, who had helped engineer the whole show. He got upset about some things and accused the Lewis team of being arrogant.

There were also a couple of really sobering moments during the build-up to the contest. The first was when 43 spectators died during a disaster at a football match between Orlando Pirates and Kaiser Chiefs. It was terrible to watch it all unfold on the television screen in my room, and a few days later we went to a blessing and cleansing ceremony at the stadium. Lennox spent quite a bit of time there speaking to relatives of the victims and I think we all felt very moved by the whole experience.

We also went to an orphanage in Soweto which had most of us holding back the tears when we saw the plight of the little kids there. Lennox's mum, Violet, seemed as upset by the whole thing as I was and put her arms around me as we both looked on in disbelief.

In the days before the contest I couldn't help feeling a little uneasy about everything, and to be honest, I said as much off the record to some of the English press guys. I agreed that Lennox was a class above Rahman, but I knew the challenger would be really fired up as he tried to cause an upset. My gut feeling was that Lewis's preparations had not been the best and he needed to be careful.

NO BALONEY

From the first round until the punch which eventually dumped him on his backside in the fifth, Lennox was given enough warning signs but he chose to ignore them as Rahman ripped his titles away. Lewis got caught in the opening round and had his mouth open and his hands dangling by his side from early on in the fight.

At the end of the fourth round Manny told him, 'You start shooting the left hooks, you're gonna knock him out of here.'

They were bold words and I couldn't help thinking back to what Pepe Correa had said to Lennox at the end of the first round in his fight with McCall: 'Forget the game plan, just go and knock the bum out.' Unfortunately it was the 'bum' who knocked Lennox out in the next round, and this time it was Rahman who had his arms raised a short time after Manny's confident words.

In the fifth round Lennox found himself against the ropes as Rahman took a step back. But instead of moving away he grinned and the challenger just walked forward and threw a big right hand punch. That was it. Lennox went crashing to the canvas.

When it was over he just kept shaking his head muttering over and over again, 'I don't believe it,' but it had happened all right and once again Lennox was an ex-champion. The first time it had happened against McCall I was in a terrible state, but it didn't feel the same against Rahman. I did feel sorry for him, but I couldn't help coming back to the fact that bad preparation and arrogance within the camp had a lot to do with it. Lennox seemed as though he'd taken the whole thing too lightly and he'd paid a heavy price for it.

I was asked to take control of the dressing-room after the fight and say a few words to everyone. I told them we'd lost and it was Rahman's night, but we had to be positive and be seen as a team. If Lennox wanted to go back and get his titles we had to do our best to make sure that happened. It was important that we said the right things and behaved with dignity.

It was a strange scene with most of Lennox's team still calling him champ. It was as if the punch that detached Lewis from his senses had also detached them from reality. The truth of the matter was Lennox was no longer the heavyweight king. The crown had been snatched by Rahman.

19. THE WRITING'S ON THE WALL

MY REACTION TO THE DEFEAT BY RAHMAN WAS VERY DIFFERENT TO THE WAY I felt after McCall.

I was upset but not in the same way as I had been at Wembley, when I was in a state of shock. This time I was more annoyed about the way the whole thing had been handled and the kind of arrogance that had cost Lennox his crown. The bottom line was that he and his new team had to take responsibility for what had happened in the ring, and his attitude clearly hadn't been right. He seemed to think he could just turn up and everything would be all right.

Not arriving in South Africa earlier was crazy as far as I was concerned, and so was getting involved in making a movie so close to the fight. The preparation just didn't seem right. Manny Steward may have a reputation as a great trainer, but I thought he needed to take a good long look at the part he played in it all.

He was looking after the heavyweight champion of the world and yet two weeks before the Rahman contest he was in Hamed's corner. I believed he should have concentrated on Lennox alone. Some years back when Manny was unhappy over some money issues we received a letter from his lawyer and in it he detailed just what

Steward had given up, in terms of work with other fighters, so that he could concentrate on Lennox. But during the time that I knew him, Manny was often out of camp on other boxing business. And for someone who had been in the game for so long, I was surprised by his attitude to the business of altitude training.

'You must understand something,' he later said. 'With people who travel internationally as much as we do, the altitude and climate does not hurt our bodies as much.' I'd never heard such bullshit in my life.

It was amazing to think that after all the fights Lennox had been involved in, his two defeats had come against nobodies. I didn't exclude myself from some of the blame. Perhaps I should have tried to talk him into retiring after the Grant or Botha fights. He'd proved he was the best in the world and he could have sat back and counted his millions.

Lennox's reaction to the defeat was different this time as well. He clearly couldn't believe what had happened to him. I think he quickly realised he'd made some mistakes in the ring, but when I visited him in the apartment he'd been staying in at the Kopanong Hotel just before I was due to fly home, it wasn't the same sort of scene it had been back in 1994. Then it had been me and him in a darkened hotel room. This time he was sitting with some friends I hadn't seen before, and his friends were smoking and drinking champagne.

I knew there was no way he would want to go out as a loser, so it was obvious the battle was on for him to try and get a re-match with Rahman. I hadn't been involved in any of the negotiations for the fight, so I didn't know the strength of the contract. It was going to be Adrian's first big test in the boxing world and it soon became apparent that he wanted some help.

In the first few days that followed the fight I was naturally asked my views by the press as to what had gone wrong and what was likely to happen. I believed it was my job to say something because it at least put a buffer between the press and Lennox. Adrian agreed with me on this, but seemed to change his tune a bit later, probably because he didn't like me voicing what I thought were a few home truths.

The silly thing was that there was a real possibility Lennox need not have gone ahead with the Rahman fight and instead focused his attention on Tyson. I had it on very good authority that the Tyson money was in place and that an agreement in principle could have been reached to get the fight done.

On the Thursday after the defeat Adrian met with Frank Warren and me at a hotel near Heathrow. We had already had another, earlier meeting, and it was clear he hoped we might be able to help him engineer a way back for Lennox. Adrian even suggested Frank could have the job as Lennox's promoter. I saw the contract for the first time and it seemed a bit of a mess. Frank's opinion was that you could drive a bus through it and not touch the sides. Needless to say, it was obvious a lot of work had to be done, because Lennox was in danger of being frozen out of the picture.

Adrian outlined the changes he thought should be made in the Lewis camp. It sounded as though he was ready to get rid of some people in the set-up and he was determined to bring Lennox back into the world title picture, but he realised he needed help. He put on a brave face, but in my opinion Adrian was way out of his depth at that stage.

We left the meeting telling Adrian we'd talk again when we had something more concrete in mind. Joe Calzaghe was due to defend his WBO super-middleweight title against Germany's Mario Veit two days later in Cardiff, and after leaving Ogun we set off with my driver for Wales. It almost turned out to be the last journey either of us made when the car had a blow-out. It was a nasty moment, but Frank managed to see the funny side of it.

'Barry Hearn's dream of becoming the biggest promoter in Britain almost came true then, Frank!' he told me.

The Calzaghe fight was going to be screened by Showtime, the TV company who broadcast Tyson's fights, and Jay Larkin was due to fly in for the contest. We formulated a plan to get everyone together under the same roof to discuss how we could sort out the Lennox Lewis situation and the re-match problem.

After the meeting with Adrian at Heathrow, Frank had phoned Jay and a conference call was eventually set up where we all agreed we would meet in Cardiff on the day of the fight. Adrian booked a suite at the Angel Hotel and brought along his new American lawyer Judd

Burstein, who had previously done some work for Frank Warren. By this time there were all sorts of stories flying around about what was going to happen, and Rahman found himself at the centre of a bidding war, helped by the fact that he didn't have a binding contract with a TV network.

Various scenarios were discussed in Cardiff, and in the end we shook hands on a proposal which was subject to having it looked over by lawyers and getting their go-ahead. The basic idea was for Lewis not to go after an immediate re-match, but instead allow Rahman and Tyson to fight, with Lennox taking on the winner. We asked Ogun if he needed to speak to Lennox about it, but he told us it was a good deal and he was happy with it.

That possible deal lasted for a matter of days before the situation changed and it continued to do so as the rival TV networks tried to get Rahman to sign with them. A few weeks later Don King entered the picture and put a whole new slant on things by signing Rahman to a promotional deal. It looked as though Lennox could be left out in the cold and I felt the whole situation had been badly handled.

I was asked about how I felt with regard to the situation and did an interview with Jim Lawton in *The Independent* where I mentioned the mess and referred to the Johnny-come-latelys in the Lewis camp. I think the words in that article and some of the others I'd used to describe how I felt in a piece with the *Express* became the writing on the wall for me.

It was pretty obvious Adrian began to think I was having a go at him and I knew that could spell trouble for me. If you underestimate Adrian he's a dangerous man. He'd come into the Lewis organisation seven years earlier as an assistant to Dennis Lewis. In the years that followed, Dennis went out of the main picture, Panos was gone and by this time I had the distinct feeling my days were numbered as well.

It seemed even more apparent in the summer when Adrian asked me to sign a new consultancy agreement, which contained a confidentiality provision in it. I let my lawyers have it and was advised not to sign. One of the main reasons for this was the fact that it left me wide open to being sacked at the drop of a hat.

Lennox eventually got the go-ahead for a second fight with Rahman after a court battle and there was also talk in the papers of a two-fight deal with Tyson being lined up as well. After a holiday in Jamaica he returned to Britain for a birthday party on 2 September. I hadn't spoken to Lennox for some time and wasn't invited to the party. Neither was Julius Francis, although he did turn up on the night having been told by Harold Knight to come along, only to be stopped at the door because Lennox didn't want him there.

The next day a press conference had been called in London to announce the Rahman fight and during the early hours of the morning Adrian left a message on my answerphone. 'What I need you to do is, in the morning, to phone Lennox. Both you and he need to have a chat and just talk some things over,' Adrian said. 'Maybe call around nine o'clock.'

When I phoned Lennox's home his mother told me he'd already left the house, and when I tried his mobile number I got his answering service, so I left a message. I also left a message with Adrian but neither of them phoned me back.

The press conference went ahead, but I wasn't there because I hadn't been asked to go and had already made plans to travel to Blackpool to see a young heavyweight. There might have been a name plate for me but the press soon picked up on the fact that I wasn't around and obviously thought it was a bit strange.

Lennox said I was technically still his manager, which seemed to raise more suspicions before later claiming to some of the media that I'd been his manager since day one and would be in his corner on 17 November, the day of his fight with Rahman in Vegas, although he added that he and I had to talk some things over.

Lewis went off to training camp and I carried on with my work at Sports Network, part of which, at the end of October, involved setting up a training facility in California for a fighter named Roman Karmazin to prepare for a world title shot against Oscar De La Hoya.

I hadn't heard anything from the Lewis camp and had been told in writing that Lennox wanted to concentrate on his preparations and that if there were any problems they should be discussed with Jerome Anderson, the football agent, who had appeared on the scene. Anderson's company, The Sport Entertainment and Media Group, had acquired Cloudmanor in June 2001. Adrian Ogun was Cloudmanor's chief executive and the company managed the boxing business affairs of Lewis. Ogun became an executive director of Sport Entertainment, with Anderson becoming more obviously involved in the Lewis team. But as far as I was concerned, the idea of me talking to Anderson instead of Lennox was like using a call centre when you really wanted to speak to the bank manager.

Out of the blue at the end of October just before I was due to leave for California I received a telephone call from Adrian. Once again the subject of the consultancy agreement came up, and I told him I wasn't happy with the confidentiality clause. When he asked me why I hadn't spoken to Lennox about it, I pointed out that the memo I'd got from Anderson basically told me not to bother Lewis.

Adrian suggested I call Jerome, but I didn't see why I should have to do that. Instead it was agreed that Anderson would contact me, and a conference call was scheduled for Friday 2 November. Anderson and Ogun were on the line from London and after talking about what my role might be if I signed the agreement and went to Las Vegas for the Rahman fight, it was time to make a decision.

There was no way I was going to sign the agreement they'd given me because it was like a slave contract as far as I was concerned, even though doing so would have given me $225,000 which was the percentage I would have earned from the Rahman fight, and there was also the prospect of a huge pay day for me if Lennox fought Tyson, which in many ways could have been my pension for all the years I'd been with him. It would have been easier to have just said yes and Anderson seemed surprised that I was willing to pass up that kind of money. I agreed it was a lot of cash, but in my view Lewis didn't really need a boxing manager any more with the way he was running things, and I told them that. It was as if they wanted me along for the ride and under control, but weren't prepared to give me any meaningful role.

It was clear to me that Lewis and I had come to the end of the road and we might as well part on good terms. I suggested I could go and see Lennox, we could then make a public statement saying we'd decided to go our separate ways after more than 12 years together, and shake hands. We talked about some sort of settlement and when Adrian asked me what kind of money I was looking for I told him a figure of $750,000.

THE WRITING'S ON THE WALL

I arrived at the amount by taking into account the money I would have got from the Rahman contest and the fact that Ogun had already talked publicly about Lennox having a couple of huge pay days against Tyson. Of course it was quite a lot of money, but I don't think it was an unfair figure in the circumstances.

Three days after the conference call a reporter from London phoned telling me he'd heard there was going to be a press conference where an announcement about me splitting with Lennox was going to be made. That same day a faxed letter was sent to me from Lennox terminating with immediate effect all arrangements for me to act as a consultant in relation to his boxing affairs. In other words he was giving me the sack. It seemed strange to me, because I was under the impression when I spoke to Ogun and Anderson that we were talking about an amicable parting of the ways.

The letter didn't even have his signature on it, instead it had been signed on his behalf, and claimed he would have preferred to meet me face to face to discuss the issue of the contract but couldn't due to the closeness of his next bout. He wished me success in the future and at the end of the letter said he'd made arrangements for my mother to go to the Rahman fight as his guest! It was unbelievable really.

After 12 years together I'd have thought he might have been able to at least pick up the phone to tell me himself, even if he was in training camp. Don't forget, I was only in California and if he'd wanted to see me I was quite prepared to hop on a plane to his camp.

When the end came for me it was all done at arm's length, just as it had been with other people over the years. I do believe that if Lennox and I could have sat down face to face I might still be in my position as his boxing manager.

I was telephoned by the British press and there seemed to be a couple of different statements coming out of the Lewis camp about why I'd gone. One said that I'd made a ridiculous cash demand and the other claimed that there was a conflict of interest because of my work with Sports Network.

'You do realise Frank was working for Frank Warren,' Lennox said. 'It is about conflict of interests.' It seemed a bit of a strange comment considering both Ogun and Lewis had raised no objections when I told them I was joining Sports Network.

The fall-out from the split rumbled on with the story occupying the back pages for days. I didn't realise what a big thing it was until I flew home from the States when the Karmazin fight was postponed because of a hand injury to De La Hoya. The newspapers seemed to have a lot of sympathy with the way I had been treated with headlines like, 'Maloney's sad reward for telling the truth', typical of the kind of treatment I got.

A little more than 24 hours after touching down from America I got a call from Bernard Clarke, telling me Lennox was about to go to court to take out an injunction that would effectively impose a gagging order, stopping me from talking to the media. It seemed to show the level of paranoia and need for control that existed in the Lewis camp. What was already a crazy situation suddenly became even crazier, as the bullying tactics of Lennox's new team reached a different level.

20. THE WAY WE WERE

WHEN I HEARD THE NEWS ABOUT A POSSIBLE COURT BATTLE I WAS absolutely amazed. I couldn't help thinking about the way things had changed during the 12 years since I'd waited at Heathrow hoping to clinch a deal to become Lennox's manager.

For most of those years I'd had a great time and enjoyed playing my part in helping Lewis reach the top, but towards the end it became a different story. The atmosphere and people surrounding Lennox had changed. Although at the split I was still his boxing manager, I really didn't have a proper role to play. There was no doubt in my mind that Adrian had slowly but surely become the real power behind the throne, and I don't think he was too unhappy to finally see the back of me.

I was the longest serving member of the Lewis team and had been there from day one. The funny thing was that even in the early days I'd never felt totally secure as his manager. I always knew there were people around from both inside the camp and out of it who were more than willing to put the knife in, but I'd survived. Levitt, Hornewer, Davenport, Correa, Dennis, Panos. They had all been part of the set-up during those 12 years and yet I'd somehow managed to stay longer than any of them.

NO BALONEY

The nicest thing about Lennox when he first arrived was the way he was prepared to muck in and get on with things. I think he just enjoyed being in Britain and starting his professional career here. He never really asked for special treatment and he certainly wasn't pampered. A few months after his professional debut he even made do with sleeping on a couch in the front room of a guy in Wales, because there wasn't a room for him at the hotel we were using during a promotion in Cardiff. The person who put him up for the night was a friend of Eric Guy, and later on he actually had a plaque placed on the wall saying, 'World heavyweight champion Lennox Lewis slept here.'

Lennox was as happy wandering around in south London eating fish and chips in East Street market as he was staying in a five-star hotel. Of course everyone changes and we move on with our lives but at that stage in his career there was a very small and closely knit team surrounding him. By the time I left there were all sorts of bodyguards and faces I didn't recognise.

After we parted company I made some comments about the fact that I'd helped to create a monster. What I meant by that was that I believed he'd changed a lot from the guy I first got to know 12 years earlier. I think some of the people around him seemed to try and take things into their own hands when they read what I'd had to say at the time and later during the build-up to his fight with Mike Tyson in June 2002.

I actually got a call on my mobile from one of them giving me what amounted to a 'warning' about what nasty things I said in relation to Lewis. I was travelling in my car to Manchester with my family for a friend's wedding, and later reported the incident to my lawyer. I can't believe for one minute that Lennox had anything to do with it, but it wasn't very nice for Tracey to hear it. Lennox and I had been through a lot together and I think there was a mutual respect. We were never bosom buddies but we had a good professional relationship and when we did socialise we had fun.

I've always thought Lennox is basically a shy person who was desperate to guard his private life like no other fighter I've ever known. That's fine, but it's not easy for the world heavyweight champion to be anonymous. He must have given countless interviews over the years, but nobody could really say they know him.

Although I worked with him for a long time and had a lot of good times and laughs along the way, we were never really close and he kept me at arm's length when it came to a lot of his life, which I think was fair enough. I must have experienced weeks in the company of Lennox and his mother over the years, but I was totally unaware that Violet had a grandchild until I read it in Lewis's own book. Knowing that neither Lennox nor Dennis had any children, it came as a bit of a surprise.

I think it was probably because he was so desperate to keep his life away from the ring private that people thought he had something to hide. The gay rumours were always flying around while I was with him, despite Lennox categorically denying them, as in the case of *The Sun* story before his first fight with Holyfield. I've seen Lennox with loads of beautiful women over the years, but he's never gone out of his way to get publicity and has always preferred to keep his private life private.

Maybe it's because of who he is that people like to have a go, and it's almost as if they want Lennox to behave more like other fighters outside the ring. But he's not like other fighters. He's made millions and you won't see him squandering his money, womanising in public or getting hooked on drugs and booze like so many other heavyweights. Lennox is a careful person by nature and someone who expects to get his own way.

I've known him keep members of his inner circle up until the early hours of the morning in training camp just so he can get his revenge in a re-match having lost at chess. He has a real need to win and succeed.

Despite what went on I've got no problem with Lennox. If I've got any kind of gripe it's simply that he never bothered to pick up the phone to me after sending that letter back in November 2001. People may ask why I never bothered to speak to him, but as far as I'm concerned I still believe I haven't done anything wrong. We've been in the same room at a couple of dinners since the split, but not spoken and I wonder whether we ever will. We're both probably as stubborn as each other.

NO BALONEY

I admit that at first I felt bitter about what had gone on and there was a temptation to start saying bad things about Lennox, but I soon realised that would be stupid and thought about the good times we'd had together during those 12 years.

Although there was a lack of contact with him, his mother Violet did pay a visit to my house to see our new little baby Libby, who was born in March 2001. It was good of her to pop over and showed once again what a nice lady she is. I know Lennox thinks the world of his mum and I can understand why. She's been a big part of his life.

I've often wondered what Lewis really thought at the time of my departure and whether he knew all the facts. In an interview which was published by a Sunday newspaper in the summer of 2002 Lennox talked about what had gone on after his defeat in South Africa and in it said that Rahman had told him, 'Your manager phoned me up trying to get a fight with me and Tyson.' Lennox also claimed that I wasn't acting in his best interests. It wasn't very pleasant for me to read and it also wasn't true. I actually got a substantial sum from the paper in question and an apology once I disputed the claim.

Lennox can be kind, but there's also a ruthless streak which runs through him, that I've seen both inside the ring and out of it. My differences with him were eventually settled and I was able to get on with the rest of my life by the end of 2001, including a family trip to Australia to see my brother Vince who has lived there for some years.

But Panos was given the knockout treatment by Lewis when they went head-to-head in New York. As I've said, Lennox ended up being awarded $8 million in February 2002 when the court decided that Panix promotions and Panix of the USA along with Panos had jointly severely defrauded Lewis in relation to the income due to him from previous bouts.

The case opened up a can of worms for Panos and Lewis had another victory in the courts towards the end of the year when he was awarded $1.175 million in damages for an action against Milt Chwasky, having accused the lawyer of failing to protect him, by letting Panos take money from his expense account.

I was never allowed in on financial settlement meetings and for a lot of the time Panos and Dennis took care of that, and after all that eventually happened it probably did me a favour. Panos and Lennox used to have long meetings together which never involved me and I often used to say to Lennox that it might be a good idea for him to have more independent legal and accountancy advice.

When the fall-out came I couldn't help feeling Panos had brought a lot of trouble on himself. During the final part of my time with him it seemed as though he was desperate to be in control of Lennox and his affairs. He talked about his relationship with Lewis once and was quoted as saying, 'I'm his adviser, his friend, his father and his mother, everything – it's a unique relationship.'

But when they split it was a very different story. Lewis and his people even employed a detective agency to investigate certain people in the Lewis team, including me and my brother! I couldn't believe it at first but it soon became clear it was true, and I suppose the move eventually paid off for him.

Even before Lennox's split from Panos it was pretty clear that Ogun was playing a much bigger part in the career of Lewis, and it really shouldn't have surprised me. When Adrian had approached me all those years earlier to talk about possibly acting for us in trying to get some sponsorship deals for Lennox and was all over us like treacle, he came across as being very smooth and slick.

It wasn't long before he was working alongside Dennis Lewis looking after the commercial aspects of Lennox's career. I remember telling Dennis one day that he ought to watch Adrian, because I felt he was trying to muscle in, but he told me not to worry and that he had everything under control. A few years later that didn't seem to be the case as Dennis was sidelined and played no real part in his brother's career.

I know Panos began to be suspicious of Ogun and the fact that he was having more to do with Lennox than he felt comfortable with, but he couldn't really do anything about it. Adrian got to know about the business side of Lennox's career and slowly started to take control as Panos got edged out. By the time Eliades went, Ogun had already made his move to gain greater knowledge about the way things worked in the boxing world. He was very friendly towards me after the

Botha fight and seemed to want to pick my brains on a lot of things.

He's a clever guy and I suppose you could say that perhaps he's achieved what he set out to do, but as for him carrying on in boxing after Lennox has retired, I'm not sure it will happen. I think he could very soon go from being Adrian Ogun, business manager of Lennox Lewis, to Adrian who? It's easy to be a big shot in the game when you have the heavyweight champion of the world, but he knows relatively little about building fighters and making the right sort of boxing decisions for a kid coming through the ranks. Adrian seems desperate to try and control things when it comes to Lennox, even down to the press, but you just can't do that with the media.

In case you haven't already guessed, I've got no time at all for Ogun, and I told him so in Cardiff during the summer of 2002 when he turned up at a Joe Calzaghe fight. He tried to be his usual smooth self, but I wasn't having any of it and those people who were within earshot will tell you that what I had to say to him wasn't particularly pleasant or complimentary.

Someone who will survive in the game is Emanuel Steward. He had already built a reputation as a great trainer before he ever got involved with Lennox and you certainly can't question the success he's had with some fighters. But they haven't all been winners and if I have to give an honest assessment of Manny, I'd say I wasn't as impressed as I thought I'd be.

Like a lot of other people I'd heard how great he was but I saw nothing from him that made me feel as though I was watching a master at work. There were plenty of times during my association with him where I disagreed with the way he went about things. The fact that he went missing from camp at times to look after other fighters and boxing business wasn't right as far as I was concerned.

From the very first day Manny could never be content with just being a trainer, he acted as though he wanted to be manager and promoter as well. I think it was his way of trying to take control when he worked with a fighter, but some of his antics during the time I knew him made me wonder why he was so highly regarded.

Although being the manager of Lennox Lewis played such a big part in my life for 12 years, my career in the game began a long time before I teamed up with him and it will go on a long time after leaving him. Boxing is like a drug and no matter how many knocks you take it's hard to just give it up and walk away. I admit the split from Lennox was not the way I'd have liked it all to end. I was there at the beginning and it would have been nice to be there at the end or at least bow out with him still being a world champion. But it wasn't to be.

In the end I missed out on Lewis regaining the title from Rahman 12 days after our split. I always thought that if he prepared right and got himself focused there was no way Lennox could lose again. On the night of the fight I was in a Sky TV studio giving my comments on the action from Vegas.

It was a strange feeling, because for the first time in 12 years I wasn't in the corner for one of Lennox's fights. When I was asked to do the show I knew it was a chance for me to get in a dig of my own if I wanted to, but on the way to the studio I realised it was a silly thing to do. I knew there was no point in me trying to phone Lewis, but instead I made a call to Joe Dunbar and asked him to wish Lennox good luck. I did feel out of things, watching all the action from such a distance, but at least my fellow pundits in the studio seemed a lot more genuine than some of the people I would have been dealing with had I swallowed my pride and signed the consultancy contract they'd come up with.

Lennox had nothing more to prove in the ring after gaining revenge against Rahman and beating Tyson seven months later. I think it would have been a good time for him to retire after disposing of Tyson. I think both of them were past their best. The thing that did surprise me after Lewis beat Tyson was the way he became the invisible heavyweight, but perhaps that was down to the new team that Lennox has around him now.

I've often been asked where I would rate Lennox in my all-time top ten heavyweights and if I'm honest I would have to say it would probably be on the fringe of that list. I don't think he really had a defining fight in his career, because although he beat the likes of Holyfield and Tyson, I don't believe either man was at their peak when they stepped into the ring with Lennox. Don't get me wrong,

Lewis always got on and fought the people who were put in front of him, and you can't ask any more than that. But when it comes to rating him alongside other world champions of the past, there's a lot of very good competition.

On the same night as the Rahman return, Scott Harrison continued his progress with another win, and a little less than a year later he provided me with one of the greatest moments in my boxing career when he became the WBO world featherweight champion.

In front of 5,000 screaming home fans at the Braehead Arena in Renfrew, Scott produced a brilliant display of non-stop aggressive boxing to take the title from the Argentinian, Julio Pablo Chacon. I was almost in tears at the end as I stood in the ring, dressed in a kilt, hugging Scott and punching my fist in the air. I had another world champion and maybe if I really needed proof that there was going to be life after Lennox that was it. There's no greater satisfaction for a boxing manager than signing an amateur and seeing him go on to become a world title-holder.

Like Paul Ingle before him, I think Scott is an exceptional fighter. In his early days as a professional Harrison would sometimes spar with Paul and on one occasion went down to Scarborough when Ingle was preparing for his first world title defence. When he went to Yorkshire Ingle had set up a ring in the Grand Hotel, which is a huge place over looking the sea. Paul was quite happy training there in front of some of the guests who were staying in the hotel, but as they watched a lot of them would be smoking and drinking as well. Scott couldn't put up with the atmosphere because he thought it just wasn't right for him.

He wasn't showing off or being precious, it was simply that he had a very strict way of preparing and I have to say that he's probably the hardest training boxer I've ever worked with, and that includes Lennox Lewis. He's quite happy to lock himself away in training camp and the work he gets through while he's there is phenomenal. Had the tragedy never happened to Paul Ingle, I think a fight between him and Scott would have been sensational.

I'm convinced Harrison could go on to be one of the best fighters this country has ever produced and he's been a joy to deal with. He was recommended to me by former world champion Barry McGuigan. When Harrison first talked about signing professionally he came to my house with his father, Peter, who trains him, and within no time we'd shaken hands on a deal. That's the sort of relationship we've had since day one, and long may it continue.

After winning the title against Chacon and producing a successful first defence against Wayne McCullough, Scott was beaten on a split points decision by Mexican Manuel Medina at the Braehead Arena in July 2003. It was the same Medina who had lost to Paul Ingle almost four years earlier. The result was a shock for Scott and for me. Harrison was a heavy favourite and I had been the one who had approved the match. In hindsight it also made me think about what Paul might have achieved had his career not come to such a tragic end. It meant that Harrison had to deal with the loss of his title, but there have been many great champions over the years that have come back as better fighters following a defeat. I believe it was a case of Scott having a bad day at the office, and as Dan Duva told me all those years ago when Lennox had lost to McCall, the only thing better than winning the title is regaining it, which Scott did in a return against Medina later in the year.

After some bad times during the final couple of years with Lennox I'm enjoying my life much more now than I have for a long time. Working with Frank again has been good for me. I have a lot of respect for him and having worked closely with him, I can now see how he was always able to stay one step ahead of us when I was with Panix.

I'm getting a kick out of working with fighters like Alex Arthur, Kevin Lear, Tony Oakey, Wayne Elcock, Graham Earl, Martin Powers, Ross Minter and Danny Hunt, and signing the best young prospects around.

There's a lot for me to look forward to and I am lucky to have finally found the kind of family life I've always wanted, with Tracey and the two children. As well as having a young family at the age of 50, I'm also a grandfather, with Emma having settled down with two kids of her own, but things haven't all been rosy with my daughter. Although I love her dearly we had a disagreement some time ago and haven't spoken for a while. I know it's something lots of parents experience with their kids and I'm sure we can eventually patch things up.

I'm not the sort of person who can ever sit still for too long. Even when I was with Lennox I began to dabble in the world of politics and almost put my name forward as a candidate in the first Mayor of London elections as an independent. When Ken Livingstone decided to enter the race, I knew he'd blow everyone else out of the water, so I never went ahead with it. But I still feel passionately about the city I grew up in and that's why I decided to stand for election earlier this year representing the UK Independence Party.

A couple of weeks after Scott's win against Chacon I had a meeting with the BBC who were interested in me getting involved in a celebrity boxing programme. The idea was for me to help train comedian Ricky Gervais for a bout against Grant Bovey. The training was due to take place over a period of weeks with the two men eventually meeting in a specially staged contest at the Television Centre in west London.

Although Ricky was the star of one of the biggest comedy hits for years, I'd never seen *The Office* and didn't even know what he looked like when I went to meet him. Tracey had seen the show and told me how good it was, but I had no idea that Ricky was such a funny man until I met him. We got on well right from the start and had a great time in the weeks that followed. I told him right from the off that I was going to train him properly and knew that the key to him winning was to make sure he was able to maintain a high work-rate and throw plenty of punches.

Poor Ricky used to get stick from me and from Eugene, whose gym we used for all the training sessions. My brother eventually moved his gym back to south London and runs Maloney's Fight Factory in the Old Kent Road. He's also promoting shows and has really got back into the sport in a big way. He actually took over from me towards the end of the celebrity boxing filming and the Beeb were delighted with the way it all worked out.

Ricky duly won his contest and as he said earlier in this book, it was an experience for him, even though Eugene and I really put him through it. When I screamed at him and said he wasn't acting like a boxer his reply made me think.

'I'm not a fucking boxer, I'm a fucking comedian and that's what I'll still be in six weeks when this is all over!' said Ricky.

That moment also made me realise something as well. I'm a boxing man. I have been ever since I first put on a pair of gloves, and I will be until the day I die.

21. THE BUSINESS OF BOXING

AS FAR AS I'M CONCERNED, PROFESSIONAL BOXING IS A UNIQUE BUSINESS and a unique sport. It is also as addictive as any drug you care to name.

Having worked in the game virtually all my life, I still find it as exciting and compulsive as I did when I was a kid in south London taking part in all those amateur contests. I've been lucky enough to earn a good living from it, but I'm convinced that even if I hadn't been able to achieve my dream of managing the heavyweight champion of the world, I would still have carried on in the sport in some way or another. Once it's in your blood it stays there forever.

The buzz I got when I first began to train, manage and promote fighters has never left me, and whether I'm involved in a Las Vegas world title fight or making sure everything goes well during a promotion at York Hall, the business of boxing is still very special to me.

I've often been asked why I love the sport and there is no easy answer. Boxing is something that captured my imagination from an early age and there's no one thing that I can point to as the reason for me getting hooked on the game. It can appear to be brutal and basic at times, but I doubt whether there is another sport around that can generate so much raw excitement.

Unless you've lived your life within boxing, it's very difficult to explain the sort of hold the fight game can have over you. There are a lot of people who think it's an easy business to get involved in as a way of making money, but that's simply not the case. If you look at people like Frank Warren and me, or before us, Mickey Duff and Terry Lawless, you realise that any success we might have had did not come overnight. You have to spend years learning your trade and getting to know the ways of the boxing world.

It's still true that if you have a fat enough cheque book and a big enough ego, you can march in and become a promoter without too much trouble, but that doesn't mean you automatically become a boxing person. It's also disturbing in some ways that you can become a trainer without any kind of qualifications for the job. Panos Eliades was a very successful businessman when he entered boxing as the backer of Lennox Lewis, but, as I've said, I always felt he never fully understood the business of boxing and the way it worked. I'm not talking about figures and money, but the whole system and what it takes to bring fighters along.

I can remember walking along a street in London with Roger Levitt some time after I became Lennox's manager and being asked for my autograph by a couple of boxing fans. Roger was quite put out that they recognised me and not him. He was the one bankrolling the Lewis operation and seemed to think it had also bought him entry into the wider boxing world. I think he liked the idea of suddenly becoming someone who would be recognised in the street, but it never really happened.

Frank Warren is the number one promoter in Britain, and having started with him in the early days and worked closely with him in the last few years, I can understand why. It's not just about being smart, or knowing a good fighter when you see one, it's also about being able to make the right deals, know the right people and build for the future. When I first met Frank all those years ago, I thought he looked more like a businessman than a fight man, but he's managed to be successful at both and has the staying power that many people thought he lacked when he first hit the scene. Like it or not, Frank and his Sports

THE BUSINESS OF BOXING

Network company are the Manchester United of British boxing and there isn't really an Arsenal or Liverpool out there to mount a serious challenge. Is that bad for the sport? I don't think so, because we happen to put on quality shows on a regular basis throughout the country. The fighters are well looked after and know they have a chance to go all the way if they have the ability. For a long time Frank and I were fierce rivals, always trying to outdo each other. Even when that was happening, I couldn't help having a sneaking regard for what he was doing, and I think perhaps he felt the same way towards me.

Splitting from him back in the 1980s was probably the best thing that could have happened to me in many ways, although I didn't see it that way at the time. It meant I had to stand on my own two feet and learn about managing fighters and promoting shows. I had the drive, ambition and that little bit of luck which eventually helped me to succeed, but it hasn't all been easy.

I struggled desperately to keep afloat when I first started, but even when I knew I was losing money by the bucketload on small hall promotions, I never once thought about giving up. I think it's even harder these days to fight your way up the ladder as a manager and promoter. If you don't have the backing of TV it's almost impossible to make shows pay, but that doesn't stop people from continuing to try, even though there are far more failures than success stories. A manager or promoter will carry on in the hope that one day the prospect they've hoped for will walk through their door. The reality is that it very seldom happens.

Even if you are a good fighter it doesn't always follow that your ability will take you right to the top. I firmly believe that unless a boxer has the right management team around him, he can struggle to make it, no matter how talented he is. Quite often an average boxer with the right people will succeed, where someone with more skill but a poorer management set-up will not do as well.

I went to a show earlier this year and watched as a young kid with a good amateur record was thrown in above his head in his first professional fight. It was a classic case of a talented boxer signing with a manager who just wasn't able to nurture the fighter and bring him along slowly. This particular boxer may have had talent, but he looked like someone who would soon become a journeyman.

It was a shame but instead of being a bright prospect, he was more likely to become someone who was brought in to offer a decent test to other boxers who had more chance of climbing to the top.

Professional boxing is a harsh business, and at the end of the day it's not just about sport, it's about money as well. But that doesn't mean to say boxing or the boxers suffer as a result, and it doesn't make it any dirtier or nastier than other professional sport. Money rules football today in a way it has never done in the past, and look at the cash involved in things like tennis, golf, baseball, basketball and horse racing.

Because it is a sport and the boxers who take part in it love the game, it still continues to produce great competition and drama. I've described boxing as theatre with blood and that's what it is. I'm not saying it's as pure as the driven snow, or that the game is as noble as some people might like the 'Noble Art' to be, but that could apply to so many other sports.

Things like cricket and horse racing have had their names tarnished by betting scandals in recent years, and there is the constant cloud of drug-taking cases hanging over athletics, but somehow it always seems to be boxing that gets singled out for having a murky image, or for the dangers involved in the sport.

Of course it's dangerous and anyone who tries to deny that would be an idiot. By the same token they would also be idiots if they didn't recognise the dangers involved in other sports and pursuits, like riding horses, driving racing cars or even playing rugby. I've never tried to justify or defend boxing, and if I ever had a son I can't say I would want him to be a fighter. But I can't see anything wrong with letting someone who does want to box step through the ropes.

There are probably three categories of fighters. The journeyman, the average domestic boxer and then those who are a bit special and can go on and win world titles. They may all start out with the same sort of dreams, but they pretty soon get a good idea of what area they fall into. Not everyone can be a Lennox Lewis, a Paul Ingle or a Scott Harrison, but I can't ever remember coming across a fighter who claimed to have been forced into becoming a professional boxer. They made their own choice and they are also the first people to admit that they know the risks involved.

THE BUSINESS OF BOXING

Boxers are some of the bravest and most genuine people you could wish to meet. Of course, there have been stories of fighters being exploited and used, and I'm sure that may still happen today in some countries, because with no single world regulating body the business is, perhaps, open to abuse.

But the idea that boxing is riddled with corruption is ridiculous as far as I'm concerned. In all my time in the business I may have come across a few dodgy characters, but there's never been any hint of things like fixed fights. There is this idea that boxing is all about gangsters and villains but it just isn't true.

I think a lot of it stems from the fact that during the 1930s in America there really was a gangster element, with mob figure Frankie Carbo effectively controlling a lot of what went on in boxing. The fight-fixing and betting scandals all added to the sinister image the sport was given. Even in the 1960s the gangster connections of world heavyweight champion, Sonny Liston, added fuel to the idea that crooks and boxing seemed to go hand in hand. When Liston lost his world title re-match against Muhammad Ali in 1965, there were cries that the fight had been fixed, even though nothing was actually ever proved.

Carbo was at the heart of the fight fixing that went on during the 1930s and 1940s and the fall-out from all of that and the involvement of the Mob did little to help boxing's credibility. The great Jake La Motta, whose defeat by Billy Fox in 1947 at Madison Square Garden stank the place out, summed things up years later. 'I'm not going to try and whitewash myself,' he said. 'I was a thief. I threw a fight. I did two terms in jail and I'm lucky I wasn't a murderer. But those rats who run boxing made me look like Little Lord Fauntleroy.'

One of the real tragedies was the story of Italian heavyweight Primo Carnera, who won the world title in 1933, but was Mob-controlled, badly exploited and robbed of thousands of dollars in purse money. When people hear about things like that it's no wonder they think the sport is corrupt and has a murky background. But all of this went on years ago, and it happened in America, not Britain.

Something that has been a problem for fighters in the States in more recent years is drugs. There have been quite a few sad stories about boxers in America getting hooked on drugs and losing their way completely. I had personal experience of one of them when I brought John Tate over to Britain in 1988. Tate had won the WBA world heavyweight title in 1979, but was way past his best when he stepped between the ropes at York Hall to take on Liverpool's Noel Quarless. By the time he faced Quarless, the former world champion's weight had ballooned to more than 20 st. With no disrespect to Noel, he wouldn't have stood much chance against Tate at his peak, but the big American lost on points against Quarless and was clearly only a shadow of the man who had once been on top of the world. I didn't know it at the time, but that fight was to be Tate's last recorded contest as a professional.

I actually spoke to Tate one day about what had gone wrong with his life and it seemed that mixing with the wrong people and getting involved with drugs had really screwed him up. He said that he suddenly found he had a whole new bunch of friends once he had become champion, and it wasn't long before Tate started sliding down the slippery slope. He never really managed to get his career back on track and in 1994 he was sentenced to three years in prison after breaking a man's jaw and stealing $14. John died in April 1998 when his pick-up truck went off the road and crashed. It was said that a tumour caused him to have a stroke and he weighed more than 30 st. at the time of his death. After coming out of prison he vowed that he would try to educate people on the evils of booze and drugs that had ruined his own life, but never really got the chance to do that or to turn his own life around.

I know of quite a few boxers in the States who have got involved in drugs and I have seen once promising careers hit the rocks. There's no doubt in my mind that some fighters do indulge in some of the softer drugs like marijuana when they're not in training for fights, although I have never managed any. Boxers have to have insurance when they're taking part in big fights, and that means having to take medicals when they start training camp. I have heard of fighters who have come up with excuses not to take tests for the medical until quite a few weeks after they have started training, which would presumably allow time for any traces of something like marijuana to be flushed from their system.

THE BUSINESS OF BOXING

It has to be said that most of the drug taking I have come across or have heard of has been for recreational use, not for enhancing performance. There have been exceptions where boxers have tested positive for steroids, although as in the case of the American Fernando Vargas, they have claimed they knew nothing about taking them.

Vargas was given a nine month ban after he tested positive for steroids after losing to Oscar De La Hoya in September 2002. As a result of the findings, Vargas fired his fitness trainer and nutritionist after claiming that someone had slipped him the drug without his knowledge.

There have been cases of drug taking with fighters in Britain, but nothing on the scale of America. Former British and European welterweight champion Kirkland Laing, whose partner gave me that clump at ringside all those years ago, had a reputation not only as a gifted boxer but also as someone who enjoyed a drink and a puff. In his day Kirk was a brilliant boxer who once beat Roberto Duran in 1982, but then he went missing from the fight scene for about a year and never managed to fulfil the potential he had.

I think booze is probably more of a problem with some British fighters and perhaps that's down to our way of life and culture. It might also have a lot to do with the sort of company they keep, and the fact that they see their mates going off down the pub when they have to sweat it out in a gym. When they're not training some fighters like to let off steam just like the rest of their friends, without remembering the fact that they're supposed to be professional athletes. There have been a few fighters who have used diuretic drugs in an effort to lose weight, and Paul Ingle was once called before an inquiry following his British and Commonwealth featherweight title win against Jonjo Irwin in 1997 after testing positive for using a weight-reducing drug, but was eventually cleared.

It would be stupid to say that drug taking doesn't happen in boxing, it does. But it also goes on in other sports and as I've said, it's usually recreational drugs and not the kind that you often hear about in athletics. Unfortunately drugs are part of our society and it's a problem that is not going to go away.

I might not have come across fixed fights during my time in the game, but there's no doubt an air of corruption has existed in the boxing world during more recent years as well. Although I believe it was no more than poor judging that robbed Lennox Lewis of a deserved victory over Holyfield in their first fight, the whole thing also happened to take place right in the middle of an FBI investigation into the dealings of the IBF world governing body which is based in New Jersey. There were allegations levelled against the organisation that money changed hands in exchange for having fighters rated in their rankings and as a result the IBF was put under federal monitoring. Its president, Robert Lee, although eventually cleared of the charge that he took $338,000 in bribes, was banned for life from boxing and also agreed to pay the IBF $50,000 in compensation. Incidents like that do the sport no good at all and just give ammunition to those people who want to have a go at boxing.

The whole question of having so many different governing bodies also does little to help the sport's reputation. I agree that it would be easier for everyone if there was just one organisation that had overall control for the game, just as FIFA does in world football. But like it or not, the simple fact of the matter is that anyone can start up a world boxing organisation. If you can then persuade enough managers, promoters and fighters to compete for your world titles and pay sanctioning fees to do so, you're off and running. I've no doubt that having so many different world organisations has weakened the sport's credibility in recent years, and I know a lot of the public would be happier if there were only a handful of champions. But from the point of view of the boxers, it has at least meant that a lot more of them have become champions and with it they gain valuable TV exposure and earn money.

The best known organisations are the WBC, WBA, IBF and WBO. I've dealt with all of them over the years and quite a few others that have sprung up. Because fighting for a world title is the ultimate for a boxer there is always a scramble with managers and promoters to get their men rated with the different bodies so that they can get a crack at the title. In order to do that you need to make sure a boxer builds a good record that moves him up the ratings.

I've often thought the ranking systems of some of the world organisations are crazy, and some of the annual conventions are nothing more than a farce in terms of the way decisions are made and the amount of influence top officials and promoters wield.

Let me just say that in many respects I don't think boxing is any different to other businesses. Like anything else, you try to stay on good terms with the people who can help you and be of use to you. I've had my run-ins with quite a few officials over the years and I've had to swallow my pride on a couple of occasions because I had to look at the bigger picture.

What has often really got to me is the way certain high-ranking boxing people are treated like royalty, and allowed to carry on doing pretty much what they want to. For example, I know of one well known boxing dignitary who would regularly expect to be given first class air travel or flights on Concorde whenever he flew to England on business, and was also provided with a suite at a hotel in London's Park Lane. This particular person also used to let it be known that he was partial to a bit of shopping, and I know of a couple of instances where promoters have had to pick up the tab for things like silk socks and camera lenses.

Boxing still operates in a very macho environment, and because of that it's no great surprise to see the busiest people at some conventions are the local 'working girls' who often congregate in the hotel lobby at the end of each day. Entertaining and visits to places like lap dancing clubs are all part of the environment, and when some boxing people travel their idea of a night out is no different to a lot of men who spend their lives working for big corporations and find themselves on business trips. They like to be entertained and enjoy having the company of women. I know of a certain young lady from New Zealand who helped out one promoter by regularly acting as an escort for certain well-known boxing figures whenever they visited London.

Sex has often played a part in the story of fighters over the years, and it has also been known to be used as a way to try and get favours from some people, or even influence the performance of boxers. There have been a few occasions where I've been offered women by people almost as a 'gift' as part of my visit to their country. It's often difficult thinking of ways to refuse without causing offence. I once grabbed the hand of my matchmaker Dean Powell when we were in

Uganda and claimed I was gay after a woman propositioned me!

In some of the old Eastern Bloc countries I've seen visiting boxers given the playboy treatment during the preparation to their fights. The idea being that if they concentrate on having a good time, they'll be less inclined to perform well in the ring.

Part of the job of a manager or promoter is to get the right matches for a prospect. It's not just a case of getting him easy fights to pad out his record, because ultimately that can blow up in your face the first time he's confronted with a tough fight. I've always believed in being cautious but at the same time I like to make sure the fights are all part of a learning curve.

You need to be able to match boxers with the right kind of opponent at the right time in their career. Sometimes that means using fighters from abroad. That's when you need a good agent who knows his stuff and can provide just the right person for the job. You want an opponent to look good and provide a test, but you certainly don't want someone to come over and knock your man out. Of course, there have always been stories about prospects being matched with real no hopers, or 'Mexican road sweepers' as some people call them. I once heard a story about the time a fighter had been sent over by an agent, and when the people staging the promotion went to pick him up at the airport, they saw that he actually had grey hair. They were worried that he'd look too old to step into the ring with the young prospect who was supposed to be fighting him, so he was whisked off to have his hair dyed black. Unfortunately, under the hot ring lights and with sweat pouring down his face, the colour from his hair started to run as well. Apparently nobody actually noticed, and the prospect duly got the win he wanted.

I'd be lying if I said I've never been guilty of making a one-sided match in an effort to get one of my fighters a win as I've tried to build a boxer's record and experience. It's not a case of fixing a fight, it's just making sure that the odds are stacked heavily in your favour. But that doesn't mean it can't all go badly wrong. Hasim Rahman was supposed to be an easy defence for Lennox and look what happened in their first fight in South Africa. More recently Manuel Medina upset the odds to take the WBO world featherweight title from Scott

Harrison in Glasgow, when most people thought the Mexican would not be able to cope with the younger champion.

That sort of thing can happen in less publicised fights as well and I recall years ago seeing Steve Pollard, who later went on to be such a successful trainer with Paul Ingle, step in at late notice and destroy one of my own fighters. Pollard was regarded as a journeyman fighter by many people, and that tag is given to an awful lot of boxers who are never likely to be world beaters, but are always fit and ready to fight at a moment's notice. More often than not they will end up as losers, and they know that in the promoter's eyes that's their job. But it doesn't mean they just go in the ring and roll over. They are proud fighters who quite often earn very decent money from the sport because they're in such demand.

I wasn't the only manager to have a fighter turned over by Pollard and I remember another frantic promoter agreeing to pay Steve quite a lot of money to step in at the last minute and save a show. He turned up as an opponent for one of the 'house' fighters who was expected to win in front of his own fans. It didn't quite work out that way with Steve ending up a few thousand pounds better off, after notching up another win on his record.

There have been complaints at times from fans who have said a show has been too heavily weighted in favour of the house fighters. There was one incident some time ago when all the winners were on one side of the fight card and the show was over really quickly because of all the easy victories. But fight fans are not stupid and if you don't provide the right kind of matches they simply will not turn up to watch a show.

The journeyman fighter is a big part of the sport the world over. They may not be world beaters but that doesn't mean they are bums who simply come to lose and take their money. All fighters have pride and even if the odds are stacked against them, they will generally go out and give it a go.

There are exceptions and I had experience of one of them on a trip to Russia. I was asked to help glove up a black American journeyman who had been brought in to face a local fighter in front of a really fanatical crowd. The ringside seats were full of some very heavy looking guys, and from the bulges in some of their jackets, it looked as though quite a few might be carrying guns. Like any fans they wanted their own man to win, and the hostile feeling had certainly not been lost on the American. As I was helping him to get ready he suddenly said, 'Man, that crowd out there sure looks ugly. They might not be wearing masks, but some of those guys make the Ku Klux Klan look like choirboys.'

I told him not to worry and just go out and fight. 'I'll go out there,' he added, 'but the moment I get hit I'm going down until I hear the sweet sound of that number ten being called by the referee!' Sure enough, he went out and did just that. The crowd loved it and he went back to the States with a decent pay day, even though he hardly broke sweat.

The Russian and Eastern Bloc boxing scene is really beginning to open up. It's very early days at the moment and a lot of places are still coming to terms with operating in a more capitalist market. It's almost like the Wild West in some places, but that will settle down and I'm convinced there will be a lot of very good boxers to come out of those countries.

Getting sponsorship in this country can still be difficult at times and some blue chip companies are reluctant to get involved in the sport even though there can be a lot of TV exposure for them when a big fight is staged. The importance of television to boxing is huge. In many ways the TV stations are the real power brokers when it comes to putting fights together, particularly in America. Stations like HBO and Showtime in America and Sky in Europe, have a lot of say in what goes on in big-time boxing.

With companies like HBO and Showtime you will often find that fighters are signed to an exclusive deal with them and consequently, some of the best matches are never made because the boxers are with rival TV stations and each wants to stage the fight. Compromises are rare, but sometimes they do happen, as in the case of Lewis and Tyson. Fights like that are huge pay-per-view events and can break all records when it comes to making money. Like it or not, Tyson is still a massive draw, even though the world knows he's way past his best.

I can't deny that boxing suffers from an image problem and sometimes it gives itself a bloody nose with incidents that make it into the newspapers for all the wrong reasons.

THE BUSINESS OF BOXING

One incident that didn't make the papers was a shooting in Salford after the weigh-in of a promotion I was involved with. It happened in November 1997 as I was leaving the Viking Fitness Centre in Salford. Ady Lewis was going to top the bill the next day in Manchester when he challenged for the European flyweight title against David Guerault, and on the same bill Steve Foster was taking on Pascal Mercier. As we were leaving the weigh-in I heard some loud bangs as Foster was getting into his car. I was promoting the show with a guy named Steve Woods and when we raced over to the car we could see four bullet holes in the side of it, but there was no sign of Foster. We later found out that it had been a case of mistaken identity and Foster duly turned up for his fight unscathed and won the contest. On the day of the promotion, the *Manchester Evening News* had got wind of what had gone on and tried to find out more from us. We played the whole thing down because nobody had actually been hurt and so they couldn't really stand the story up. But they did manage to come up with a good headline the day after Foster had beaten Mercier. It read: 'Foster gets a shot at British title'.

Back in 1994 I was involved in a promotion at Watford that resulted in a riot. Robert McCracken beat Andy Till to take the British light-middleweight title on points, and although Robert had nothing to do with the trouble, some of his supporters got a bit out of hand and the whole thing became pretty frightening as people ran for cover.

Whatever venue you're in, when trouble breaks out in the crowd, it doesn't take long before everything is in chaos and people start to panic. It wasn't a nice situation and when something similar happened a few years later in Peterborough I decided more drastic action needed to be taken. As some fans staged a running battle and chairs flew through the air, we managed to get some pictures of the people involved and I decided to put the photos in the local newspaper in an effort to shame them. I also vowed that none of those found to be involved in the trouble would ever be allowed to come to my shows again.

Last year there was more trouble at York Hall following one of Audley Harrison's fights, when former WBO world heavyweight champion Herbie Hide got involved in some pushing with a spectator and chairs went flying as fans scattered in all directions.

Hide had a bit of a history of volatile behaviour having wrestled with his opponent Michael Bentt in London in 1994, and he also had a go at another heavyweight, Danny Williams, during a press conference a few years later. But he was fined just £500 by the British Boxing Board of Control for what happened at York Hall, while Harrison who was not involved in the actual pushing incident, was fined £1,000.

In my opinion, the BBBC do a good job of regulating the sport in this country, but in so many ways they seem to lack any teeth. I'm sure they must often appear to the outsider as the Board of No Control, because they seem to lack the same sort of authority a body like the Football Association has, and are perhaps too worried about having to fight possible legal action if some people don't like what they are doing.

Of course, things like a riot are always going to make headlines, but in general terms boxing has figured less and less on the sports pages in recent years, which is a shame. I believe the game is flourishing and the shows around the country that I'm involved in on a regular basis for Sports Network are sell-out affairs. Eugene has done well with sell-out shows at small hall venues, despite the fact that none of them get TV exposure.

But sports editors seem less inclined to devote space to boxing unless it's for a big-name fighter. I've also noticed a change in a lot of the people who actually cover the sport in the media. When I first got involved in professional boxing, you pretty soon knew all the writers and broadcasters because they were the regular people covering shows. That's not the case any more and some of the people who enjoy their trips abroad to cover fights, and are happy to be wined and dined during the build-up to a world championship contest, are the very same people who will then knock the sport a few weeks later.

The real boxing writers are different and they have the same kind of passion and love of the game that I do. They know what they're talking about and even though I've had blazing rows with a lot of them over the years, I still respect their views and enjoy their company but they seem to be a dying breed.

They're all part of the business which I've enjoyed and been fascinated by since I first became involved in it. It's by no means perfect but then it would be boring if it was. No matter what happens I think boxing will survive because it has learnt how to

THE BUSINESS OF BOXING

adapt, and I'm convinced it will continue to be around for a very long time to come.

It takes a very special kind of courage for anyone to step between the ropes and take part in a contest, and you can never really predict the way things will turn out for fighters. I was reminded of that by Ed Robinson after Harrison's loss to Medina. As I've said, Ed used to be my press officer and now works for Sky as part of their boxing team. He was as upset by Scott's defeat as I was and told me he still has a boxing bill hanging on his wall with his name on it from the days he tried his hand at having a professional contest when he worked for me.

On the same bill are names of other fighters whose careers took very different paths: Scott Harrison is on the poster, along with Matt Brown, who boxed in two British title fights, Paul Ingle, Richie Edwards, who committed suicide, Benny May, who ended up serving a term in prison and P.J. Gallagher, a former featherweight champion whose career was cut short in its prime due to a medical condition. They all started out with their hopes and dreams and they all had a love for the game that perhaps only boxing people can fully understand.

For me, boxing isn't just a sport and it isn't just a business. It's a way of life.

22. END OF AN ERA

WHEN LENNOX DECIDED TO ANNOUNCE HIS RETIREMENT FROM THE RING, IT signalled the end of an era in heavyweight boxing. He did it a little less than eight months after what proved to be the 44th and last professional fight of his career, when he overcame Vitali Klitschko to stop the challenger on cuts in the sixth round.

It certainly wasn't his best display and, in fact, most people thought he was losing the contest until gashes around Klitschko's left eye meant blood started to pour all over the ring at the Staples Center in Los Angeles. Despite a lacklustre display from Lennox, though, I still felt he showed a true champion's heart to make sure he won the contest and remained world heavyweight champion.

He'd always maintained from day one that he would know when to bow out, and it was no great surprise to me when he finally made his decision to retire, holding a press conference in London to make the announcement and, at the same time, taking the opportunity to thank all of his boxing team. It was also no real surprise that, despite being with him for 12 of his 14 years as a professional, I didn't get a mention in the speech he gave. I watched the whole proceedings from the comfort of a Sky TV studio and I was immediately asked by people if I was hurt at not being thanked by Lennox, but I could honestly say that I wasn't.

It had been almost three years since I was last part of Lennox's team for a fight and we'd both moved on since then. To me, it was like getting a divorce, and we'd both taken different paths with our lives.

I don't have anything against Lennox Lewis and I really don't think he has anything against me. We haven't spoken since the split but that's just the way things are.

Despite not being involved with him, I still took an interest in the fights he had after we parted company. As I've said, I think it would have been a good time for Lennox to retire after he beat Tyson, but, at the same time, I could see why he decided to carry on. Klitschko stepped in as a replacement for Canadian Kirk Johnson, who injured himself in the build-up to a proposed fight with Lewis. I was amazed at the amount of problems that the big Ukrainian caused for Lennox in the fight, although I think that many of Lennox's problems were self-inflicted.

Lewis went out with a real kamikaze attitude, as far as I was concerned, and just seemed intent on taking Vitali out as soon as he could. All the reports before the contest suggested that Lennox was in great shape for the fight, but he soon started to look laboured and got caught far too often. Klitschko is a big, upright fighter and I'm sure that if Lennox had stuck to some basic principles, like boxing behind his jab, Lewis's class would have told and he'd have taken the challenger apart. Instead, he really had to dig deep to eventually come up with the goods, but it didn't leave the impression that Lennox was on top of his game. It doesn't matter how good you are, or what sort of success you've had as a fighter, Father Time will always catch up with you.

I believe that the way he boxed in the Klitschko fight was one of the main reasons why Lewis decided to call it a day. Knowing the way he thinks, he probably analysed the fight and came to the conclusion that, although his mind might have wanted to continue, he knew deep down that he probably didn't want to put his body through the torture of a training camp for six or eight weeks. Having achieved all he had in his career, and with the win against Tyson behind him, I don't believe Lennox had the same interest in the fight game that he once had.

Do I believe his farewell speech was the final chapter in his distinguished career? I think it should be, but I think he may still have left the door ajar. One thing is for sure, Lennox would never return to the ring unless he was absolutely satisfied in his own mind that he could come out of retirement and beat someone like Klitschko, who took the WBC version of the crown in April with an eighth round win against Corrie Sanders

Lennox dominated the heavyweight scene for 12 years and when he left, it created a vacuum. The titles split, and it gave the other fighters an opportunity to come along and claim a piece of the action. Instead of someone like Lewis being recognised as the one true heavyweight champion of the world, there was suddenly a situation where the division had four major champions.

Ironically, I think the lack of real quality in the heavyweight scene at the moment could benefit someone like Audley Harrison. As far as I'm concerned, he's a pretty ordinary fighter, but when the division is so thin, the opportunity is there for some fighters to take advantage of the situation. The possible problem from Harrison's point of view is that he may have to give up some of his independence in order to get a crack at one of the titles.

From my own point of view, I'm just sorry that injury and politics have prevented Georgi Kandelaki from taking a more active part in proceedings, because, at this moment in time, he has just the sort of pedigree and ability that could take him onto the world stage.

Heavyweight boxing has always excited me. On a domestic level, it was nice for me to be involved, as a consultant, with the success story of Matt Skelton. Although well into his 30s, he won the British and Commonwealth titles in only his 13th professional fight, just 19 months after making his professional debut.

Matt was a fighter I looked at in the gym and, because of his age and lack of experience, I decided not to take a gamble on him. But that wasn't the case with Eugene. He believed Matt could be a champion and was proved right when Skelton won the titles by beating Michael Sprott in the last round of their fight. It means the

Maloney boys have both played a part as managers of British heavyweight champions, and it was particularly satisfying for me to see Eugene getting the credit for the job he'd done.

Having spent a lifetime in boxing, I've come to realise that the game is full of ups and downs. It can make you feel as though you're on top of the world one moment and then send you tumbling. It's never pleasant seeing one of your fighters lose, particularly if you have really high hopes for them, and that's why Scott Harrison's loss to Media was so hard to take. On the night, Scott was never able to produce the kind of non-stop performance his whole game is based on and it was a bitter blow when he lost the WBO world featherweight title. He claimed he'd felt ill before the contest, and there was no doubt something was wrong, but once it had happened the main aim was to get a re-match.

I had to sit down with Scott and his father to explain that, although his purse for a return wouldn't be as much as he'd like (because the mandatory challenger had to be paid to step-aside), it gave Harrison the chance to get his title back at the first attempt. Getting your hands on the world championship belt means a lot more in the long run than being frozen out of the picture. It didn't take long for Scott to agree, and when Frank Warren put the whole thing together in November 2003, Harrison came up trumps with a win in the 11th round. There's no better feeling for a boxing manager than having a world champion, and, as I've said, seeing a fighter regain a title is very special.

Sport in general, and boxing in particular, has played such a big part in my life. I'm pleased to have achieved so much and experienced so many great times, and having my hands on the world heavyweight championship belt was an unforgettable moment. As crazy as it sounds, though, I was just as thrilled to get my hands on another sporting trophy earlier in 2004, when I was asked to put together a team of celebrities and fans to represent Millwall in a challenge match against an equivalent Manchester United team a few weeks before the two clubs met in the FA Cup final. I couldn't have been happier as my lot ran out 5–2 winners against their counterparts from United at the Millennium Stadium in Cardiff, and I got to collect the real FA Cup.

END OF AN ERA

It was a dream come true for me as a football fan and, in many ways, it's the same with boxing. I'm just a fight fan from the streets of Peckham who learnt his trade and was lucky enough to see so many of his dreams come true.

INDEX

INDEX

INDEX

INDEX